Scottish Mountaineering Club
District Guide Books

THE NORTHERN HIGHLANDS

General Editor: A. C. D. SMALL

DISTRICT GUIDE BOOKS

Southern Highlands
Central Highlands
Western Highlands
Northern Highlands
Islands of Scotland
Island of Skye
The Cairngorms
Southern Uplands
Mountains of Scotland

Munro's Tables

SCOTTISH MOUNTAINEERING CLUB
DISTRICT GUIDE BOOKS

THE
Northern Highlands

by Tom Strang

THE SCOTTISH MOUNTAINEERING CLUB
EDINBURGH

First published in Britain in 1974 by
THE SCOTTISH MOUNTAINEERING TRUST

Copyright © 1975 by the Scottish Mountaineering Club

First Edition 1924
Second Edition 1936
Third Edition 1953
First Edition New Series 1970
Second Edition New Series 1975
Third Edition New Series 1982

ISBN No. 0 907521 04 5

Printed in Great Britain by Hugh K. Clarkson & Sons Ltd.,
Young Street, West Calder, West Lothian EH55 8EQ, Scotland

CONTENTS

ILLUSTRATIONS

PLATES

TEXT DIAGRAMS by *J. Lunday, J. Renny and K. V. Crocket*

Sketch maps in each chapter opening by James Renny.

ACKNOWLEDGEMENTS

In common with both the 1970 and 1974 editions of the Northern Highland Guide Book, this latest edition relies heavily on the wealth of original information contained in earlier publications and in the Scottish Mountaineering Club Journals. I would particularly acknowledge the work of E. W. Hodge, whose 1953 Guide Book greatly expanded upon the original editions by W. N. Ling and J. Rooke Corbett and facilitated the production of subsequent volumes.

The Cambridge University Mountaineering Club and the Corriemulzie Mountaineering Club published interim Guide Books in 1958 and 1966 respectively, both of which provided a rich source of information on the districts they covered. To the editors, M. J. O'Hara (C.U.M.C.), and the late P. N. L. Tranter and the late A. R. M. Park (C.M.C.), acknowledgement is given.

The more recently published Area Rock Climbing Guide Books are constantly referred to throughout the text as sources of reference. I would give special acknowledgement to the authors, Ian G. Rowe (Vol. I—Letterewe and East Ross), and D. G. and R. W. L. Turnbull (Torridon, Achnasheen and Applecross).

Once more I must re-affirm my great indebtedness to the late Tom Patey for his invaluable advice and information given during the compilation of the 1970 edition—much of this remains very relevant.

Over the years, Peter MacDonald has made freely available his own wide knowledge of the Northern Highlands, and in this latest edition he has collaborated with David Jenkins to produce a selective list of recommended climbing routes. For all his help and constructive criticism I would like to express my special thanks.

Jim Renny has revised the series of maps which appear at the beginning of each section. As before, these are of the highest quality and invaluable assistance was received in their original preparation from Graham Tiso, Hamish M. Brown and Peter MacDonald. In this respect also, acknowledgement is given to J. C. Donaldson, author of the first revised edition of Munro's Tables and co-author with Hamish

M. Brown of the 1980 revised edition on which are based the heights shown both in the maps and throughout the text. Line drawings by J. Lunday once again appear throughout the text, and a special line drawing by K. Crockett is also included. Many bodies willingly gave information of a specialised nature for inclusion in this and in earlier editions. These include: The Nature Conservancy, The Red Deer Commission, The Forestry Commission, The Scottish Right of Way Society, The Mountain Bothy Association, The Grampian Speleological Group, The Ordnance Survey, The Countryside Commission, The National Trust for Scotland, The Highlands and Islands Development Board, The Scottish Mountain Rescue Committee and the Northern Constabulary.

The Geology of the Mountains is a reprint of the work of L. W. Hinxman taken from the earlier edition of the Guide Book. Ray Burnett is given credit for his help in compiling a selected Bibliography, and John MacLennan, Plockton, gave invaluable help with Gaelic placenames.

A major problem in any production of this nature, is that of finding suitable photographic coverage. This latest edition proved to be no exception, and for their tremendous help in this I am deeply grateful to Tom Weir, Hamish MacInnes, John Cleare, Jack Selby, Campbell R. Steven, M. J. O'Hara, Peter MacDonald, K. M. Andrew, Alex Gillespie, The Scottish Field, Donald J. Bennett and P. Hodgkiss.

Donald Bennett and Peter Hodgkiss have also given invaluable assistance with both technical advice and in the selection of suitable material—no easy task. Alex Gillespie I must mention for the vast amount of background photographic work which he performed so patiently. I would also like to express my appreciation to all those contributors of photographs and slides which were not finally selected for use—on technical grounds only.

The final presentation of the manuscript was done under great pressure and with great efficiency by Mrs. Jean Muirden to whom I would express my great appreciation.

Finally, I would like to express my gratitude to the General Guide Books Editor, Alex Small—always patient with delays and always ready with a cheerful and helpful comment.

INTRODUCTION

1. Area

The area covered by this guide to the Northern Highlands of Scotland includes the mountains of the northern half of Ross-shire, the whole of Sutherland and the south-west corner of Caithness.

The southern boundary follows for its greater part the line of the Dingwall-Kyle of Lochalsh Railway, that is from Dingwall at the head of the Cromarty Firth, by way of Garve and Strath Bran to Achnasheen, and westwards by Glen Carron to the Atlantic seaboard.

2. The Mountains

The Northern Highlands contain some of the most spectacular mountain scenery on the Scottish Mainland, characterised by the comparative remoteness of the area as a whole and by the isolation of the individual peaks. It is worth noting that of the twenty-one regions of outstanding beauty described by Mr W. H. Murray in his survey for the National Trust for Scotland—*Highland Landscape*—six are located in the area of the guide. These are Applecross, Ben Damph and Coulin Forests, Torridon, Loch Maree, Strathnasheallag and Fisherfield Forests, Inverpolly and Glen Canisp Forests.

The area is covered by sections 13, 14, 15 and 16 of Munro's Tables, which list 37 mountains over 3000 ft. (914m) and 30 subsidiary tops. In addition, sections 13, 14, 15, 16 and 17 of J. Rooke Corbett's Tables list 42 mountains over 2500 ft. (762m) and under 3000 ft. (914m). Where it is considered appropriate, these also are included in the chapter headings.

Mountains of lesser height, unlisted by either Munro or Corbett, but which are nevertheless of special significance, are also covered in the text.

3. Maps

1:10,560 O.S. Maps—(6" to one mile)

The area of the Guide has now been completely resurveyed and the sheets have been published. With the exception of some coastal sheets, these are square, with sides representing 5 kilometres. They have little value to hill-walkers.

1:25,000 O.S. Maps

The greater part of the area of the Guide has now been covered by the 2nd Series which is based on 1:10,560 and 1:10,000 surveys. The sheets cover an area 20 kilometres east to west by 10 kilometres north to south—twice the area of the 1st Series.

1:25,000 Outdoor Leisure Maps

These contain a wealth of information in English, French and German—Youth Hostels, Camping and Caravan Sites, Footpaths, Mountain Rescue Posts, Telephones, Boundaries and Access Paths are all shown. Significant paths are picked out by strong green symbols in 2nd Series maps. Two maps, printed back to back, cover the Cuillin and Torridon Hills.

1:50,000 O.S. Maps

This replaces the 1 inch to the mile maps and the whole area is now covered by the 2nd Series. These maps are essential. The following sheets apply to the Guide:
No. 9—Cape Wrath, No. 10—Strathnaver, No. 11—Thurso and Dunbeath, No. 12—Thurso and Wick, No. 15—Loch Assynt, No. 16—Lairg and Loch Shin, No. 17—Strath of Kildonan, No. 19—Gairloch and Ullapool, No. 20—Beinn Dearg, No. 21—Dornoch Firth, No. 24—Raasay and Loch Torridon, No. 25—Glen Carron.

1:250,000 O.S. Maps (Routemaster Series)

The whole of the Northern Highlands is covered by Sheet No. 2 of this series. This is invaluable for gaining an overall impression of the area.

Bartholemew—National Map Series—1:100,000

These contoured sheets are a useful supplement, especially for general expedition planning. The area of the Northern Highlands is covered by the following sheets:

Sheet No. 54—Skye and Torridon.

Sheet No. 55—Moray Firth.

Sheet No. 58—Ullapool and Cape Wrath.

Sheet No. 59—Dornoch Firth.

Sheet No. 60—Caithness.

Grid References

In the text of the Guide the location of places is sometimes given as a full National Grid reference relating to the 1:50,000 O.S. Maps. These are inscribed as—for example—NC 319202.

4. Transport

Rail travel is limited to the eastern and southern borders of the area; the scenic Kyle Line, which serves the communities between Dingwall and Kyle of Lochalsh, being the most useful of the two for access to mountain country. Its continued existence is unfortunately still in the balance. The north line from Dingwall to Wick is of more limited use to the would-be mountain traveller.

The road system in the area is now a good one, with improvements continually being made. It does not at all justify the fearful travellers' tales which one often hears in connection with Highland roads. The private car is still the most convenient method of travel to and between suitable centres, and for those who prefer cycling, some of the better kept cross-country paths are possible short-cuts.

For those without their own form of transport, it is possible, but less convenient, to use the system of local transport to travel between centres. The publication by the Highland and Island Development Board—*Getting Around in the Highlands and Islands*—gives fully comprehensive and up-to-date information on all forms of travel within the region. This includes ferries, buses, local hires, and planes and trains where applicable. It is obtainable from the Highlands and Islands Development Board, Bridge House, 27 Bank Street, Inverness IV1 1QR, or from the Tourist Associations of Ross-shire, Sutherland and Caithness. Current price—70p plus 30p postage. Highly recommended.

5. Accommodation

With the continuing growth of the tourist trade throughout the

Highlands, the amount of accommodation available, especially in the remoter mountain areas, has increased considerably.

Hotels

Those hotels conveniently located from the climber's point of view are usually established favourites with the fishing fraternity also. Consequently, over the summer months, they are normally well-booked. Many also tend to be seasonal, and close down during the winter months. Because of this, it is usually safer to check up beforehand as to availability in order to avoid disappointment.

Many of the hotels in the north still live up to the old Highland tradition in terms of hospitality, and the standard is generally high. However, it is probably wiser to be guided in choice on the strength of a personal recommendation.

A comprehensive register of Hotel and Boarding House Accommodation is to be found in the Scottish Tourist Board publication—*Where to Stay in Scotland*. Equally worthwhile companion volumes are—*Self Catering Accommodation in Scotland* and *Scotland for Caravan Holidays*. All three volumes can be obtained from the Scottish Tourist Board, 23 Ravelston Terrace, Edinburgh EH4 3EU.

Bed and Breakfast

Bed and Breakfast accommodation can usually be found close to most of the mountain areas. The prices are generally reasonable and the standard good. Even where no advertisement is displayed it is worth while enquiring, as most of the local population are now prepared to accommodate the overnight visitor. The most useful sources of information are the excellent and up-to-date lists published by the various local Tourist Associations. These can be obtained from the Local County Tourist Officers at the following addresses:

Tourist Office, Wick, Caithness—Wick 2596
Tourist Office, Dornoch, Sutherland—Dornoch 400
Tourist Office, Muir of Ord, Ross-shire—Muir of Ord 433
Tourist Office, Gairloch, Ross-shire—Gairloch 2139

These lists cover Guest-houses, Bed and Breakfast, and Caravan Hires. Caravan and Camp-site information will also be supplied on demand.

In addition, the Northern Times Publishing Co., Main Street, Golspie, (Tel. No.—Golspie 215), produce annual Tourist Guides for the three districts in the area of the guide—Ross-shire, Sutherland and Caithness. These contain a wealth of information of all forms of accommodation, and are very good value.

Hostels

The Scottish Youth Hostels Association have two useful publications giving full details of Hostel provision in the North. These are: *The Northern Highlands* and the *S.Y.H.A. Annual Handbook*. Hostels tend to be concentrated along the North and West coastline. Many of them are fairly small and require prior booking, and it is necessary to check each season on winter closing dates.

Bothies

The area abounds in disused steadings and croft houses in various degrees of repair, which are often well situated from the mountaineer's point of view. Some of those are already recognised climbing bothies, and their use has been authorised by the estate-owner, with few restrictions. Others have been used on dubious authority, and consequently local relationships have suffered. Where bothies are mentioned in the text, this does not imply permission to use them, and in the interests of the good local relationship it is emphasised that such permission should be obtained in advance.

The Mountain Bothy Association has done sterling work here, as in other regions, both in obtaining owner's permission to use, renovate and maintain old buildings of this type.

The Association is a charity formed in 1965 with the object of maintaining simple unlocked shelters in remote country for the use of walkers, climbers and other outdoor enthusiasts who have in common a love of wild and lonely places. Membership is open to all who are prepared to give of their time and effort to help save the old bothies from ruin.

Further information can be obtained from:
The Membership Secretary.
Richard Butrym.
Tigh Beag.
Macleod Homes.
North Connel, Oban, Argyll.

Camp-sites

The Northern Highlands abound in pleasant, uncluttered camp-sites, a fast disappearing phenomenon elsewhere in the country. Where these are near houses, it is always diplomatic to seek permission—this is seldom withheld without good reason. On certain estates, care should be taken in the choice of sites during the stalking season. The official dates are 15th July-15th October, but most estates concentrate the greater part of their shooting from the beginning of September to the end of the statutory period.

Shelter Stones

In many parts of the Northern Highlands there exists a wide choice of natural forms of shelter. To attempt to list these would be impossible—their location and use must be left to the initiative of the individual explorer. The majority take the form of caves and shelter stones, the latter especially prevalent amongst the great boulder-fields of Torridonian sandstone. Once a certain familiarity with a particular area is gained, the use of a tent soon becomes unnecessary.

6. Hill Track and Drove Roads

The intricate network of hill-tracks which covers the area of the Northern Highlands, provides the mountain traveller with the key to a vast unspoiled wonderland of rolling moorland, lonely glens, dark hill lochans, and isolated peaks.

The development of lines of communication in a wild mountainous region is greatly influenced by natural physical obstacles, and consequently every hill track had a sound reason for its existence. The Highland population in the distant past can hardly be said to have been road-minded. The frequency of inter-clan foray and cattle reiving often made inaccessibility desirable, and their own clandestine routes would hardly have been advertised.

According to a local minister writing the Statistical Account of his parish at the end of the 18th Century—'Travelling it must be owned is difficult and disagreeable, there being no roads, but such as the feet of men and cattle have made'—and of the country as a whole—'The most inland parts are nothing but a vast group of dreadful mountains, with their summits piercing the clouds, and divided only by deep and narrow vallies, whose declivities are so rugged and steep, as to be dangerous to travellers not furnished with guides'.

As in all mountainous country, the tracks followed the most natural line along the driest ground of the straths, avoiding peaks and crossing watersheds by the lower bealachs at the head of glens. In this country of a thousand lochs, water supplies were of great importance and chosen with care, especially along those routes which were to become established as drove-roads.

Droving and the subsequent development of the main drove roads which were to form the basis of the present day main communication system of the area was a natural outcome of the Highland way of life. By its physical formation and climatic pattern, the area, like other parts of the Highlands is a vast natural grazing land, and in the days before the advent of 'The Great Sheep', cattle were the main tangible form of wealth. The system of Land Tenure led to a great proportion of the population having grazing rights with resultant overstocking. The primitive and limited form of agriculture practised made it essential that stocks should be drastically reduced annually, since it was impossible to produce enough winter feeding for the whole of the Summer herds. There was always a demand for cattle in the south; cattle provided their own transport to the marts; consequently droving was a natural economic outcome, and remained so for nearly 400 years, until the latter part of the 19th century.

Droving seemed to suit the nature of the Highlander with this background of clan forays and reiving, and the ability to endure hardship over great distance was bred into them. A Memorandum covering the Highlands in 1746, speaks of cattle thieving among the people as—'the Principal source of their barbarity, cruelty, cunning and revenge (which) trains them to the use of arms, love of plunder, thirst for revenge'.

Scott's assessment of the Highlander's aptitude to the craft of droving is more sympathetic—'the Highlanders in particular are masters of this difficult trade of droving, which seems to suit them as well as the trade of War. It affords exercises for all their habits of patient endurance and active exertion. They are required to know perfectly the drove roads which lie over the wildest tracks of the country, and to avoid as much as possible the highways which distress the feet of the bullocks and the turnpikes which annoy the spirit of the drover; whereas on the broad grey or green track which leads across the pathless moor, the herd not only may move at ease and without taxation, but, if they mind their business, may pick up a mouthful of food on the way'.

These 'broad grey or green tracks' were the ecnomic links from the North and West to the East and South. Beauly Tryst—Faill na Manachaim—was the greatest market for cattle from Caithness,

Sutherland and Ross-shire, and remained so until 1820 when the mart moved to the neighbouring township of Muir of Ord.

Here too converged the cattle herds from the Outer Island, which were brought by sea then often thrown overboard to swim ashore at Poolewe, Aultbea, Gruinard and Ullapool along the western seaboard of Ross-shire.

Droving has long passed from the economic life of the area, but many of the present roads still follow the line of the old drovers' routes through the glens, in part if not as a whole. The present road from Poolewe to Kinlochewe takes the south shores of Loch Maree, while the old drove road followed the north shore and can still be followed. From Gruinard, the drovers' route by way of Strath na Sheallag and the Fannichs to Achnasheen, can still be followed by well-marked tracks. But the road which marks the southern boundary of the guide, from Loch Carron to Dingwall, follows exactly the line taken by the drove road, as does the present road to Ullapool and the West, and from Bonar Bridge on the A9, to both Lochinver and Laxford Bridge in the north-west of Sutherland.

Those tracks which provided lateral communication between Strath and Strath from West to East, across, the line of glen and mountain were never developed to the same extent as the drove routes. With local needs and habits continually changing, many no longer serve their original purpose, but although no longer used to the same extent as before, they can still be followed, and provide for the walker both access to mountains, and worthwhile expeditions in themselves.

Many of the more remote tracks are partially grown over and neglected, but those which lie in the sporting estates are usually well-maintained for stalking purposes, frequently marked by cairns, and in some cases cyclable for part of their way. This is especially true in the north of Sutherland and in Wester Ross.

To list in detail the numerous cross-country tracks still in use would detract from the pleasure of exploration. The walker may choose a combination to suit conditions and personal ability. It will be the policy in the text to indicate tracks of particular use and cross-country routes of special interest and beauty.

Rights of Way

It would seem logical at this point to broach the controversial subject of the law of Rights of Way in Scotland—a law which can affect at some time or other all who use the mountains for their pleasure.

By definition—A public right of way is a right of passage, open to the public at large, over private property, by a route more or less defined. It is a burden on the property in favour of the public, the solum or ground traversed by the route remaining the property of the proprietor, subject to the public's right of way. Roughly speaking they may be categorised as vehicular routes, drove roads and footpaths, and the greater right includes the lesser: motor vehicles may be used on routes previously used by wheeled traffic, e.g. a cart track; a drove road implies right of way for horseman, but a footpath does not.

Not all of the existing established rights of way were drove roads. 'Kirk' and 'Coffin' roads are also common—the former being a road to the church, e.g. the road from Alligin along the north shore of Inner Loch Torridon past Alligan Lodge, the latter being roads to the nearest graveyard. Indeed, all public rights of way have their origins in a public need for a route from one place to another for a specific purpose in the course of normal everyday life whether vocational, religious, or recreational. It should be noted that local planning authorities now have statutory powers to establish public rights of way.

The essential elements of a public right of way at common law are: (a) it must have been used for a continuous period of not less than forty years; (b) the use must be a matter of right and not attributable to mere tolerance on the part of the proprietor; (c) it must connect two public places, or places to which the public habitually and legitimately resort; and (d) it must follow a route more or less defined.

At the time of writing, the Ordnance Survey do not show Rights of Way on O.S. Maps of Scotland as is the case in England. However, principal rights of way have in many cases been signposted and then recorded on maps for the attention of local authorities. In due course this could form the basis of a composite register of ways which can be published.

In 1845, the Scottish Rights of Way Society was founded, and re-constituted in 1946. Its objects are the preservation, maintenance and defence of rights of way throughout Scotland. Over the past century it has done much to preserve our great heritage of rights of way. They exhort the public to assist their efforts by using these rights of way which have been handed down, and indeed were sometimes fought for, by our forefathers. At the same time, they emphasise that in the course of following these tracks through the glens and over the mountains, regard should be given to all those who make their living on the hills and that the countryside may be preserved from further human pollution and desecration with litter.

The Scottish Rights of Way Society have published a concise booklet—*A Walker's Guide to the Law of Right of Way in Scotland*—this is obtainable from the The Secretary, Scottish Rights of Way Society Ltd., 32 Rutland Square, Edinburgh EH1 2BZ. Further information on all aspects of the subject of rights of way may be obtained from the Honorary Secretary, Mr D. H. McPherson at the above address or at 6 Abercromby Place, Edinburgh EH3 6JX—031-556-3942.

7. Rock, Snow and Ice Climbing

The potential of the Northern Highlands as a climbing area has been seriously explored only comparatively recently. The remoteness of the area as a whole was a major drawback in the earlier years, and many promising crags remained virtually untouched. With little information filtering out, few climbers were tempted to spend time in exploration. Those who did were amply rewarded, and the increase in activity throughout the region over the part twenty or so years has produced a wealth of routes at every standard of difficulty. Perhaps the most fruitful 'finds' in this latter era have been on Foinaven, in the far north of Sutherland, Beinn Dearg in the Inverlael Forest, the Fannichs, the mountains of Letterewe, beyond Loch Maree, and in the Applecross peninsula, with its great winter potential. While there is still scope for further exploration, the chance of finding any major new crag has rapidly diminished.

The Scottish Mountaineering Club has produced (to date) two Climber's Guides relative to the Northen Highlands. These incorporate extensive lists of new routes as well as the original climbs which were recorded in earlier editions of the District Guide, and in various Mountaineering Club Journals. They have expanded upon the very valuable interim Guides (now out of print) published by the Cambridge University Mountaineering Club (1958) and by the Corriemulzie Mountaineering Club (1966).

Volume I—Letterewe and Easter Ross—I. G. Rowe—covers the area from Fannich mountains, south of the Garve-Ullapool road, to Strathoykell on the border with Sutherland, together with the areas of Fisherfield and Letterewe, collectively known as Carnmore.

Volume II—Torridon, Applecross and Achnasheen—D. G. and R. W. L. Turnbull covers the area formed by the Achnasheen—Lochcarron—Poolewe roads, bounded on the west by the sea.

A companion volume—a Selective Guide to the Northern Highlands—(including the areas covered by Volume I and II)—is also visualised. This would also include selected climbs on the mountains of the far-north of Ross-shire and of Sutherland.

Within the text, detailed descriptions of climbing routes have either been eliminated, or greatly curtailed, in order to avoid duplication with the current series of climber's Guide-books. In general, the policy has been to indicate where and when routes have been climbed and to credit the party making the first ascent. The exception to this is mainly in those areas which are not included in either of the two existing Climber's Guide-books—mainly in Sutherland.

A selection of routes, chosen both for their individual worth and to cater for a wide varity of standard, is included in the Appendices. The usual grading for rock climbs in Scotland has been used, i.e. Easy, Moderate, Difficult, Very Difficult, Severe and Very Severe. 'Left' and 'Right' refer to the climber facing the rock.

The separate winter classification is as follows:

Grade I—Straightforward, averaged-angled snow gullies, generally showing no pitches under adequate snow cover. They may, however, present cornice dificulty.

Grade II—Pitches encountered in gullies, or gullies with high-angled or difficult cornice exits. The easier buttresses which under snow present more continuous difficulty.

Grade III—Serious climbs which should only be undertaken by parties with good experience. Reaches technical standard of Severe.

Grade IV—Routes which are either of sustained Severe standard or climbs of higher difficulty which are too short to be classed as Grade V.

Grade V—Routes which give major expeditions and are only to be climbed when conditions are favourable. Technical standard Very Severe.

8. Ski-ing

There is no organised ski-ing of the 'downhill only' variety such as has developed in the older established Scottish winter sports centres, but during most winters, many areas within the Northern Highlands offer excellent sport for skiers.

Ski-ing is often possible from the beginning of December to the end of March, suitable slopes being reasonably sheltered from wind and weather. Snow conditions can be surprisingly good, but the comparative low level increases the chance of a quick break-up of fields following a thaw.

The most likely areas are: Ben Klibreck, Seana Bhraigh and the surrounding area, Beinn Dearg (Ross-shire) especially from the Inverlael side, the whole area of the Fannichs, the area around Forsinard, north of Kinbrace on the railway line to Thurso, many of the Eastern glens which stretch inland from Helmsdale down to Golspie, and finally, Ben Wyvis.

Ben Wyvis has undoubtedly the greatest potential for future development, and a detailed survey of the large snowfield in the south-east corrie overlooking Strathpeffer has been carried out over a number of years. This is Coire na Feith Riabhach (or Coire na Fearaich)—the corrie of the Grey Bog—unnamed on the O.S. map. It has been found to be a good snow-holding area on smooth terrain with excellent shelter. The corrie's gentle concave profile provides adequate ski-ing up to intermediate standard with a more limited scope for the expert. The Highland Regional Council have approved provisional planning permission for the development of an all-the-year-round leisure centre, ski-resort and cable lift, rack railway including loop line and station on the Dingwall-Kyle line.

The proposed mountain—rack railway would start from a point on the Dingwall-Kyle railway some 50m east of the railway bridge over the Peffery Water (N.H. 469607) and below Raven Rock summit. From here to the summit of Ben Wyvis by way of the upper slopes of Glensgaich, Cnoc na Each Mor, Coire na Fearaich and the S.W. spur of Ben Wyvis—a total distance of 9.3 km.

The illustrated prospectus written by Mr John Murray, and published by Monument Press, Abbey Road, Stirling, covers this imaginative, and obviously practical scheme, in fascinating detail.

Reasonable access to ski-ing on Ben Wyvis is at present possible from Garbat, 8km (6m) north of Gorstan junction, near Garve. The way lies through the forestry plantations on the lower slopes of the mountain, and then by way of the Bealach Mor between Wyvis and Little Wyvis round the shoulder of An Cabar into the snow corrie.

Throughout the whole area it is often most practicable, as in other parts of the Highlands, to combine ski-touring with winter climbing. The possibilities here are considerable. To those looking for further information on basic requirements for this, a most complete and satisfying form of mountaineering, 'Scottish Mountains on Ski' by Malcolm Slesser is recommended reading.

9. Cave Exploration

Opportunities in this field occur in three main areas, all in Sutherland.

Around Durness on the north coast of the county, the Smoo Cave is the largest and best known, figuring not unnaturally in several local legends concerned with the supernatural. Further exploration has been done in the sea caves at Balnakeil and further inland at Ach a'Chorrain.

At the east end of Loch Assynt, the strip of Cambrian dolomite near Inchnadamph offers greater scope for investigation. The main area is along the course of the Traligill river and its tributaries with easy access from Inchnadamph hotel by track along Gleann Dubh. The main systemn—Cnoch nan Uamh, N.G.276206—has three entrances and 500m. of recorded passages and is the largest cave known in Scotland.

Slightly to the south, the course of the Allt nan Uamh has also been the site of worthwhile investigation and further complexes have been uncovered. Here occurs the famous Bone Cave—N.G. 269170—excavated 1889 by Doctors Peach and Horne and later in 1927 by Messrs Callender, Cree and Dr J. Ritchie. These have been established as the most northerly habitation of Palaeolithic Man in Britain. This area is now part of the Inchnadamph Nature Reserve and comes under its regulations. The honorary warden can be contacted at Stronechrubie for further information.

The most southerly of the three main cave areas occurs at Knockan, near the Sutherland border with Ross-shire. The limestone area to the east of the villages of Elphin and Knockan is largely drained by the Amhainn a'Chnochain which passes underground at Uamh an Tartair—N.G. 217092—above a dry waterfall. Two other likely pots here—Uamh Poll Eoghainn, N.G. 205094 and Tobhar na Glaise, N.G. 210105—have also been investigated. The Grampian Speleological Group are amongst the most active in the area of Knockan and Inchnadamph, and are responsible for much of the current investigation and documentation of the caves and pots in the area. For those seeking further information on the subject, their publication (occasional only), 'The Caves of Assynt' is well worth obtaining, giving details and maps of all locations within the area. The club have a hut a Knockan village, which is also a Cave Rescue Post. Enquiries can be made to Mr A. L. Jeffreys, 8 Scone Gardens, Edinburgh EH8 7DQ.

10. Wild Life and Conservation

The area of the Northern Highlands provides a wide variety of natural habitats, still containing a wealth of specimens covering the whole range of indigenous Flora and Fauna, despite centuries of Man's misuse and depredation. They form an invaluable part of our National Heritage and have begun to receive more serious attention than previously. Many of those areas have now become National Nature Reserves under the control of the Nature Conservancy. Here preservation and ecological studies, the basis of conservation, are carried on, and while the Reserves are by no means the only areas where the natural life of the country can be observed at close quarters, they are usually the location of a particularly wide cross-section of species or of some special interest.

In the area of the Guide, most of the Reserves are located in the more mountainous regions, a fact which should increase their interest to the mountain traveller.

These Reserves are located as follows:

Allt nan Carnan Reserve a mile long, 18 acre stretch of thickly wooded gorge north-west of Lochcarron village in Wester Ross. Rich in plant life.

Rasaal Reserve covers 202 acres across near the head of Loch Kishorn on the road from Loch Carron to Sheildaig, and here can be found one of the few natural types of Ashwoods in Scotland and the most northerly in Great Britain. The floor of the wood which is growing on a limestone pavement is remarkable in that it has a peculiar hummocky surface, rich in mosses.

Beinn Eighe Reserve in the Torridon area of Wester Ross was declared in 1951 and became the first National Nature Reserve in Britain. Comprising 10,507 acres it contains one of the few remaining remnants of the old Caledonian Forest which once covered large areas of the North of Scotland. The preservation and study of this

Caledonian Pinewood is one of the main projects of research carried out at Anancaun Field Station just north of Kinlochewe.

The Coille na Glas Leitire Nature trail on the south shore of Loch Maree gives an opportunity to see many of the Reserves features and wild-life.

As well as Otter, Wild Cat and Fox, the animals of the reserve include the rarer Pine Marten. Deer management is carried on in liaison with neighbouring estate proprietors.

In 1967, the 14,100 acres of Torridon Estate, including some of Scotland's finest mountain scenery, was accepted by the Inland Revenue and placed under the care of the National Trust for Scotland. To this was added a few months later the 2000 acres of Alligan Shuas adjoining its western boundary.

Between them the National Trust and the Nature Conservancy control an area some 20 km E-W and 6.5 km N-S including Beinn Alligin, Liathach, Beinn Dearg and Beinn Eighe.

Information about the Reserve can be obtained from the warden at Anancaun Field Station, and the National Trust have an Information Centre in Glen Torridon.

Corrieshalloch Gorge. The gorge adjoins the roadside near Braemore Junction on the Garve-Ullapool road. The 13 acre reserve is a magnificent example of a box-canyon with special interest in its plant and tree life—especially mosses. The walls of the gorge are mostly between 30m and 45m high, attaining 60m approaching the well-known Falls of Measach.

Inverpolly Reserve on Ross-shire's northern border with Sutherland, covers 26,827 acres including 816 acres of woodland and three summits over 600m—Cul Mor, Cul Beag and Stac Polly. There is a diversity of habitats, loch, stream, bog, moorland, woodland, scree, cliffs and summits. Pine Martens can be found here among the animals of the area and Golden Eagles can be seen. On the islands of Loch Sionascaig are untouched relics of primitive Birch-Hazel woodland. The reserve is rich in plant life and on the east boundary at Knockan Cliff the now classical exposure of the Moine Thrust is of special attraction to the geologist. The Reserve is the second largest in size in Britain and is managed jointly by the Conservancy and the landowners. There are two wardens—one at Strathpolly and one at Knockan Point—while visits to the reserve are not normally restricted, contact should be made beforehand, especially in the case of parties of more than six, going on to the Drumrunie part during the stalking season—15th July-15th October.

The following obviously sensible restrictions apply to all visitors to the Reserve—no fires, no camping, no dogs, no litter. The surrounding hills carry a considerable stock of North Country Cheviot Sheep and, particularly during the lambing season—Late April—Late May—uncontrolled dogs can cause havoc. Contact can be made as follows:

Warden, Strathpolly.—Tel. No. Lochinver 204.

Warden, Knockan.—Tel. No. Elphin 234.

Inchnadamph Reserve covers 3200 acres between the East end of Loch Assynt and Ben More Assynt, the highest mountain in Sutherland. It is of great geological and botanical interest, lying as it does at the western front of an area of disturbed Durness Limestone and ringed round by outcrops of the Glencoul, Ben More and Moine thrusts.

Work on the reserve is aimed at preserving the interest of the limestone formations and at a study of the varied plant life. Peculiar to the reserve is a type of willow scrub common in Scandinavia but rare in Scotland and on the driest limestone areas Mountain Aven (Dryas Octapetala) is abundant.

The effects of traditional land-use practices—sheep grazing and rotational heather burning—are also the subject of research on the reserve.

The Allt nan Uamh bone caves lies within the reserve boundaries. Permission to carry on any scientific work here, or elsewhere on the reserve is required from the Nature Conservancy, 12 Hope Terrace, Edinburgh, 9.

Visitors to the reserve should contact the part-time warden at Stronchrubie, by Inchnadamph. Tel. No. Assynt 208.

Invernaver Reserve covers 1363 acres near the mouth of the River Naver in the North of Sutherland. It is remarkable for the variety of habitats it contains within its relatively small area, including those of blown sand, and for its boreal plant communities, the finest in the North of Scotland. The mingling of species of montane and oceanic affinities is an added attraction. There is also an unusual development of Juniper scrub on peat which is within reach of the blown sand. Greenshank, Red-throated Diver, Ring Ouzel and Twite all breed within the reserve.

Strathy Bog, lying just eight miles south of Strathy, on the north coast of Sutherland, the 120 acre of bog is the best example of low-lying blanket bog left in its natural state in the country. It has unusual structural features and a wealth of bog-plants.

Handa Bird Reserve, famous as a sea-bird sanctuary, is a 766 acre island lying close inshore off the N.W. coast of Sutherland, one and a half miles by sea from Tarbet and three miles N.W. of Scourie. It was established as a reserve by the Royal Society for the Protection of Birds in 1962 by agreement with the proprietors. It is renowned for its magnificent sandstone sea-cliffs rising sheer for 400 ft. while the Great Stack of Handa covered with nesting sea-birds in summer poses its own peculiar problem to the rock-climber. The island was inhabited until 1848, when potato famine influenced the seven families to emigrate to America. The ruined crofts can still be seen, but the only inhabitable house is a reconditioned bothy which accommodates six. There are no restrictions on day visits but permission to camp or to book the bothy must be made throughout the R.S.P.B. Office, 21 Regent Terrace, Edinburgh 7. Only members of the society, or of the Young Ornithologists Club can use the bothy, but camping is free. In the interests of nesting birds no dogs are allowed on the island.

The survey of breeding birds on the Island is extensive, and many others breed, or can be seen in, the vicinity. A 6-inch to the mile map extract of the Island and detailed information sheet can be obtained from the warden by post—price 5p—or from the Edinburgh Office.

Handa has a full-time resident warden during the period April to September. He is in full charge of the Island, and ensures that visitors adhere to the regulations laid down. Boats to Handa can be hired from Tarbet or Scourie—except on Sundays. Boatmen to contact are: Mr A. Munro (Jnr), Tarbet, Foindle, By Lairg, Sutherland.—Scourie 2126. Mr W. MacRae. 61 Seaview Tarbert. Scourie 2156. Mr R. Macleod, 15 Scouriemore, Scourie, Sutherland.—Scourie 2140.

A system of flag and smoke signals has been devised for emergency communication between the island and the mainland at Tarbet. Instructions are to be found on the noticeboard in the bothy. The nearest doctor is Dr I. D. Pennie.—Scourie 2206. Isle Martin, which lies in Ardmair Bay, a few miles north of Ullapool, has recently been gifted to the R.S.P.B. and is now listed as a reserve. Information can be obtained on application by letter to the Warden, Warden's House, Isle Martin. The R.S.P.B. Field Officer of the northern area is Mr Roy Dennis, 'Landberg', Kessock, Ross-shire. Tel. No.—Munlochy 368.

The Red Deer Commission

The Commission was set up under the Deer (Scotland) Act 1959 with the general functions of furthering deer conservation and control, and of keeping under review all matters relating to red deer. Of its twelve members, five represent farming, forestry and crofting and two represent the Nature Conservancy. A well-equipped field staff works under the Field Officer on the practical work—taking census counts, calf marking and helping estates with their annual culls and the all-important work of investigating and dealing with complaints of marauding deer.

The Commission meets regularly to receive reports on the work of the field staff and to discuss all aspects of deer conservation and control. The broad problems of land use, the effects of forestry planting programmes, legislation and scientific research on red deer in Scotland all feature in its discussion. Its interests are wide and the Commission have long been aware that the sport of deer stalking often conflicts with that of mountaineering and that addicts of each sometimes get irritated. The view of the Red Deer Commission is that, given reasonable courtesy and consideration by both sides, there is no need for such conflicts.

In an attempt to improve the situation they have published the following list of suggestions with relative background information.

First, to the hill walker, it is pointed out that shooting deer is not merely an expensive sport. The red deer is one of the finest wild animals in our island. When the last wolf in Scotland was killed, deer were left without a natural predator. But their numbers must be kept under control, otherwise the animals themselves suffer from insufficient food and are more likely to cause loss and damage on agricultural land. Hill stags are at their best for shooting only for a comparatively short period. They carry little fat until the growth of their antlers is complete, usually about mid-August; after this they rapidly gain weight until the onset of the rutting season, which reaches its climax in mid-October when most of the big stags have lost condition and their meat is of poor quality. Consequently every effort has to be made to kill the proper numbers between mid-August and mid-October.

The Commission feel, therefore, it would be in the general interest if all organisations connected with the tourist industry, and in particular those which provide information for climbers and hill walkers, would stress that those who wish to go to the hills from mid-

August to mid-October should first, if possible, ascertain if stalking is being carried out in the area, and if so, whom they should contact—stalker, factor, owner or tenant—to enquire where they can go without interfering with stalking. It is hoped that most hotels, boarding houses, youth hostels and local information offices will be able to provide information on this.

On most estates no attempt is made to restrict access by walkers and climbers, except when stalking is in progress. Visitors are able to make use of the paths which saves them fatigue and enables them to cover greater distances than they could otherwise. Often these paths were made for deerstalking, so it is considered reasonable to ask visitors to make enquiries before using them during the stalking season.

To Owners and Tenants of deer forests and other shootings and their employees, the Commission urge that they should, so far as possible meet all enquiries and requests that are courteously made and where they cannot agree to the route which the party enquiring wishes to take they should suggest an alternative. It cannot be expected that those visitors whose requests meet a blank refusal to allow them to walk anywhere in the forest, will continue to seek permission: they can hardly be blamed if they do not consider that it is worth while. Good will is lost; they give up asking and go as they please.

Even the widest publicity in tourist pamphlets, Youth Hostels' notices and Club Journals does not reach all visitors who go to walk or climb on the hills, and in some places roadside notices could be helpful. These should be worded to seek the co-operation of the visitor by making it clear that while they are welcome to reasonable access, they are requested to call at the stalker's house before going to the hill between the dates when stalking normally starts and finishes on that estate.

Notices that are worded solely with intention of intimidating and deterring visitors from entering the forest are not helpful towards securing good will without which co-operation is impossible.

The presence of a Youth Hostel or Climbing Club Hut on or close to a deer forest is apt to be regarded as a serious disadvantage by stalking interests. This need not, and should not, be the case; it has been found in several places that where relations are good between the local stalkers, hostel wardens, and members of climbing clubs, there is seldom any cause for complaint.

The classic text on the wild-life of the Northern Highlands is 'The Highlands and Islands' by F. Fraser Darling and J. Morton Boyd, now published in the New Naturalist series by Collins (1964), and the following bodies also produce interesting publications on the subject.

The Nature Conservancy, 12 Hope Terrace, Edinburgh 9.

The National Trust for Scotland, The Secretary, 5 Charlotte Square, Edinburgh 2.

The Red Deer Commission, Elm Park, Island Bank Road, Inverness.

The Countryside Commission for Scotland. Battleby, Redgorton, Perth. Tel. No. (0738) 27921.

11. Geology

The Mountains of the Northern Highlands fall naturally into three main groups, according to the nature of the rocks of which they are composed:

1. Unaltered or Slightly Altered Sedimentary Rocks—Old Red Sandstone, Cambrian Quartzite, Torridonian Sandstone.
2. Metamorphic Rocks—Archaean Gneiss, Schists, Slates, Quartzites etc., of the Central Highlands.
3. Igneous Rocks—Granite and Porphyry.

Sedimentary Rocks

1. *Old Red Sandstone*—This formation rarely attains any considerable height above sea-level. Morven (2313 ft., 705 m) in Caithness is one of the few exceptions. They are composed of conglomerate arranged in regular and nearly horizontal layers, are smooth and conical in outline, and offer few if any features of interest to the climber.

More remarkable are the deep and narrow gorges, with vertical walls rising in some cases to a height of nearly 200 ft., that have been cut by streams along the parallel joints of Old Red Conglomerate. The best known of these is the Black Rock of Novar on the way to Ben Wyvis.

Caithness—Morven and Maiden Pap
Sutherland—Ben Griam.

2.*Cambrian Quartzite*—This rock is slightly altered and hardened siliceous sandstone and follows the same line of country as the Torridon Sandstone. It usually occurs as a thin capping on the mountains of the latter formation stealing up the slopes to the summits, or in isolated patches crowning to the warm red-browns and purples of the under-lying sandstone. In only a few cases does the quartzite compose the whole or greater part of a mountain. The notable examples of this are Foinaven and Arkle in the Reay Forest of Sutherland, the eastern peaks and ridges of Beinn Eighe in Torridon, and in some of the hills of the Coulin and Achnashellach Forests.

The rock is hard, splintery and full of joints, and consequently breaks up readily into sharp angular fragments of all sizes which stream down the hillsides in long scree slopes. Where the angle is especially steep, the instability of these screes can make traverse or ascent a slow, awkward operation and care has to be taken not to send the whole slope in motion. Where the angle is too steep to retain the debris, precipitous escarpments such as those that surround the northern corries of Beinn Eighe are formed and these are usually shattered and untrustworthy. Instability is the prevailing character of the quartzite mountains of the west, a fact which should be borne well in mind when climbing on them.

Sutherland	Meall Sgribhinn	Beinn Spionnaidh
	Foinaven	Arkle
	Glas Bheinn	Breabag
Ross-shire	Beinn Eighe	Sgurr Dubh
	Hills of Coulin and Achnashellach Forests.	

3. *Torridonian*—There are no mountain forms in Scotland more striking in appearance than those found in the belt of Torridonian Sandstone that stretches along the western coasts of Sutherland and Ross-shire from Cape Wrath to Applecross and Loch Carron.

The regular parallelism of the beds, and the steady dip of the gently inclined and often horizontal strata, combine to produce that architectural character for which they are so remarkable.

Long lines of mural precipice which sometimes as on Suilven almost encircle the mountain; rounded and terraced bastions, and pinnacled ridges. are constant features of these mountains. The summits vary greatly in character, from the flat top of Beinn Bhan in Applecross, to the spiry cones of An Teallach or the sharp serrated ridges of the Fasarinen on Liathach and the smaller Stac Polly.

The terraced cliffs are cut at frequent intervals by vertical joints, which give rise to steep gullies. These often form channels for the streams that rise in the higher corrachs and pour down the face of the mountain in a succession of waterfalls. When dry, the gullies form chimneys of excessive steepness, usually terminating below in long stone shoots. The climbing where possible is good. The rock is firm and reliable and rarely slippery, while holds and ledges are plentiful, though the latter may be encumbered with loose rocks fallen from above. Suitable belay points, however, tend to be scarce.

The pinnacles afford plenty of good rock-scrambling, and chimneys, presenting every degree of steepness and difficulty, abound.

Sutherland	Quinag (2 peaks capped with Cambrian Quartzite)
	Canisp (capped with Cambrian Quartzite) Suilven
Ross-shire	Cul Mor (peaks capped with Cambrian Quartzite)

Ross-shire (continued)

Cul Beag   Benn More Coigach group
Stac Pollaidh
An Teallach (3 eastern spurs capped with Cambrian
                     Quartzite)

Sail Mhor	Beinn a'Chlaidheimh
Beinn Tarsuinn	Beinn Dearg Mhor
Slioch	Mullach Coire Mhic Fhearchair
Sgurr Ban	Beinn Eighe
Liathach	Beinn Dearg
Beinn Alligin	Baosbheinn
Beinn Damph	Beinn Bhan (Applecross)
Sgorr Ruadh	Maol Chean-dearg
Beinn Liath Mhor	Fuar Tholl

Metamorphic Rocks

The great majority of the Scottish mountains belong to this group. The Archaean or Lewisian Gneiss occupies a considerable area in the west of Sutherland and Ross-shire and forms the whole of the Outer Hebrides. On the mainland it seldom rises to any great height. Ben More Assynt and Ben Stack in Sutherland and the fine group of mountains on the north side of Loch Maree are the most noteworthy belonging to this formation.

The gnarled and corrugated nature of this ancient rock, and the absence of drift from the lower slopes, give a peculiarly rugged character to its hills. Their sides are usually broken up into a succession of rounded bosses and craggy steps; but occasionally fine vertical precipices are developed, such as those that fall from Beinn Lair to the Fionn Loch. The exceeding toughness and uneven surface of the gneiss make the climbing everywhere reasonably safe.

Lewisian or Archaean Gneiss

Sutherland	Ben Stack	Ben More Assynt
Ross-shire	A'Mhaighdean	Beinn Airigh Charr
	Beinn Lair	Beinn a'Chaisgein Mor
	Glasbheinn	Sgurr a'Gharaidgh

Highland Schists (Flaggy Gneises, Mica schists, Quartz schists etc.—of indeterminate age)

Sutherland	Ben Hope (Mica and Hornblende schists)	
	Ben Hee	Klibreck
	Ben Armine	Meall Horn
Ross-shire	Fionn Bheinn	Moruisg
	Beinn Dearg	Hills of Freevater Forest
	Ben Wyvis	

The Fannichs

Sgurr Morr
A'Chailleach   Mica schist
Sgurr Breac
Beinn Liath Mhor
Sgurr nan Clach Geala   Mica and Quartz schist
Meall a'Chrasgaidh

Igneous Rocks

The only Igneous rock in the district is the granite of Ben Loyal and Strath Halladale.

Sutherland Ben Loyal
            Beinn Stumanadh

12. Mountain Rescue

The Northern Constabulary are responsible for the co-ordination of Mountain Rescue operations within the area of the Guide.

In the event of an accident, contact should be made with Police H.Q. in Inverness—Tel. No. Inverness 39191.

The Police Co-ordinator is Sgt. K. MacKenzie, who is also organiser for the Search and Rescue Dogs Association.

The Police will, if necessary, take the responsibility for calling in the Mountain Rescue Team from R.A.F. Kinloss, which also operates in this area.

The following civilian volunteer teams also operate within the area:
> Assynt Mountain Rescue Team.
> Dundonnell Mountain Rescue Team.
> Torridon Mountain Rescue Team.

Contact with these can be made through the Police, or as follows:

Assynt Mountain Rescue Team
Mountain Rescue Post—Inchnadamph Hotel—Ref. NC 252216.
> Telephone No. Assynt (057 12) 202.

Post Supervisor—Mr G. Morrison.
> Telephone No. Assynt (057 12) 202.

Team Leader—Mr J. Ross.
> Telephone No. Assynt (057 12) 209.

Dundonnell Mountain Rescue Team
Mountain Rescue Post (Assembly Point principally)—Dundonnell Hotel—Ref. NH 090881.
> Telephone No. Dundonnell (085483) 204.

Post Supervisor—Mr Florence.
> Telephone No. Dundonnell (085 483) 204.

Team Leader—Mr W. Neate.
> Telephone No. Aultbea (044 582) 204.

Torridon Mountain Rescue Team
Mountain Rescue Post.—Torridon Youth Hostel—Ref. NG 903558.
> Telephone No. Torridon (044 587) 282.

Post Supervisor— The Warden
> Telephone No. Torridon (044 587) 282.

Team Leader—Mr C. Rose, Heather Cliff, Alligin.
> Telephone No. Torridon (044 587) 256.

Other locations where equipment is held:

Police Station, Rhiconich, Sutherland—Ref. No. NC 255523.
Supervisor—Officer i/c.
> Telephone No. Kinlochbervie (097182) 222.

Police Station, Thurso.
Supervisor—Officer i/c.
> Telephone No. Thurso (0847) 3222.

Police Station Ullapool.
Supervisor—Officer i/c.
   Telephone No. Ullapool (0854) 2017.

Bridge End Stores, Aultbea—Ref. NG 873890.
Supervisor—Mr W. Neate.
   Telephone No. Aultbea (044 582) 204.
NB—**Always check locally—The location of a post is sometimes changed.**

Additional Help

Search and Rescue Dogs Association—The call-out organiser is Sgt.
K. MacKenzie. Work—Police H.Q. Inverness.
Tel. No.—Inverness 39191.   Home—1 Canal Road, Inverness—
Tel. No.—Inverness 38109.
Dog Handlers in the area are:
Dr M. C. MacInnes   Glenelg 272
A. Jackson   Gairloch 2017
J. Barlow   Tongue 256
K. MacKenzie   See above.

Scottish Cave Rescue Organisations—organiser is A. L. Jeffreys, 8
Scone Gardens, Edinburgh 8. Cave rescue calls should be made via
Edinburgh Police—Edinburgh 1212.
   Help is always obtained from local sources in the case of emergency
and it is hoped that any climbers in the vicinity will accept the
traditional obligation to offer their services to the person in charge of
the operation.

Public Telephones
   It is sensible to locate their position from your map before setting
out. They are not too frequent in the more remote parts of the area,
and where none is indicated, private phones may be the only
alternative.

Doctors
   Nearly all of the medical practitioners in the area are involved in

wide-spread country practices—consequently they are not always immediately available. In order to save valuable time in an emergency, contact is best made through the police.

Mountain Rescue Committee

The Mountain Rescue Committee Handbook—Mountain Rescue and Cave Rescue—is published annually and contains much valuable information.

Any query regarding Mountain Rescue in Scotland should be made to the Committee.

Secretary—Mr E. Grindley, Nurses House, Glencoe, Argyll.

13. Place Names

The rule adopted here, as in other sections of the S.M.C. Guides, is to follow the Ordnance Survey spelling of place names throughout. The accuracy of some of the O.S. forms is disputed by scholars competent to speak upon Gaelic philology and local usage, and several cases in point are noted in the letterpress. It would, however, be impossible in a guide book to embark upon this very specialised field, and the O.S. spellings are therefore adopted, though not as being necessarily correct in every case.

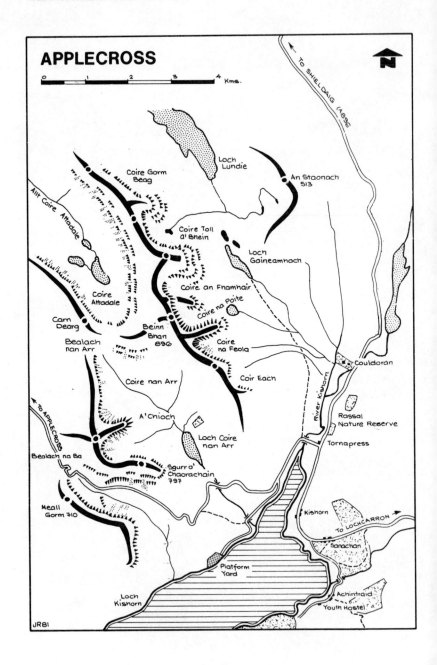

Applecross

(1) **Beinn Bhan** (896m) N.G. 804450.
(2) **Sgurr a'Chaorachain** (792m) N.G. 797417.
(3) **Meall Gorm** (710m) N.G. 779409.
MAP: O.S. 1:50,000 (2nd Series) Sheet No. 24—Raasay and Loch Torridon.

The Applecross Peninsula forms the extreme south-west corner of the area of this guide to the Northern Highlands of Scotland. Fish-tailed in shape, it is bounded on the north by Loch Torridon and on the south by Loch Carron and Loch Kishorn. The 25km long western seaboard faces across the Inner Sound to the Islands of Rona, Raasay and Scalpay, beyond which rise the mountains of Skye. The eastern boundary is formed by Glen Shieldaig through which passes the main road from the village of Lochcarron to Shieldaig and Torridon. A.896. This main road rises steeply westwards from Lochcarron, then passes down through the deep gorge of the Amhainn Cumhang a'Glinne into Kishorn village (named Sanachen on the O.S. map)—a distance of 6.5km. The attractive little community scattered around the head of the bay has changed somewhat in character over recent years with the advent of the oil rig construction camp, as have many of the other previously isolated villages in the area.

There is a Youth Hostel at Achintraid, 2.5km to the south, and this can be reached by road from Kishorn or by track from the Lochcarron-Strome road. This latter passes through Forestry Commission land and can be difficult to follow in places.

The daily mail bus service from Lochcarron to Shieldaig is a useful means of public transport.

The road turns north along the side of Loch Kishorn and reaches Tornapress junction at the tidal head of the loch in just under 2 km. From the ruins of Courthill House, which lie by the roadside half way between Kishorn and Tornapress, there begins a fine series of views on to the cliffs of Meall Gorm and Sgurr a'Chaorachain, rising proudly across the waters of the loch.

From Tornapress the road into Applecross is one of the highest motor roads in Britain. It swings southwards at first along the west side of the loch, then rises relentlessly around the lower slopes of Beinn Bhan, crossing the Russel Burn at the mouth of Coire Lair, which separates Beinn Bhan from Sgurr a'Chaorachain. Still rising steadily, it continues to traverse upwards between Sgurr a'Chaorachain and Meall Gorm, passing above the north side of the Allt a'Chumhaing, and giving magnificent views of the great terraced faces on either side of the glen. The final section on to the summit of the plateau is accomplished in a spectacular series of four hairpin bends up the head wall of the glen, giving the road a distinctly Alpine character. The pass at the head of the glen is known as the Bealach na Ba—the Pass of the Cow—and at this point the road reaches a height of 626m. From the plateau the road drops less steeply towards the village of Applecross on the bay at the head of the Applecross river, giving a sweeping view westwards of the mountains of Skye across the dead crater, Dun Ca'an, on the island of Raasay. From Applecross village, the motor road passes southwards through several small communities to Toscaig, and here more or less finishes.

The daily steamer service between Toscaig and Kyle of Lochalsh has, unfortunately, been discontinued.

Untill recent years, the road across the Bealach na Ba was the only motor road into the Applecross Peninsula and was quickly blocked by snow in winter time—effectively cutting off the whole area from the outside world. Nowadays, the long-awaited north coastal route is complete—it leaves the A896 just south of Shieldaig and winds its way along the north and west coastlines by way of Kenmore and other scattered communities to join up with the old road at Applecross village itself. In its initial stages the road is scenic, but improves in quality as it progresses.

A footpath follows the valley of the Applecross River to its head, then crosses over the pass below Croicbheinn at a height of 370m from where the right-hand branch leads down to the head of Loch Shieldaig. It is too far from the mountains to be of much use however, and the words of the minister who wrote the statistical account of the area in 1792 are still largely true—"neither public road or footbridge from one extremit of it to the other. . . . The foot traveller is guided according to the season of the year, what course to take, over rugged hills, rapid waters, and deep marshy burns. Besides here, as in all the adjoining parishes and Western Isles, the computation of miles is merely arbitrary, always terminated by a burn, cairn, well, or some such accidental mark, which renders them so remarkably unequal that it is impossible to reduce any given number of these imaginary miles to a regular computation''.

The village of Applecross, built along the bay of that name, more or less the centre of the western coastline of the peninsula, is the most populated of the numerous small crofting communities which are dotted along the coastal fringe, and like these, has been left with a mainly ageing population. This pattern of inhabited coastline and deserted interior becomes only too common as one travels through the north. The villages of Applecross were the last footholds of the native inhabitants who were evicted from their croft holdings inland to make way for the sheep and the deer. Crofting and fishing still forms the basis of life here but still the coastal crofts are falling empty faster than there are young people to take them over. The area lies almost entirely within the Wills Estate, which previously, along with tourism and some forestry work, provided the main alternative forms of employment. This situation has changed for the time being with the development of the oil construction rig at nearby Kishorn. The Dockland Settlement West Highland School of Adventure at Hartfield House, near the village, is now closed down.

The charm and isolation of Applecross attracts an ever increasing number of visitors each year, and one can understand how this has always been known as the Sanctuary—indeed the Gaelic name is A'Comaraich, meaning Sanctuary, and in ancient times this was a place of refuge for fugitives, recognised as such by the Church until the times of the Reformation. In the old church-yard at Cruarg, on the north side of the river, lies buried Saint Maelrubha, who gave his name to Loch Maree, further inland. He ruled as Abbot here for almost 50 years in the 7th century, and his influence extended over a wide part of the inland area of Ross-shire. The sandstone Celtic cross which stands at the gate of the churchyard is probably the one which previously marked his grave. Local legend has it that if you take a handful of earth from the grave of Saint Maelrubha you will always return again safely to the Sanctuary of Applecross.

The mountains of Applecross form an elevated plateau of Torridonian sandstone which lies in the south-eastern part of the peninsula, rising more or less gradually from the north-west, and falling to the east in a series of deep corries with steep, terraced cliffs and fine buttresses. The main tops lie to either side of the Bealach na

Ba (626m) and the summits can easily be reached from here without dropping lower than 580m. The plateau is relatively flat, but the boulder strewn surface gives remarkably rough walking throughout. From many points the view westwards across the entire length of the mountain ranges of Skye is by far the most exhilarating, although in all directions the view is extensive and spectacular.

Meall Gorm (710m)

Meall Gorm lies to the south of the Bealach and its summit is quickly reached from the road in the just under half a mile. The ridge extends for a mile south-eastwards towards Loch Kishorn, falling in imposing cliffs to the north and east above Allt a'Chumhaing. These are frequently split by deep gullies and wide stone-shoots, and are well terraced and vegetated. Seen from the road below the hairpins, a broad, broken buttress with a shorter, terraced buttress on its left, forms the right flank of the Meall Gorm cliffs. These have no recorded routes, and are separated by a scree gully from the next triangular buttress, Wedge Buttress, which in turn butts onto the more prominent, and more extensive, Cobalt Buttress. Cobalt Buttress, sometimes known as Blue Buttress, has on its immediate left, a steep narrow terraced column—Blue Pillar. There is a broad gully to the right of Wedge Buttress.

Mono Blues (210m) Grade III, (M. C. Geddes, B. P. Hall, A. McIntyre and J. Porter, 24th March, 1978,) follows the next gully to the right of this.

Cobalt Buttress was first explored in summer, 1953, by J. M. Taylor, C. G. Thomson and R. P. U. Tait, giving a 180m route of Moderate standard. The winter ascent in February, 1970, by I. Clough, G. Drayton and C. Young, was rated as Grade III, starting about 30m up to the right from the toe of the buttress, just above the toe of Wedge Buttress. *Rattlesnake,* 140m Severe (P. Macdonald and A. R. M. Park, 15th May, 1965) follows the obvious line of corners running up the centre of the buttress. The line is well seen in plate IV. On the wall between *Rattlesnake* and the *Blue Pillar* is *The Smooth Creep,* 90m. Very Severe (S. J. Carrol and P. Macdonald, 4th September, 1971). A scramble up the preliminary tiers leads to the foot of a smooth vertical corner about halfway along the wall. The start is marked by a cairn. The *Blue Pillar,* the steep and narrow buttress to the immediate left of Cobalt Buttress, gives 150m of climbing. The summer route (A. G. Nicol and T. W. Patey, May,

1953) is graded Very Difficult; the winter route—Grade IV—was first climbed by Joe Brown and T. W. Patey in February, 1958.

Blaeberry Corner, 105m. Severe. (W. D. Brooker and A. J. D. Norton, 1955), lies on the broad buttress to the left of the Blue Pillar,and is separated from it by a broken-up buttress. It is in three vertical tiers, the route being on the left side on clean, sound rock. The winter route—Grade IV (J. Horsefield, B. Jones, K. Spence, P. Thomas, February, 1971)—follows the same line, with a difficult middle pitch.

The corrie leading up to the Bealach na Ba has a steep step in its floor halfway up. At this point the cliffs of Meall Gorm form a long buttress, whose toe descends into the step. To the right lies a wide gully—Easy Gully.

Way Out—210m. Grade II, R. Robb and S. Young (both solo) February, 1980—is the least obvious and farthest left route on this face.

On the buttress right of Easy Gully is *Stonner Falls*—90m, Grade III/IV, (P. Anderson and K. Murphy, 5th February, 1980). This follows a rightward trending gully topped by a large cascade of ice resting on a broad terrace running the width of the face. This is the most easterly recorded route to date on the Meall Gorm cliffs.

Sgurr a'Chaorachain (792m)

Sgurr a'Chaorachain lies on the north side of the Bealach na Ba. The summit is flat, and curves south-eastwards to Loch Kishorn, sending broken slopes down towards the roadside on its south and south-eastern flanks. On the east side are two fine spurs of terraced sandstone cliffs. The main summit of the mountain stands at the base of the south spur and a subsidiary top of 774m stands 1.2km north-west along the main ridge, at the base of the north spur. Both tops can be climbed without difficulty from the road at the top of the Bealach, 800m to the west.

Any expedition along the north spur of the mountain should be undertaken with caution. Exposed, vegetated cols links the spur's five tops. If weather conditions are at all bad these can become a serious hazard to hill-walkers. In addition, both flanks of the spur drop steeply. The south-east face, which drops into the wide corrie separating the north and south spurs, is vegetated and broken. The north-west face is a series of broken, rocky buttresses.

The north spur terminates in the mountain's finest and best known

33

feature—A'Chioch of Sgurr a'Chaorachain. This is reached from the road at the mouth of the glen by following the Russel Burn to Loch Coire nan Arr from where a slanting line leads upwards to the foot of the buttress. For walkers, a pathless way leads onwards along the Allt Coire nan Arr over the Bealach nan Arr into Coire Attadale, between Beinn Bhan and Carn Dearg, and thence to the valley of the Apple-cross River.

Coire Attadale is known locally as the "Sanctuary"—probably by reason of its steep, boulder-strewn flanks, which can be seen to provide a natural protection. The west side of the corrie,-rising to the summit of Carn Dearg, is both steep and rugged. The east side gives 4.8km of slightly easier walking along the lower slopes of the long northerly spur of Beinn Bhan before connecting with the path to Applecross already mentioned.

A'Chioch, the 330m terminal tower of the north spur, is connected with the main mass by a narrow col, from which prominent gullies seam both flanks to the corrie floor. From the scree fan of the south gully, a broad heathery ledge, Middle Ledge, cuts horizontally to the right across the face. This Middle Ledge, along with the Nose of A'Chioch, are main landmarks on the south-east face. A second ledge, Upper Ledge, crosses the middle part of the face some 25m higher up.

The first climb on A'Chioch was made by Dr Collie (1906) and has been described in earlier editions of the Guide. It begins at 334m on steep grass and rounded rocks up a shallow chimney. Several other parties starting from Middle Ledge followed the same general lines. *Glover's Route*—105m. Very Difficult, (Glover and party 1908)—starts from the first grassy bay about 30m east of the gully. A series of chimneys was climbed past the left end of Upper Ledge to the next higher ledge. This was traversed right until a way upwards could be made without serious difficulty.

In August, 1961, T. W. Patey and C. J. S. Bonnington pioneered what has become one of the classic routes in Applecross—*Cioch Nose,* which in its original form gave 180m of climbing at a sustained standard of Very Difficult. As a route, it has been described as 'the finest of its category on Torridonian Sandstone'. The start is from Midway Terrace at the first of two breaks some 18m or more to the left of the true nose of the buttress (well to the right of Collie's Route). Since the route tends to keep to the edge of the nose throughout, it affords some superb situations.

Cioch Nose Variation Start—27m. Very Difficult, (H. MacInnes and T. W. Patey)—proves a better start to the original climb, beginning to the right of the normal route at a short crack where Middle Ledge becomes defined again.

Cioch Nose Direct—(T. W. Patey and H. MacInnes,) 135m. Severe, 1968—improves on the original line. It starts from Middle Ledge immediately underneath the Nose, at a big mossy dièdre. Along with *Cleavage*. 150m. Very Severe. (R. Hobbs and C. W. Dracup, June 1968) on the Lower Tier (below Middle Ledge)—it gives 300m of climbing to the summit of the buttress.

Cioch Nose—Super Direct 170m. Very Severe, (J. E. Howard and C. Rowland, May 1970) follows the obvious line of grooves and crack from the foot of the Cioch to Midway Terrace—it lies to the left of Cleavage. Combined with Cioch Nose Direct, it has been considered one of the longest and finest rock climbs in Britain.

This south-east face of A'Chioch is well explored, and has several other fine routes ranging in difficulty from Very Difficult to Very Severe. Starting on Middle Ledge, to the left of the Nose are: *Sideburn*—80m. Severe, (G. Anderson and A. Ewing, Summer 1968)—this starts from the second grassy bay up the buttress bounding the bay on the right; *Parting*—105m. Severe, (A. Ewing and F. Harper, July, 1970)—starting 6m left of the left-hand end of the low roof overhanging Middle Ledge; *Gritstone Grooves*—105m. Severe, (R. F. Allen and M. Allen, 25th May, 1969)—starting immediately left of the low overhanging roof mentioned previously. To the right of the start of Cioch Nose Direct is *Cioch Corner*—120m. Very Severe, (C. W. Dracup and R. A. Hobbs, 25th May, 1969). *The Maxilla*—135m. Very Severe, (R. A. Hobbs and C. W. Dracup, 3rd June, 1968)—starts 18m right of the Nose, at the first break right of Cioch Corner. *The Mantissa*—135m. Very Severe,(R. J. Archbold and D. Dinwoodie, October 1975)—has the same first pitch for 18m as the previous climb, then follows a line tending to the right. *African Waltz*—90m. Very Severe, (A. S. MacDonald and R. Popham, 14th April, 1971)—starts from the Upper Ledge. This is reached by climbing the first pitch of the Nose, and follows a line immediately left of the Nose. *Snothard*—85m. Very Severe, (C. W. Dracup and R. A. Hobbs, May 1969)—follows the line of grooves 6m to the left of the chimney on Cioch Nose.

The north face of A'Chioch gives two routes. *North Wall,* 285m. Hard Severe (T. W. Patey and G. B. Leslie, J. M. Taylor and J.

Morgan, May 1952). The lower section is open to variation. The upper section above Middle Ledge is 135m. The climb starts from the north-east corner of the lowest rocks. *Lap of the Gods,* 150m. Very Severe (R. How and J. R. Sutcliffe, 25th May, 1969) starts well to the right of the North Wall. It is suggested that the start is best reached by traversing the Middle Ledge into North Gully and then scrambling up the gully to the point where it becomes a steep, open chimney.

From the connecting col of A'Chioch, a steep wall rises up onto the north spur proper of Sgurr a'Chaorachain. Climbed directly, the wall is Severe—*Upper Connecting Rib* (T. W. Patey, G. B. Leslie and J. M. Taylor, 31st May, 1952). This was used by the party as a continuation of their North Wall route. Altenative routes are (a) starting up a groove at the extreme left-hand edge and then traversing right on to the face higher up (Difficult), or (b) climbing up a groove round the corner of the left, on the wall of the gully. The gully route taken by the original parties here is almost universally condemned as being foul and unpleasant.

Beyond the north face, exploration by T. W. Patey in 1952 revealed a recessed corrie with five great buttresses. Four of these have given routes ranging in length from 135m to 300m, and varying in standard from Difficult to Severe. The buttresses are numbered from left to right. No. 1 Buttress gives a 300m route *Jupiter,* Mild Severe. No. 2 Buttress has two routes, *Sinister* 150m. Very Difficult, and *Dexter* 150m. Difficult. No. 3 Buttress has an apparently impregnable centre, but the right grassy flank has been descended. No. 4 Buttress gives a 135m Difficult route, *Totem,* and No. 5 Buttress has a 150m. Severe route. *The Turret.*

The *Fourth Gully* from the left—between Totem and Turrent Butteresses—has been climbed. 150m. Grade IV. (C. Rowland and A. C. Cain, February, 1977). After the initial ice pitch, a huge cave is reached at 60m. The steep pillar on the right is climbed (crux) to easy slopes above. Continuing to where the gully forks, the left fork is taken. This leads to two short, awkward pitches and a final slope.

The south face of Sgurr a'Chaorachain has a considerable exposure of steep sandstone, but most of it lacks great continuity. Climbing is mainy concentrated on six steep ribs which rise from the roadside on the way up to the Bealach na Ba, at a point nearly opposite the waterfall. The leftmost rib, starting a mere 30m above the road, gives the original route here—*Sword of Gideon* 105m. Very Severe (T. W. Patey, October, 1961). Starting from the base of the rib, easy climbing for 45m leads to a wide ledge below the big wall which is the feature of the route—still considered to be the finest on these crags. All six ribs give climbs, the standard throughout being Severe—Very Severe. Their proximity to the roadside probably accounts for the increased activity on these crags, and it is considered that they have now reached saturation point with regard to new lines. There are now about twenty recorded routes and a number of one pitch variations to Sword of Gideon. The nature of the crags makes anything less than fully detailed route descriptions rather confusing, and the climbs are covered fully in the *Climbers' Guide to the Northern Highlands Area,* Volume II.

Beinn Bhan (896m)

Beinn Bhan is the highest point on the great sandstone plateau of Applecross, and lies on its north-eastern side. The summit is flat, and is easily reached from the Bealach na Ba, along the north-west flank of Sgurr a'Chaorachain and the intervening Bealach nan Arr (610m). Alternatively, the long south-east ridge rising from Loch Kishorn can be climbed without difficulty in any conditions. The western slopes fall gradually into the basin of Coire nan Arr which separates Beinn Bhan from Sgurr a'Chaorachain, but to the east, the mountain presents four magnificent corries separated by narrow precipitous sandstone spurs. From north to south these are: Coire nan Fhamhair (The Giant's Corrie), Coire na Poite (Corrie of the Pot), Coire na Feola (Corrie of the Flesh), and Coire 'Each (Horse Corrie). Terraced cliffs fall sheer into the middle two corries and there is no easy way down into them. Even in winter conditions, however, the head of Coire nan Fhamhair can be descended. A fifth corrie, unnamed on the O.S. map, presents a steep north-east face towards Loch Lundie from below point 2765. This is Coire Toll a'Bhein—the Corrie of the Hole of the Skin.

A good track leads into the corries from the west side of the bridge over the Kishorn River, towards Loch Gaineamhach. It keeps rather low down on the moors but can be left at any convenient point and a direct line taken upwards into the corries. Lochan na Poite lies at a height of 376m at the foot of Coire na Poite, and several hundred feet higher, two tiny lochans lie on top of a rock barrier which forms the lip of the inner corrie. Immediately behind these rises the (364m) wall of Beinn Bhan, its steep slabs broken by occasional vertical rifts and narrow terraces. The corrie is enclosed by narrow ridges with precipitous sides, their outer ends forming the great castellated buttresses which are prominent features of the mountain. The right-hand buttress is A'Phoit and the left is A'Chioch (of Beinn Bhan). The ridges can be gained by scree-slopes behind the terminal buttresses but there are difficulties in getting from there onto the summit. The general angle of the upper wall where A'Chioch joins it is at least 60 degrees and the individual slabs are steeper.

The *Upper Connecting Ridge of A'Chioch* is an unpleasant, exposed scramble in summer, in winter conditions it is Grade II (T. W. Patey and J. Brown, 1968). The *Upper Connecting Ridge of A'Phoit* is a Severe climb by any direct route (T. W. Patey, 1961). At the col behind A'Phoit one is confronted by three tiers of sandstone barring the way to the easy, more broken ridge above. These could possibly be turned on the left by a long and tedious detour on loose grass. The first sandstone tier is climbed centrally for 10m, then climb shattered blocks on the left to a wide ledge below the third tier. From here the best way looked to lie 10m left of the true nose by a clean holdless inset crack. This ends in a wet overhang, but a cramped move right across a loose flake on the slab leads with surprising suddenness to the top of the tier.

The winter route here was climbed by B. E. Goodwin, J. E. Rieve and D. Tierney, February, 1971, Grade IV.

The corrie face of A'Chioch is a grand wall of overlapping rock. Its *North Buttress* which falls towards the lower lochan was climbed by S. Paterson and D. J. Bennet, starting near the foot of a prominent chockstone gully forming the left boundary of the buttress. It gave 150m of Mild Severe climbing, trending to the right.

A'Phoit presents an unclimbable face to the corrie but the Lochan na Poite face gives 150m of climbing (Very Difficult) starting from a cairn at the foot of a short, severe wall leading to a fine 18m slab. The route then trends left and finishes back to the right and can hardly be called a genuine climb as the face is broken by ledges but with good pitches. This was first climbed in 1948 by Messrs. Parker and Young.

The *North Gully of A'Chioch* was climbed by J. Wood and I. Rettie. This is a short gully which lies just within the entrance to Coire na Poite on the wall of A'Chioch. There is a big pile of rubble at the entrance, and one climbs on loose scree broken by five chockstones, each of moderate difficulty. A pinnacle divides the gully, and the route goes left up a grassy wall. The final 35m pitch is a difficut, steep scramble. The winter ascent by A. Fyffe, M. C. MacInnes and Miss

M. Alburger, March 1969, was Grade II.

Well to the right of North Gully and high in the centre of the north face of A'Chioch is a prominent ice-filled chimney, often found to be in condition. This is *Dormouse Chimney* Grade IV (M. Foreman and J. Moreland, 4th February, 1980). The lower section leading to the Chimney may be avoided by a traverse along a good ledge from the corrie floor. Above the Chimney, an escape can be made rightwards on easy snow slopes.

The left-hand back corner of Coire na Poite contains two classic snow gullies. *March Hare's Gully*—300m. Grade IV (C. J. S. Bonnington and T. W. Patey, 1st March, 1969) is the left-hand one of the two. Its top is at the point where A'Chioch connecting ridge meets the summit plateau. There are at least ten definite ice pitches. Its companion piece—*Mad Hatter's Gully*—has also been climbed (M. Freeman and G. Stephen, 1st February, 1976) 135m Grade IV/V. The lower half of the gully is a wide, deep snow channel which is followed easily for 150m to where the gully proper starts. Steep ice grooves initially lead to an overhang which is passed by a left traverse to a ledge. A wall led to another ledge leading diagonally rightwards to gain the gully.

The buttress immediately to the left of March Hare's Gully is *Alice's Buttress*—330m Grade III/IV (R. C. Archbold and J. C. Higham, 11th February, 1978). Starting on the left side of the buttress toe, the line follows a snow ramp diagonally right to a point overlooking the gully (40m)—trend diagonally left, then climb more or less directly to a rock band at 230m. Beneath this, a traverse left leads round a nose, then go up steeply to gain the crest on the right. This is followed to meet the upper connecting ridge 45m below the plateau.

To the right of Mad Hatter's Gully is a prominent ice-fall—*Silver Tear*—300m Grade V (N. Muir and A. Paul, 12th February, 1977).

The Wall of the Early Morning Light—420m Grade IV (H. Horsfield, B. Jones, K. Spence and P. Thomas, February, 1971)—takes a central line up the back wall of the corrie. Starting at the centre of the face, it gives one of the longest routes to date along with *Moonshine* 400m Grade V (D. M. Jenkins and C. Stead, 19th February, 1978). This latter route starts below the central ice-falls on the back wall, which is climbed direct to a rock barrier at 180m. A traverse left for 45m leads into a rightward trending groove. This is followed to regain the previous line.

The left-hand wall of Coire nan Fhamhair is perhaps the most continuously steep cliff of its height on the Scottish mainland. Despite this, there are only two recorded routes here. *The Chimney*—270m Grade III (A. Nisbet and B. Sprunt, 17th February, 1979). This is the prominent steep and narrow chimney left of the very steep main cliff. The lower section overhangs continuously, and rarely, if ever, holds much ice. Consequently, this ascent involved 180m of detour along sensational snow ledges into the upper part of the Chimney. The first of the three ice pitches which followed was the crux. *Die Riesenwand—Giant's Wall* 450m Grade V (A. Nisbet and B. Sprunt 26-27th January, 1980)—takes the line of least resistance on the face between The Chimney and a huge, overhanging corner tucked away on the side of the Upper Connecting Ridge of A'Phoit. It is reported that poor protection and bewildering exposure lend an air of excitement and confirms this as an outstanding route. It was thought that the bivouac may be unnecessary in future ascents.

Coir 'Each, the most southerly of the corries of Beinn Bhan, now has three recorded routes: *Deep Gully*—195m Grade IV (D. M. Jenkins and P. F. MacDonald, February, 1978)—is the deep snow gully in the centre of the corrie. There is a large ice pitch at two-thirds height. *Skidmark Buttress*—180m. Grade III (R. Robb and S. Young, 7th February, 1980)—climbs the buttress immediately left of Deep Gully, starting at the foot of a wide groove. *Hors d'oeuvres*—150m. Grade III (P. Anderson and K. Murphy, 5th February, 1980)—follows the rightmost gully on the main face, taking a direct start.

There has undoubtedly been increased activity in Coire na Feola over recent years, but none of the routes done have been put on record so far.

With the majority of recorded climbs to date still centering around Coire na Poite, it would seem obvious that the full potential of Beinn Bhan has still to be realised. The possibilities were clearly indicated by the late T. W. Patey, one of the most active explorers in the Northern Highland area, whose comments in the 1970 S.M.C. Journal are worth preserving:- "The mountain harbours in its three great eastern corries an uninterrupted two mile succession of 180m-360m crags whose resources have scarcely been tapped. There is also a hidden far northern corrie of which little is known. The Beinn Bhan crags in area and conformation are more impressive than Corrie Arder of Creag Meaghaidh and the number of potential winter lines is perhaps doubled. The winter prospects are exciting with scope for "at least thirty Grade IV-V routes of around 300m. Because of the coastal environment, the winter climbing season is short, but snow comes more quickly into condition for climbing so that, by and large, opportunities for good ice climbing are not really much less than elsewhere."

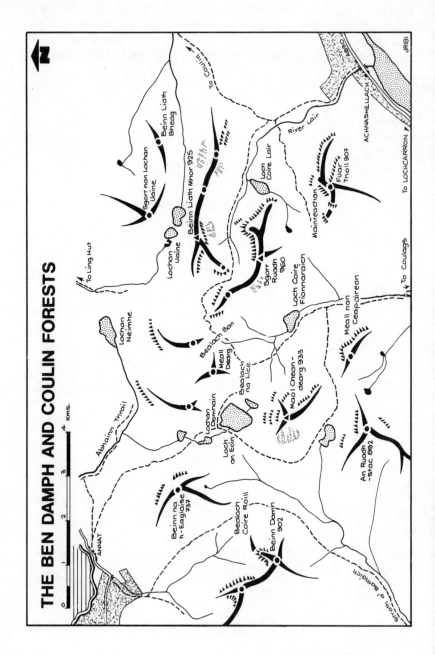

THE BEN DAMPH AND COULIN FORESTS

The Ben Damh and Coulin Forests

(1) **Beinn Damh** (902m) N.G. 893502
(2) **Maol Chean-Dearg** (933m) N.G. 924498
(3) **An Ruadh-stac** (892m) N.G. 922481
(4) **Sgurr Ruadh** (960m) N.G. 959504
(5) **Fuar Tholl** (907m) N.G. 975489
(6) **Beinn Liath Mhor** (925m) N.G. 964519
(7) **Sgorr nan Lochan Uaine** (873m) N.G. 969531
(8) **Sgurr Dubh** (782m) N.G. 979558

MAP: O.S. Sheet No. 19 Gairloch and Ullapool, Sheet No. 24 Raasay and Loch Torridon, Sheet No. 25 Glen Carron.

The mountains of the Beinn Damph and Coulin Forests lie between Glen Torridon and Glen Carron, along the southern boundary of the area of the Northern Highlands. On the west side they are separated from the Applecross peninsula by Glen Shieldaig, and on the east side they reach the line of Loch a'Chroisg and Glen Docherty, bordering on the area of the Fannichs.

The area is conveniently ringed by good motor roads which greatly facilitate the approach to the mountains. In addition, the four main villages are located on each of the corners, and these provide good facilities for accommodation, provisions, garages and other service.

Achnasheen is the main road junction from the east, and here the road from Dingwall divides for Kyle of Lochalsh and Gairloch. It is also the railhead for the latter and for Torridon. The south fork of the road leading by way of Achnasheen to Lochcarron has been largely reconstructed but several sections still remain more or less single track.

Lochcarron is an attractive village on the north shore of the loch, the largest of several small communities which stretch from Strathcarron to Ardaneaskin, and a good centre for the exploration of the mountains. The main road to the south cuts off from the

Lochcarron road some 3km east of the village. From this junction the road to Strathcarron station now continues along the south side of Loch Carron to link up with the old road at South Strome. The ferry which previously operated from North Strome, 6.5km west of Lochcarron village, no longer functions.

The road from Lochcarron north to Shieldaig has been described in the previous chapter, with its superb views into the great corries of Beinn Bhan on the Applecross Peninsula, and eastwards across the summit of the principal mountains dealt with in this chapter.

The new stretch of road east from Shieldaig to the head of Loch Torridon gives increasingly splendid views of the whole Torridon Range. It skirts the tops of numerous little bays and inlets whose names are characteristically Gaelic in origin. Farther north along the coastline, the Gaelic word 'Ob' gives way to the Norse 'Geo', showing the extent of the Viking influence along this western seaboard of the Highlands.

Just past the tiny village of Annat, at the very head of Loch Torridon, there is a junction with a branch road which passes along the north side of the loch before rising and falling spectacularly into the isolated crofting/fishing village of Diabeg. There is a new Youth Hostel here near the National Trust Information Centre. It should be noted that the Glen Cottage, 1.5km east along Glen Torridon, no longer provides bunk-house accommodation. It is also advisable to make enquiries locally regarding camping availability anywhere in the Torridon glens.

The Scottish Mountaineering Club's Ling Hut stands on the south shore of Lochan an Iasgach. It is reached by a track which leaves the road 2km to the east of Glen Cottage, opposite the entrance to Coire Dubh of Liathach and Beinn Eighe. The key is available to Club members on application to the Honorary Hut Custodian. At present this is Mr J. Anton, 'Sandpiper', 1 Craigdarroch Drive, Contin, by Strathpeffer, Tel. No. Strathpeffer 686.

The village of Kinlochewe marks the north corner of the area and is itself an excellent centre for all the surrounding mountain groups. There is a caravan and camp site at the road junction in the centre of the village, and another maintained by the Nature Conservancy at Taagan Farm, close to the main road, at the head of Loch Maree. This latter is intended for overnight stays only. Beinn Eighe towers above the village to the west, and the view along Loch Maree, with Slioch standing on its north-east shore, is superb.

The main mountain tops of the area lie within three great estates—Ben Damph, Coulin and Achnashellach—the latter is now governed mainly by the Forestry Commission. The area immediately behind Loch Carron in the south-west corner is further split amongst other smaller estates, but contains few mountains of note.

Lochcarron was established as a fishing community at the end of the 18th century and its importance in this capacity lasted into the 19th century. This has now declined, and boats generally operate from Kyle of Lochalsh. The completion of the Dingwall-Kyle of Lochalsh railways in 1865 brought a period of revitalisation to the area for a time, and it is interesting to note that this was included in the prophesies of the Brahan Seer in the early 17th century. He forcast that 'Every stream shall have its bridge, balls of fire will pass rapidly up and down Strath Peffer and carriages without horses shall leave Dingwall to cross the country from sea to sea'—A fair description of what came to pass. The land is now mainly under deer and sheep and the interior lies uninhabited.

Lochcarron has benefited greatly from an economic point of view with the development of the Kishorn construction yard. Prior to this, estate and forestry work, subsidised by crofting and the passing tourist trade, formed the main pattern of livelihood—a pattern all too familiar throughout the north.

An exceptionally fine system of cross-country tracks cover the area making for relatively easy access to the principal mountains from all directions and providing the hill walker with a variety of rewarding routes. The general line of the tracks is from north to south, connecting Glen Carron with Glen Torridon, but most of these interconnect in their middle stretches, providing lateral communication as well.

Beinn Damh (902m)

Beinn Damh is the most westerly of the mountains of this group and can be climbed without difficulty from Loch Torridon Hotel. The summit lies 4.8km south of the head of Loch Torridon and is the highest point on the 3km ridge whose western flanks rise steeply from the shores of Loch Damh. An estate road is seen to follow the foot of the slopes along the loch-side for almost 4km but the gate at the main road 800m east of Balgie Bridge is locked for private cars and the best approach to the mountain is by the track from Loch Torridon Hotel. The track leaves the road by a wicket gate beside the bridge over the

Allt Coire Roill and rises through a magnificent pinewood along the steep sides of the gorge through which the river drops in a series of fine waterfalls. Once above the tree line, the rounded dome of An Ruadh-stac looms up beyond the far end of Coire Roill, framed by the precipitous north-eastern ridge of Beinn Damh and the southern slopes of Beinn na H'Eaglaise (734m). The main track continues for 4km over the Bealach Coire Roill and then swings round the foot of the south end of Loch Damh. The bothy here is locked, and the track leading back north along the loch-side connects with the motor track to Balgie. A branch leads westwards on to the road through Glen Shieldaig.

The way on to Beinn Damh is by way of the right fork of the main track, which leaves just after the treeline and winds up steeply onto the saddle between Sgurr na Bana Mhoraire (687m) and the main top. This is marked by cairns for part of the way, but these are hardly necessary. To the left of the saddle is a wide scalloped corrie, between the main ridge and Creag na h'Iolaire. This is broken and stony but has no great continuous rock face. Creag na h'Iolaire, on the northern spur of Beinn Damh, has one recorded climb. The crag is large, impressive and rather overgrown. The route, *Aquila,* 105m. Severe (J. L. Hardy and G. Halleyard, August 1967), starts at a pinnacle belay on the lower of the two terraces that cross the crag low down. The route follows the light coloured rib bounding the crag on the left.

The ridge steepens considerably onto the summit, from where a steep, craggy shoulder drops north-eastwards into the Bealach Coire Roill. It is possible, with care, to descend the shoulder on to the bealach, but if need be an alternative descent can be made down the high corrie enclosed by the shoulder and the east face of the main ridge. This is distinctly awkward and unpleasant, involving negotiating a way through unpleasant scree slopes in the upper part of the corrie and descending a series of steepish sandstone walls in the lower part. The east face of Beinn Damh has some interesting sandstone faces, broken by deep chimneys and gullies, which could well be worth further exploration.

Maol Cheann-Dearg (933m); **An Ruadh-stac** (892m) and **Meall nan Ceapairean** (655m)

The compact group of tops formed by Maol Cheann-Dearg, An Ruadh-stac and Meall nan Ceapairean can be reached equally well

DONALD BENNET

1. *A'Chioch of Sgurr a'Chaorachain*

2. *At the Summit of Bealach na Ba*

3. *The Terraced Sandstone Cliffs of Meall Gorm; the Blue Pillar is the narrow ridge on the left*

DONALD BENNET

4.   *Coire na Feola in summer;*

5.   *And in winter*

PETER MACDONALD

DONALD BENNET

6.   *On the Cioch Nose of Sgurr a'Chaorachain*

from Annat at the head of Loch Torridon, or from the road bridge at Coulags, 7.6km, north-east of Lochcarron.

The track from the cottage at Coulags is a recognised right of way to Torridon and eventually joins with the Annat track on the north side of the Bealach na Lice, between Maol Chean-Dearg and Meall Dearg (640m). The main track follows the right-hand side of the Fionn Amhainn from the road bridge at Coulags. There is another indistinct track from the prominent lay-by on the west side of the bridge but this should be ignored. It soon runs out, and the river can only be forded with difficulty at the first big bend, in order to rejoin the main track.

The river rises in a series of rocky basins along the west side of the track and is crossed 2.4km from the road by a wooden bridge or, alternatively, by the conveniently placed line of uniformly square stepping stones just below. The track is well marked throughout and now rises steeply into the inner Coire Fionnaraich. There is a locked bothy 800m from the bridge, with an open, semi-derelict stable which could be used for shelter in emergency. Past the bothy, the curious forefinger of stone on the right-hand side of the path is Clach nan Con Fionn—The stone of Fingal's Dogs—allegedly where the giant Fionn tethered his stag-hounds when hunting in the glen. Beyond this the track forks, the main track continuing over the head of the corrie, and a branch climbing steeply to the west to a height of 580m onto the flat saddle which connects the three mountains on this side of the glen.

From the saddle, the track is seen to continue downwards along the west side of Maol Cheann-Dearg, past Loch Coire an Ruadh-stac. From the floor of the U-shaped corrie which holds the loch, it disappears round the northern side of Maol Cheann-Dearg to reach its junction with the Bealach na Lice track at the north end of Loch an Eoin. From this junction, the track continues north-westwards between Beinn na L'Eaglaise and Meall Dearg to Annat, at the head of Loch Torridon. The approach from the Annat side to the north face of An Ruadh-stac probably requires less effort and provides equally fine views of the mountains. The saddle is the junction of the summit ridges of all three tops and gives an easy means of ascent. The mountains are generally of Torridonian sandstone interfolded with Cambrian quartzite.

The summit of Meall nan Ceapairean rises a further 61m to the south-east of the saddle, and though steep and rocky on its eastern side above the Coire Fionn path, is mainly of interest as another view-point for the mountains lying on the east side of the corrie and to the south across the Attadale forest. From here Fuar Tholl and Sgurr Ruadh are seen as a continuous ridge which never drops below 610m, sweeping round northwards into the Bealach Ban. Beyond them rises the summit of Beinn Liath Mhor, 5km, and more distant across the intervening Coire Lair.

Two short buttress climbs are reported on the quartz cliffs on the east side of this south-east ridge, the standard being Difficult and the climbing pleasant. The two biggest buttresses are about 122m. The left-hand buttress is *Ketchil Buttress* (H. M. Brown and D. Macnab, 29th December, 1969). The right-hand buttress is unnamed, but found to be cairned, and probably has been climbed.

The north-west ridge leads on to Maol Chean-Dearg, with preciptious faces to the north and to the east above the head of Coire Fionn. The ridge is easily climbed onto the summit; the western flanks above Loch Coire an Ruadh-stac have no noteworthy rock faces and provide reasonable access. The view from the summit across onto the ridges of Torridon is panoramic, and given clear visibility, the peaks of the Letterewe Forest beyond Loch Maree can be easily picked out.

Maol Cheann-Dearg gives some climbing on its steep north side which overlooks Loch an Eoin. A conspicuous light-coloured quartzite cliff starts some 150m above the loch-side. This has a horizontal ledge one-third of the way up, and two big leftward leading ramps resembling staircases near the top. *No Birds,* 100m. Very Difficult (K. Schwartz, 1st August, 1971), starts below the right-hand staircase. *But Midges,* 110m Severe (Miss M. Horsburgh and K. Schwartz) starts below the left-hand staircase. Also on this north side of the mountain is *Hidden Gully* (H. M. Brown, R. J. Rankin and R. Aitken, 22nd December, 1968). The right side of the 300m gully forms the edge of the north face. It is reported that in good conditions it would give a Grade II climb with fine situations.

An Ruadh-stac (890m)

The south-west ridge from the saddle leads onto An Ruadh-stac, which, unlike the remainder of the mountains surrounding it, is composed mainly of quartzite. The way to the foot of the summit ridge leads past one of those lively deep-coloured lochans which one comes to expect in every mountain col in the north. From here the ascent looks forbiddingly steep but at close quarters presents a scrambling route over large quartzite blocks. In winter these require care. The south-east face is of long slopes of highly polished quartzite which give a more interesting scramble on to the summit.

The north face of the mountain is by far the most rewarding and rises in two tiers of 100m giving excellent rock for climbing with an abundance of holds. Two routes are recorded here. *North Face* 180m Very Difficult (T. W. Patey and C. J. S. Bonington, August, 1960), starts at a prominent slabby rib just left of an obvious white scar on the lower tier. This gives 90m of delightful climbing. The direct continuation was by-passed and the start of the climb on the upper tier lies 30m to the left, going diagonally leftwards for 45m to a big recess and a spike belay. Exit on left side of recess then straight up for 30m to easier rocks and scrambling. *Foxtrot* 180m Mild Severe (D. Stone and B. T. Hill, 21st August, 1967) lies to the right of North Face route on an ill-defined buttress of ribs and grooves to the left of a large black cave on the bottom terrace.

The descent from the mountains back to Coulag is best made by retracing the track. A line down the west side of the south face of An Ruadh-stac involves circumnavigating some awkward rock walls and the way is further blocked by the deep ravine of the Allt Ruigh Sleigheich, 1.6km south-east across the lower hill-side. It is best to follow the wire fence directly down the north side of the gap to the Fionn Amhainn in the Coulag glen. It is difficult to cross over to join the main track and one is forced to take a rather boggy line along the west bank of the river to the bridge.

Fuar Tholl (907m) and Sgorr Ruadh (958m)

Fuar Tholl rises conspicuously above Achnashellach station at the head of Glen Lair and, along with Sgorr Ruadh, forms a 5km ridge (whose crest never drops below the 610m contour) running north-westwards between Coire Fionnaraich and Coire Lair. The climb on to the saddle between the two mountains can easily be made up the steep grassy western slopes rising from Coire Fionnaraich, but this holds little interest. The best approach is from Achnashellach station, 4.8km east of Coulag Bridge. There is a private hostel 1.6km to the east of the station, where accommodation is available for climbers. The hostel lies on the south side of the road and is open all year. A side road leads past the keeper's house, crossing the railway line a few metres west of the station platform. The track into Glen Lair branches west through the young trees; an unsurfaced motor track branches right through a wooden gate. This will be described later. The track leads up through the wild magnificent scenery of Coire Lair, following the course of the River Lair along its right-hand side. The river follows a turbulent course down through a deep narrow gorge, broken frequently by waterfalls and bordered by distorted pine trees. It is a formidable barrier to cross and one is advised to keep to the well surfaced tracks. After 2.4km of steady climbing, the path reaches a junction at the wide mouth of the upper corrie. A right-hand fork leads up on to the saddle between Carn Eite and the main Beinn Liath Mhor Ridge, then continues eastward along the Easan Dorcha to meet with the motor track previously mentioned.

Sgorr Ruadh has an impressive north face which throws out several distinct buttresses separated by narrow couloirs. The most northerly of these, Raeburn's Buttress, is the highest, and forms the skyline on the approach fom Glen Lair. This is separated from the two more southerly buttresses by a wide couloir whose steep upper section is usually corniced in winter. The longest of the two southerly buttresses is named Academy Ridge. Next to it is *Robertson's Buttress,* with a steep intervening gully named Robertson's Gully. The last named buttress gave the earliest route on the mountain. It was ascended, partly by rocks and partly by the gully on the right, by A. E. Robertson in 1898.

Robertson's Gully—80m Grade IV (A. Nisbet and N. Spinks, 31st January, 1976) was climbed direct through a series of chockstone filled chimneys to a deep cave half way up. This was avoided on the right and the gully re-entered by the higher of two traverse lines above the cave.

Academy Ridge has 300m of climbing (Very Difficult) pioneered by the Inverness Academy Climbing Club in 1948. The lower section is scrambling; the buttress proper starts at 518m and the upper section narrows, giving more difficult climbing. A high corrie with a wide couloir at the back separates Academy Ridge from Raeburn's Buttress. Three gullies here give climbs. The narrow, well-defined gully on the left is *Post-Box Gully* 180m Grade II (A. Fyffe, March, 1969). The narrow gully to the right of the couloir is *Brown Gully* 105m Grade II (A. Fyffe, 1969). *Easy Gully,* Grade I (J. Cleare and P. Gillman, 1969) lies half-way across the right-hand wall of the corrie, just to the right of an isolated pinnacle.

High on the left wall of the Central Couloir, just below and opposite Brown Gully, is a large, two-tiered ice-fall which forms below a narrow gully. This is *High Gully* 120m Grade III (M. Hillman and A. Nisbet, 1st February, 1976). The route climbs the ice-fall and gully, avoiding the upper step on the right and entering the gully by a chimney.

Raeburn's Buttress, 360m Difficult, was first climbed in April 1904 in winter conditions by H. Raeburn and E. B. Robertson. The lower rocks are extremely steep but can be avoided by the chimney on the left for 25m. The ridge is regained by a ledge traverse to the right, 90m of difficult climbing follows to a col from which easier rocks lead to the summit plateau. The top of the mountain lies 800m north-west, across a dip of a hundred or so metres.

Raeburn's Buttress Direct Grade IV (W. D. Brooker and S. H. Wilkinson, 20th December, 1967) takes a line up the steep profile of the buttress as seen from the Coire Lair approach path. A chimney lying just right of centre divides the steep face. The line of the climb began at an embayment just right of a small tongue of broken rock at the lowest rocks.

Raeburn's Buttress occupies the angle between the north-east and north faces of Sgorr Ruadh and is seen in profile with a steep north-east wall, bounded on the right by a deep, scree-filled gully. Behind this is *Upper Buttress,* 210m. Very Difficult (I. H. Ogilvie and P. M. Francis, 1955). The winter ascent, 270m Grade III (P. Nunn and A. Riley, February, 1972) was thought to be probably partly in common with the original route. This is the last considerable rock face in the glen. On the left edge of the buttress a series of overhangs, and on the right, are steep rocks and a prominent pinnacle—*The Frivolous Pinnacle* (Very Difficult). Between these is a face, rather less steep, broken by a series of vertical cracks. The line goes up a 3m corner near the overhangs, then traverses 15m to the cracks. It continues more or less straight up the buttress with slight traverses. The north wall of Raeburn's Buttress was climbed in 1961 by T. W. Patey—*Splintery Edge,* 120m Very Difficult. A deep chasm separates Raeburn's Buttress from Upper Buttress and the wall of Raeburn's Buttress, which hems in this chasm on the left, is nearly vertical for well over a hundred metres. The rock is very shattered and there is less scope than might be apparent. The route comes out exactly at the subsidiary top of Sgorr Ruadh, the culminating point of Raeburn's Buttress proper.

The main track continues for 5km, crosses the head of the corrie, and traverses the north side of the ridge back into the head of Coire Fionnaraich by way of the Bealach Ban. This joins with the right-of-way track previously described leading through the Bealach na Lice to Annat, in Glen Torridon. The west fork of the Coire Lair track leads steeply upwards onto the 671m saddle between Fuar Tholl and Sgorr Ruadh and from here either summit is easily reached.

Fuar Tholl radiates three spurs, one north, one south, and one south-east. These contain the mountain's main rock features. The south-east ridge has a precipitous *Nose,* prominent from lower Coire Lair. This was climbed in 1961 by T. W. Patey, giving a 150m route (Very Severe). It was found to be exposed and vegetated throughout and offered no escape. An alternative line here, more or less up the centre of the buttress, gives a steep, sustained climb on excellent, clean rock (D. Dinwoodie and B. Lawrie, S.M.C.J. 1973). The right-most section of the south-east spur is seamed by three parallel gullies. The rib to the left of the left-most of these has been climbed—*The Pile* 120m Grade II (P. Christie and P. Macdonald, 24th January, 1971).

High above the south-east and the south spurs, immediately below the summit of the mountain, is a small corrie with continuous 150m cliffs on its west flanks. These are the South-East Cliffs, first climbed in 1933 by Messrs. Ludwig and Maclennan, the standard then being Severe. (In the Climbers Guide to the Northern Highlands, Vol. II, the nomenclature has been amended and this feature is now called the Upper Cliff. New climbs on Fuar Tholl reported in recent S.M.C. Journals still retain the old name, South East Cliff). The cliffs have several routes recorded between 150m-200m ranging in difficulty from Very Difficult to Hard Very Severe.

All but one of these were climbed by H. MacInnes and party, 1969. The most recent route recorded is *Fuar Folly* (R. J . Archibald and D. M. Nichols, 19th February, 1978) noted as 225m Grade V—climbed on hard snow. The routes are described in detail in Vol. II of the Climbers Guide to the Northern Highland Area.

The small buttress on the right hand end of the face—*Right End Buttress*—gives 75m of climbing. The buttress can be climbed anywhere; the standard varies between Difficult to Severe, according to the line taken. First recorded by M. Boysen, 1969. The winter route starts right of the lower rocks, right of a huge over-hanging chimney—165m Grade III (W. S. McKerrow and D. M. Nichols, 22nd February, 1976).

Between the north and south-east spurs lies the Mainreachan Buttress—a superb buttress of terraced sandstone which is seen to hang perpendicularly above a tiny lochan on the north face of Fuar Tholl. The climbing here is generally considered to be amongst the best on sandstone to be found anywhere in the country. The original route here—*Enigma Route,* Severe (W. J. Cole, J. R. Marshall and I. Oliver 1952)—is on the outer, north-east face, starting at the left end of the lowest terrace. To the left of this are three grooves. The first of these gives a 75m climb (Very Severe)—*Nimrod* (G. Anderson, J. R. Brumfitt and P. Macdonald, 3rd August, 1968). The route does not continue beyond the terrace, from where one can walk off. The second groove, the lower section of which was first climbed in the early 1960s by C. S. M. Doake and P. N. L. Tranter, gives *Nebula* 150m Severe (D. Barr and P. Macdonald, 17th June, 1971).

To the right of the *Original Route,* starting at the cairn near the right-hand end of the lowest terrace on the outer face, is *Sleuth* 220m Mild Very Severe (I. Clough and H. MacInnes, 1969). This is the longest line on the buttress. Moving further to the right on this face, a series of parallel, leftward-slanting gangways give the start of three fine routes climbed by M. Boysen and D. Alcock in 1969—*Investigator,* 140m Hard Severe, is a steep and exposed climb on the right-hand end; *Snoopy* 190m Hard Very Severe, starts near the middle of the face; *Sherlock* 210m Very Severe, starts at the third gangway, below and parallel to Snoopy.

The more recently recorded routes here are: *Direct Route,* 180m Severe, and *All the Way,* 150m Hard Very Severe, both climbed by R. Sharp and G. Shields, June 1972. Both were said to be of a more direct nature than earlier lines.

Direct Route starts at the right-hand end of the nose at a recess which continues as a groove. *All the Way* starts on the shelf below Investigator and takes a direct line to the obvious nose at the top of the cliff, finishing as the last pitch of Investigator. *Private eye* 180m Hard Very Severe (M. Boysen, P. Braithwaite and P. Nunn, April, 1974) climbs the buttress in the centre, through an obvious black cave at half height. The start is down to the right of Snoopy at the next gangway trending leftwards.

Beinn Liath Mhor (924m)

Beinn Liath Mhor forms a 3.2km ridge along the north side of Coire Lair and can be easily climbed from the branch track to Easan Dorcha, already mentioned. It is of more interest geologically than from a climbing point of view. Here, the Red Torridonian sandstone and White Cambrian quartzite have been folded together in a complex pattern which can be traced on the rather bare sides of the mountains. The buttress to the west of the long gully trailing down into Coire Lair provides a moderate route of sorts, but more recent exploration of other outcrops here report on them as providing better sport.

The ridge can be included in a circuit over the tops of Sgorr Ruadh and Fuar Tholl, giving a long, high-level walk of over 14km with a steep drop of 457m into the bealach at the head of the corrie. Here the small rock tower can be climbed or turned on the left at the discretion of the individual, but care should be taken in any choice of route down from the Beinn Liath Mhor ridge from below the summit. Several parties have got into difficulties here.

An alternative expedition is to include the ridge in a traverse over the summits of Sgorr nan Lochan Uaine (865m) and Sgurr Dubh (782m) These form a 5km broken ridge running at right angles from Beinn Liath Mhor towards Loch Clair in Glen Torridon. They can either be traversed in conjunction with the latter mountain, or climbed directly from the road through Glen Torridon whence they rise in a series of broken sandstone terraces. To the east they enclose the three open corries which form the sanctuary of the deer forest, and to the west a track from the Ling Hut follows their lower slopes up onto the bealach at the head of Coire Lair. This is shown as stopping some 2½km short of the bealach but in fact reappears intermittently further on. The ascent of the ridge gives a fine view west of the heathered ridge and eastwards across to the mountains on the south side of Glen Carron.

There is one vehicle road crossing the area to the east of the principal mountains, but this is private for the greatest part of the length. From Achnashellach station it crosses the Coulin pass and then follows the River Coulin down along the wooded shores of Loch Coulin and Loch Clair to reach the Glen Torridon road at a point 5km west of Kinlochewe. The Achnashellach Forest is now controlled by the Forestry Commission, but the Coulin Forest is in private hands, and through vehicle traffic is not permitted. There is a locked gate across the road on the Coulin Pass. In addition, a section of the road, just past the first bridge at the Achnashellach end, has been washed away and, although repaired, is not considered to be road-worthy by the Forestry Commission who hold that section of the ground. The proprietors have agreed upon a right-of-way for walkers, and the path should on no account be omitted from any exploration of the area. The views through the trees from the lochs onto the white-quartzite capped peaks of Torridon are magnificent and provide one of the finest spectacles in the Northern Highlands. The old right-of-way track to Kinlochewe continues along the north side of Loch Maree past Letterewe to Poolewe, once a main port for the cattle trade from the Outer Isles. Roy's Military Survey Map of Scotland, 1747-55, records the route. The map was unpublished, but can be consulted in the British Museum. It presents a valuable source of information on old roads and tracks in the Highlands.

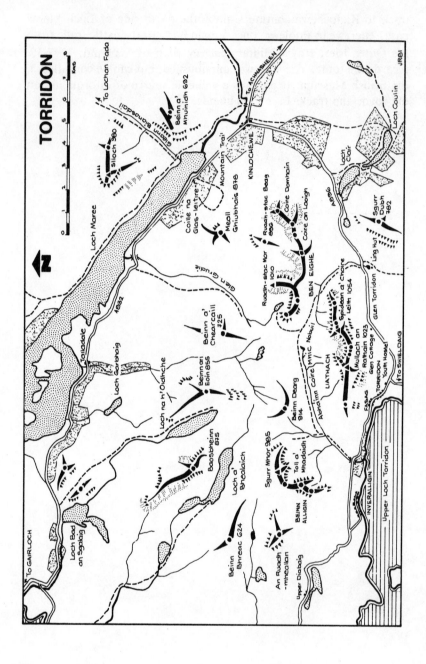

3

Torridon

(1) **Beinn Eighe** (1010m) N.G. 952612
(2) **Liathach** (1054m) N.G. 929579
(3) **Beinn Alligin** (985m) N.G. 866613
(4) **Beinn Dearg** (914m) N.G. 896608
(5) **Baosbheinn** (875m) N.G. 871654
(6) **Beinn an Eoin** (855m) N.G. 905647
(7) **Beinn a'Chearcaill** (725m) N.G. 931638

MAPS:O.S. 1:50.000 (2nd Series) Sheet No. 19—Gairloch and Ullapool, Sheet No. 24—Raasay and Loch Torridon, Sheet No. 25—Glen Carron.
O.S. 1.25.000 Outdoor Leisure Map—The Cuillins and Torridon Hills.

This chapter deals with the mountains to the north side of Glen Torridon, lying in the Torridon and Flowerdale Forest—an area which has been frequently described as 'exhibiting more of mountain beauty than any other district of Scotland, including Skye'. Here the majestic sculptured sandstone first encountered in the easten cliffs and corries of Applecross is on a greater and more majestic scale, further enhanced by the distinctive quartzite capping which forms a great broken skyline along the length of the southern ridges.

The area is bounded on its east side by the length of Loch Maree, and to the west and south-west by Loch Torridon. The northern boundary stretches from the west side of Loch Maree to the head of Loch Gairloch.

The main mountains of Torridon lie within the south-eastern corner of the area and are easily approached by the two main roads which pass north and west from their junction at Kinlochewe.

The road west through Glen Torridon to the head of the loch has already been described. From the road junction before Torridon village, it branches towards Loch Carron giving easy access from the south. Past Torridon village, a branch road continues along the north shores of Loch Torridon as far as Diabeg, a crofting-cum-fishing village with a wonderful setting on the bay formed by Loch Diabeg, an inlet of Loch Torridon. The origin of the name Diabeg is obviously Norse—'Djup-vik' (or 'Deep-Bay') and although the Vikings never really settled in this part of Wester Ross they certainly raided the coastline here. Shieldaig on the south side of Loch Torridon also shows the Norse influence in the origin of its name—'Sild-Vik' (or 'herring bay'). The road stops here, but a path continues around the coastline for 11km to Red Point, giving a worth-while walking route. The way goes past Craig where there is a Youth Hostel in an isolated cottage half a mile inland, approachable only by moorland path. Even cyclists would find this hostel difficult of access. From the crofting village of Red Point a motor road leads on towards Gairloch.

The road north from Kinlochewe follows the side of Loch Maree for more than 16km through some of the most picturesque scenery in an area renowned for its scenery. From either side of the loch, great mountain ridges rise upwards; to the west those of Torridon and to the east those of Slioch and Beinn Lair. The view is especially fine aproaching Kinlochewe from the head of Glen Docherty on the way from Achnasheen; it is unfortunate that this has been marred slightly in recent years by the rather ugly low slung electric cables which have been strung along the roadway.

The shoreline of Loch Maree was at one time entirely wooded, but now only remnants of the Old Caledonian Pine Forest remain. The north shore, which was once covered with oak trees, was burned long ago to provide fuel for the iron smelting industry carried on here around 1700. The track along the north shore from Letterewe was used by smelters to carry fuel and is a long established right of way. The Pine Forest along the south shore lies within the Beinn Eighe Nature Reserve, and here the study of regeneration of the existing forestland is one of the main projects.

Loch Maree itself is named after the Celtic Saint Maelrubha, who lies buried in Applecross churchyard. The Saint's influence here was very strong, and the Holy Isle Maree, one of the many lovely wooded islets along its northern reaches, has a well which is supposed to cure insanity. As late as 1858 the treatment was applied to a 'mad' woman who became a raging lunatic afterwards. In 1868 the same treatment cured a male lunatic. Coins were struck into a sacred tree beside the well as an offering to the spirits, and even Queen Victoria observed the custom on her visit here in 1877. The rites carried out on the island until well into the 17th century were a strange mixture of Christianity and Paganism, involving the sacrifice of bulls to Saint Maelrubha.

These practices caused great concern to the Church and feature frequently in the old records of the Presbytery of Dingwall. The local smith, who killed the bull, was always given the head in payment—an old Druid Rite.

Beinn Alligin

(1) **Meall an Laoigh** (885m) Un-named on 1:50.000 map; 5.6km W.N.W. of Torridon N.G. 857598.
(2) **Tom na Gruagaich** (992m); 660m N.N.E. of 1. N.G. 859601.
(3) **Sgurr Mhor** (The highest peak, also known as **Sgurr na Tuaich** or **Hatchet Peak**) (985m) 1.3km N.N.E. of 1 N.G. 866613.
(4) **The Rathains of Alligin** (866m) 800m N of E from 3.

Beinn Alligin is the most westerly of the Torridon group, and though its proportions fall slightly short of those of Beinn Eighe and Liathach, its splendid ridge contains several fine individual features which makes the traverse of the mountain a good introductory exercise for the longer and more varied expeditions provided by the former two.

The ridge of Beinn Alligin curves inland above the new road from Torridon to Diabeg to form the west side of Coire Mhic Nobuil. The new road to Diabeg climbs above the old road to Torridon and continues westwards for over 1½km to cross the Amhainn Coire Mhic Nobuil by a stone bridge. This marks the start of the easiest approach to Beinn Alligin, Beinn Dearg and the north side of Liathach. A convenient car-park has been constructed beside the bridge and the starting point is prominently signposted.

A track leads up through the pine trees on the right-hand side of the river to a wooden bridge just above the junction of the Allt a'Bhealaich. The left-hand fork now follows the right-hand side of this stream north towards the Bealach a'Chomhla between Beinn Alligin and Beinn Dearg, crossing a second bridge higher up, and continuing along the left-hand side of the water into the pass on the 381m contour. The right-hand fork from the first bridge leads eastwards between Beinn Dearg and the northern corries of Liathach, and eventually links with the track through Coire Dubh from the Glen Torridon road. The track onto the pass gives good walking and the 4km from the road is easily covered in just over one hour.

The traverse of the Alligin ridge from this north-east end makes what is undoubtedly the most interesting expedition. The eastern spur can be climbed by its south-east corner to the sky-line. This involves some scrambling, but alternative lines involving no rock-work can easily be found. The way along the ridge is now well marked, and between here and the main top, Sgurr Mhor, passes over the 'Horns of Alligin'. These three rocky pinnacles offer a pleasant variation and give no great difficulty but, if need be, they can be by-passed at a lower level across the steep grassy slope on the south side. Two easy winter climbs are recorded here on the Horns of Alligin. *Deep South Gully*—250m Grade I—is the deep gully on the north-east face. It goes up to the gap between the first and second horns—the first horn is the lowest one, at the south-east end. *Deep North Gully*—250m Grade II—is the other deep gully going up the gap between the second and third horns.

Between Sgurr Mhor and Tom na Gruagaich, the Cleft of Beinn Alligin plunges down into the corrie of Toll a'Mhadaidh for a depth of 549m. The west wall of the Cleft has areas of clean rock which could give climbing; the east wall is entirely vertical. The corrie itself contains a remarkable deposit of gigantic boulders, some of which reach fantastic proportions. Continuing along the ridge, the traverse southwards over Tom na Gruagaich and Meall an Laoigh is straightforward. The views from here extend from Ardnamurchan to Cape Wrath and from Skye to the Outer Hebrides, as fine as one can obtain from any point in the area.

In contrast to its northern and eastern aspects, Beinn Alligin falls down to the west towards Diabeg in a series of long grassy slopes which continue round on to the southern end of the ridge. If need be, these can be descended. The usual line down is by the way of the steep slope between Tom na Gruagaich and Meall an Laoigh, following the stream which falls into Coire an Laoigh. This bends to the east at its lower end and it is advisable to leave it at an appropriate point to take a direct line cross-country back down to the bridge over the Amhainn Coire Mhic Nobuil.

It is strongly advised that parties inexperienced in serious mountaineering should not attempt descending from the summit ridges of Beinn Alligin into the Toll a'Mhadaidh. A safe escape route from the summit of the mountain is to descend the main ridge a short distance in a southerly direction past the Cleft until the ridge levels off. From here, turn westwards and descend the large open, steady-angled, grassy corrie which forms the western flank of Sgurr Mhor. Continue down to the 610m contour and its mouth, and then contour the base of the mountain, first in a south-west, then in a southerly direction, across trackless terrain to reach the deer fence. From here the line of the road is in sight. It is also worth remembering that the mountain is prone to avalanche in winter.

Beinn Dearg

(1) **Main top** (913m) 4.8km N. of Torridon N.G. 896608
(2) **Stuc Loch na Cabhaig** (852m) 800m N. of 1. N.G. 891616
(3) **Carn na Feola** (761m) 2km E. of 1. N.G. 915611.

Beinn Dearg lies across the Bealach a'Chomhla to the east of Beinn Alligin and, like that mountain, tends to be over-shadowed by the neighbouring ridges of Liathach and Beinn Eighe. It is easiest approached by the track leading from the road bridge over the Amhainn Coire Mhic Nobuil already described and from here the south and west sides rise in a continuous precipitous escarpment which at first glance seems impregnable. Fortunately, the walls are breached in several places by rock gullies and, while these offer a way onto the summit ridge with varying degrees of difficulty, caution should be exercised at all times. The ridge leads eastwards over a rocky tower to its eastern end and the descent to the watershed at the head of Coire Dubh Mhor is made by threading a way through the out-crops of the south-east slope to join the Coire Dubh track to Glen Torridon. An alternative descent can be made from the summit cairn on the south side by any of the three chimneys which cut the line of the escarpment at this point. The spurs between these offer a detour to the side when the gullies themselves become too perpendicular. From the ridge there are exceptionally fine views into the nearby northern corries of Liathach.

In poor visibility, Beinn Dearg should be approached with caution. Sound navigation is required to negotiate a route around the sandstone exposures and in adverse weather this is not a hill for an inexperienced party.

Baosbheinn (875m)

Baosbheinn, an equally fine mountain, lies in the Flowerdale deer forest 4km to the north of Beinn Alligin and Beinn Dearg. Like the neighbouring peak, Beinn an Eoin (855m), it loses much of its individuality by reason of its proximity to the greater ranges in the southern part of Torridon. The approach is normally made from the road to Gairloch along Loch Maree, starting at a point 6½km north from Loch Maree Hotel where a bridge crosses a neck of water between Feur-Loch and Loch Bad an Sgalaig. A track leads south-eastwards towards Loch na h'Oidhche for some 6.4km and the climb onto the ridge of Baosbheinn on the west side, or that of Beinn an Eoin on the east, can easily be made from the north end of the loch. Both mountains reach their highest point at the south end of their respective ridges and fall down steeply in that direction. There is an estate maintained bothy—Poca Buidhe—at the south end of Loch na h'Oidhche on the slopes of Beinn an Eoin—this is usually kept locked. Baosbheinn has a prominent cliff face on its southwest side, under the top west of the summit, but this appears so far to have been considered unclimbable.

Beinn a'Chearcaill (724m)

Beinn a'Chearcaill lies on the opposite side of Strath Lungard from Beinn an Eoin and the approach route to both mountains can be made by a path from the roadside opposite Loch Maree Hotel. This follows the west side of the River Talladale through forestry plantations for almost 3.2km before petering out. From here there is a choice of line on to either summit ridge. Beinn a'Chearcaill is probably best approached, however, by the better-known track from Grudie Bridge which leads towards the north corries of Beinn Eighe. All three mountains provide fine view points for the surrounding area; the outlook from Beinn a'Chearcaill across onto the great rock buttresses of Coire Mhic Fhearchair on Beinn Eighe being especially noteworthy.

Liathach

(1) **Stuc a'Choire Dhuibh Bhig** (914m) N.G. 942582
(2) **Bidein Toll a'Mhuic** (833m) N.G. 941581
(3) **Stob a'Coire Liath Mhor** (983m) N.G. 933581
(4) **Spidean a'Choire Leith** (1054m) the highest point; 3.6km E.N.E. of Torridon N.G. 929579
(5) **Am Fasarinen** (927m)—a range of pinnacles lying S.W. of 4. N.G. 924575
(6) **Mullach an Rathain** (1023m) 1.6km W. of 4. N.G. 912577
(7) **Northern Pinnacles** (953m) N.G. 914579
(8) **Meall Dearg** (855m) Close N.E. of 6 but across the Northern Pinnacles N.G. 917582
(9) **Sgorr a'Chadail** (700m) 2.4km W. of 6 N.G. 894580.

Liathach is the name given to the whole range of seven tops which stretches for almost 8km from west to east along the north side of Glen Torridon. Like Beinn Alligin, it is now under the management of the National Trust for Scotland. On its eastern flank it is separated

PETER MACDONALD

7. *Crux Pitch of Mad Hatter's Gully; Beinn Bhan*

8.   *The Mainreachan Buttress of Fuar Tholl*

DONALD BENNET

9. *Fuar Tholl from Glen Carron*

10. *Sgorr Ruadh, Lochcarron*

11. *At the head of Loch Torridon looking towards the Achnashellach Hills and Beinn na H-Eaglaise (Right)*

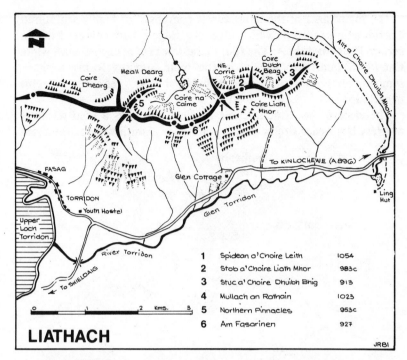

1	Spidean a'Choire Leith	1054
2	Stob a'Choire Liath Mhor	983c
3	Stuc a'Choire Dhuibh Bhig	913
4	Mullach an Rathain	1023
5	Northern Pinnacles	953c
6	Am Fasarinen	927

LIATHACH

JR81

from Beinn Eighe by Coire Dubh. Its western ridge drops down towards the head of upper Loch Torridon and on the north-east side it is separated from Beinn Alligin and Beinn Dearg by Coire Mhic Nobuil.

The steepness of the southern slopes is greatly accentuated by their proximity to the road from Kinlochewe through Glen Torridon which passes right along the foot of the ridge and consequently fore-shortens the view. From this side, the summit can be reached by several routes with varying degrees of difficulty. There are described later.

The north side of Liathach is undoubtedly the most magnificent. Here the ridge drops down into three fine corries; Coire Dubh Beag—to the north-east above Coire Dubh; the north-east corrie from the main top, Coire Dubh Mor; and Coire na Caime—The Crooked Corrie. The latter is the finest feature on the range. It is bounded on the east by the north ridge leading from the main top, Spidean a'Choire Leith. To the west, by the ridge from Mullach an Rathain to Meall Dearg, conspicuously broken by the Northern Pinnacles. Its headwall is backed by the jagged skyline of the Fasarinen Pinnacles.

The main mass of the mountain is composed of highly-sculptured Torridonian sandstone which gives the ridge a rosy coloured tint in certain light conditions. The four highest peaks are capped with white Cambrian quartzite, which on the main summit forms a sharp symmetrical cone of loose angular blocks requiring careful negotiation.

The eastern top, Stuc a'Choir Dhuibh Bhig, has a bold terminal buttress but easier slopes on the south side. South-west of the main

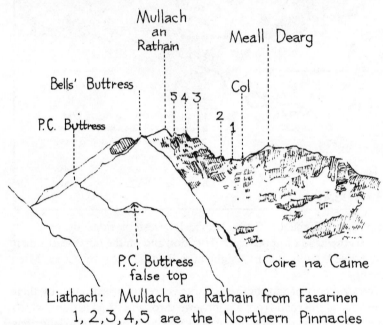

Liathach: Mullach an Rathain from Fasarinen
1, 2, 3, 4, 5 are the Northern Pinnacles

Fig. 1. North Face of Liathach.

summit, the ridge narrows for almost half a mile over the Fasarinen Pinnacles. In summer these are of no great difficulty, requiring only a good head. There is a certain amount of exposure on the north side of the pinnacles but there are plenty of good holds to compensate. In good conditions this section can be avoided if need be by a path on the south side at a lower level; in winter the pinnacles usually have to be taken direct.

From Mullach an Rathain a north-east spur leads over the jagged Northern Pinnacles of Liathach to Meall Dearg. The Pinnacles require a certain amount of rock climbing technique and should be left strictly alone by parties with no such experience. The spur can be misleading to ridge-walking parties in the event of poor visibility and its existence should be kept well in mind. The main ridge westwards from Mullach an Rathain is now uniformly broad and grassy and gives no further difficulty. There is an easy descent by the north-west slope from Sgorr a'Chadail to the Coire Mhic Nobuil path and thence to the road bridge.

Suggested Routes on to the Liathach Ridge:

1. The most used starts from the Torridon road, between the bridge over the Allt a'Choire Dubh Mhoir and Glen Cottage, making more or less directly to a point just west of Stuc a'Choire Dhuibh Bhig. There are no difficulties between here and the main top.

2. Up the east side of the stream which descends due south of the main top.

3. Via Coire Leith, south-east of the main top. The rock terraces are skirted on the left and the route requires some degree of judgment.

4. By the course of the Allt an Tuill Bhain due south of Mullach an Rathain. The approach from the road past the camp site in the pine trees leads up over sloping sandstone pavements into a wide grassy corrie. Grassy tongues penetrate the upper screes and lead onto the ridge.

5. By the prominent stone-shoot leading up onto the summit ridge to a point 400m west by south of Mullach an Rathain. This and the previous route are also useful means of descent. The upper portion of the stone-shoot is now greater loosened and requires care if used by a party.

6. The south-east ridge of Mullach an Rathain gives a fine, slightly exposed scramble onto the ridge. The upper 150m is especially interesting and is broken by several small pinnacles. This upper section could be graded Moderate and requires some care, but any difficulties encountered can be avoided to the east.

7. Up the scree slope at the head of Coire Dubh Beag to the main ridge between Stuc a'Choire Dhuibh Bhig and Bidein Toll a'Mhuic. This is reached by the track through Coire Dubh from the road bridge.

8. By a continuous scree-slope to the north-west of Spidean a'Choire Leith which runs up from Coire na Caime. This can be approached by either the Coire Dubh track or the track from Coire Mhic Nobuil.

9. The north-west slope onto Sgorr a'Chadail from the Coire Mhic Nobuil.

Descent from the ridge requires great care—especially so in winter or in bad visibility. The steep south side has few easy exits. The quickest descent from the summit of Spidean a'Choire Leith is to descend the boulder field arête of the main ridge eastwards to the first col (or notch) before reascent has to be made. From this col a small steep scree gully is descended by its true right (west) flank into the floor of the basin of the upper 'hanging' Coire Leith.

In summer, one should cross the floor of the basin eastwards to strike the rim of the rock band which isolates the upper corrie from the larger one below, approximately at mid-point—where it is at its least height. This point is now prominently cairned. The rock band should be descended here by a 3m vertical scramble of no difficulty. One must now traverse the grassy terrace (separating the upper rock band just descended from one immediately below) for several hundred metres in an easterly direction until it is possible to thread the lower rock band and ultimately pick up a zig-zag cairned path in the lower corrie.

In winter, the descent from the upper 'hanging' corrie may be greatly facilitated by suitable snow conditions. There is a continuous small gully-line (a stream-bed in summer, and not attractive as a route) falling from the south rim of the coire almost to the lowest slopes bordering the road. Given sufficient snow of the right texture, this is a remarkably efficient descent route.

From Mullach an Rathain, descend to the west via a line of cairns, to the head of the large stone shoot already mentioned as dropping into Torridon village. Alternatively, continue to Sgurr a'Chadail and thence down to the Coire Mhic Nobuil track. From the East Top, follow the main ridge over the easternmost top to the point where the rock changes from quartzite. Fifteen metres of scrambling (faint path) lands one below the highest cliffs. Steep open slopes on the south flank of the mountain lead to the Coire Dubh track.

The north face of Liathach offers the best prospects of rock-climbing. The north ridge of Spidean a'Choire Leith gives a Moderate route onto the summit if the difficulties in the middle section are taken direct.

The ascent of Mullach an Rathain, via Meall Dearg and the Northern Pinnacles, gives a fine, though somewhat indirect ascent onto the mountain. The approach from the road into Coire na Caime and the foot of the Meall Dearg ridge takes about two hours. The climb on the north flank of Meall Dearg starts to the right of a small water-course and follows a steep, narrow shelf diagonally from right to left up the middle of the north face—180m Moderate. 'The Northern Pinnacles' are extremely shattered and are covered with large unstable blocks. There are five of them, giving a straightforward, pleasant climb. The last pinnacle is climbed straight up, then a little slab is traversed just below the top. The winter route here is excellent, the first pinnacle being reached by way of a narrow, easy gully on the north-west.

From the Coire na Caime side the gullies between the Northern Pinnacles give several winter lines. Numbered from bottom to top, the wide gully to the left of the fifth pinnacle, between it and Mullach an Rathain, is *Left-Hand Trinity Gully*. The climb was mainly on ice—90m Grade III (M. Robson and A. Delafield, March, 1955). The gully between the fourth and fifth pinnacles is *Central Trinity Gully*—105m Grade II (D. Stevens and R. Urquhart, March 1955). This gave two ice pitches. *Right Hand Trinity Gully*—120m Grade III (D. Stevens and R. Urquhart, March, 1955) lies between the third and fourth pinnacles.

At the back of Coire na Caime, the 150m buttress which faces across to the Northern Pinnacles at the entrance to the inner corrie, is known as *Bell's Buttress*. The original line here by Dr and Mrs J. H. B. Bell in 1947, gave 90m of Severe climbing. It can be varied considerably, being easier on the left.

The gully immediately left of Bell's Buttress is *Vanadium Couloir*—300m Grade IV (A. Paul and D. Sanderson, February, 1979). The route is obvious from the Coire Dubh path.

The traverse of the Fasarinen Pinnacles has already been described. There is only one recorded rock route here. Seen from Coire na Caime there are six pinnacles, the third one being a pointed tower. *Dru*—105m Severe with 45m scrambling (D. J. Temple and P. G. Crabb, 1959)—starts from the lowest point of this.

Two of the gullies between the pinnacles have been climbed in winter. *3rd Pinnacle Gully*—120m Grade II (D. Stevens and R. Urquhart, March. 1955)—is the gully between the second and third pinnacle, counting from the left. After 75m, a traverse left along a snow ledge led into a subsidiary gully which was climbed to the main ridge. *4th Pinnacle Gully*—120m Grade II—is the gully between the third and fourth pinnacles, the left-hand one of two gullies forming a 'V'. A straightforward climb with several good short ice-pitches.

The stepped buttress immediately west of the Fasarinen Pinnacles is known as *P.C. Buttress*—210m Difficult (R. S. Horseman and H. K. Hartley, June, 1939). The lower terraces are found to be easy, but the buttress narrows in its upper part, and the route goes up a precipitous tower on the right centre, with some loose rock.

On the south side of Liathach, two routes are recorded, one on either end of the ridge. At the west end of the mountain, the crag below the summit of Sgorr a'Chadail has *Reflection Wall* 75m Very Difficult (W. J. Cole and J. R. Marshall, 4th August, 1952). This route is on the right-hand end of the crag, from a cairn. *Triceratops*—90m Very Difficult (R. W. L. Turnbull and D. G. Turnbull, August, 1970)—is on the high band of cliffs at the extreme eastern end. Where the cliffs peter out, 180m to the left is a short conspicuous gully, the entrance flanked on both sides by pinnacles. The route takes the right bounding edge.

In contrast to the comparatively limited scope for summer climbing on Liathach, the northern corries hold the promise of an abundance of winter lines.

The back wall of Coire Dubh Beag has a long, straight gully— *Footless Gully* 150m Grade IV (C. Rowland and A. S. Rowland, February, 1977). The first pitch is a vertical chimney. There are five pitches alternating with easy slopes.

An earlier route here followed the long, slender gully on the rocky hillside to the right of the corrie—*Hillwalk* 300m Grade II 1966. The North East Corrie—Coire Dubh Mor has two recorded routes. *George* 240m Grade III (I. G. Rowe and Miss M. Kelsey, February, 1967). This is the gully immediately to the east of the north spur of Spidean a Choire Leith. *Poachers Fall*—180m Grade V (R. McHardy and A. Nisbet, February, 1978)—is a more serious and technical climb. It is on the large ice-fall which forms at the back of the corrie.

The South-East Buttress of Spidean a Choire Leith has also been climbed. This gives *Pyramid Buttress*—180m Grade IV (D. Jenkins, C. Rowland and M. Webster, February, 1977). The route follows the skyline seen on the front cover of the Climbers Guide to the Northern Highlands Vol. II—Torridon, Achnasheen, Applecross by R. W. L. and D. G. Turnbull, which details all recorded routes in the area.

The winter traverse of the Liathach ridge should only be tackled by an experienced and well equipped party. This is an especially fine expedition. The description of this in *Undiscovered Scotland* by W. H. Murray (London 1950) is recommended reading. It should be emphasised that nobody should venture on Liathach in winter conditions unless they are already experienced and competent in the use of crampons and ice-axe. The main ridge is frequently comparable, in places, to an Alpine arête.

Beinn Eighe

(1) **Ruadh-stac Mor** (1010m) Highest point and N.W. Spur of Beinn Eighe N.G. 951612
(2) **Sail Mhor** (981m) West end of Beinn Eighe N.G. 938605
(3) **Coinneach Mhor** (975m) N.G. 944600
(4) **Spidean Coire nan Clach** (972m) N.G. 965597
(5) **Sgurr Ban** (971m) N.G. 974600
(6) **Sgurr an Fhir Dhuibh** (963m) N.G. 982600
(7) **Creag Dubh** (914m) East end of Beinn Eighe N.G. 986608
(8) **Ruadh-stac Beag** (896m) 2km N.N.E. of 4. N.G. 973614. Over a dip to 640m
(9) **Meall a'Ghiubhais** (886m) N. of 8 over a dip to 366m. N.G. 976634

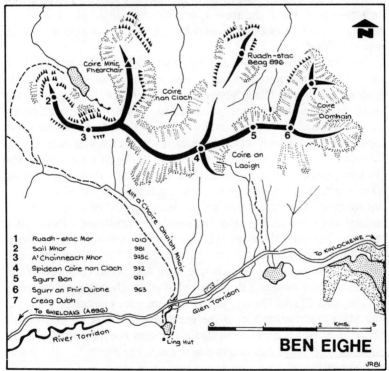

Beinn Eighe is the collective name given to the whole of the magnificent mountain range lying just south-west of Kinlochewe and Loch Maree, which, with its equally fine neighbour, Liathach, rises up to fill the entire length of the north side of Glen Torridon. It is separated from the latter mountain by Coire Dubh, and on the north-west its boundary is marked by Glen Grudie and the line of the Allt Coire Mhic Fhearchair. From any direction Beinn Eighe is seen to be uniformly steep and imposing. Gracefully curving ridges link its peaks; the whole effect being accentuated by the distinctive white covering of quartzite which almost entirely blankets the summit. This is one of the main points of difference between Beinn Eighe and Liathach. The steady but gentle eastward dip of the strata which allows the Torridonian sandstone to form nearly all of Liathach, only brings it to ridge level on Beinn Eighe at the col between Sail Mhor and Coinneach Mhor at its western end, and takes it almost completely out of sight before the east end of the ridge is reached, even more so on the south than on the north. Consequently, most of the slopes on Beinn Eighe are of quartzite scree, although on the wider and flatter parts towards the west end, a mossy covering makes for easier walking.

The south side of Beinn Eighe is in full view from the Glen Torridon road, from the summit ridge of Sail Mhor at its western end to Spidean Coire nan Clach above Loch Bharranch. This part of the range no longer comes under the National Trust for Scotland, being, like the remainder of the mountain lying to the east, part of the Beinn Eighe Nature Reserve. Consequently, parties climbing here should observe the restrictions laid down by the Nature Conservancy. The resident warden can be contacted at Anancaun Research Station, 800m north of Kinlochewe, for any information governing the area of the Reserve. The north side of the mountain is of more complex pattern than the south, and includes the mountain's finest rock features. The main ridge drops in this direction into three great corries enclosed by spurs. The most easterly is Coire Toll a'Ghiubhais (Fir tree hole); separated by Ruadh-stac Beag and Meall Ghiubhais from the central corrie—Coire Ruadh-stac, of which the uppermost section is Coire nan Clach. Finally, at the western end, enclosed by Ruadh-stac Mhor and Sail Mhor, is the great amphitheatre of Coire Mhic Fhearchair, which contains in its inner recess the magnificent Triple Buttress; one of the finest climbing areas in the Northern Highlands.

This north-west corner of the mountain is easily its finest section, and the view from Loch Coire Mhic Fhearchair, or from the summit of Beinn a'Chearcaill, should not be missed. The upper buttresses of quartzite stand on a plinth of sandstone rising to almost half the total height of 305m, the two strata being separated by a 'Broad Terrace', lower and more continuous in its eastern extent, so that East Buttress is two-thirds composed of quartzite while West Buttress is almost half Torridonian sandstone. Broad Terrace is an easy scramble, used as an approach to climbs on the upper parts of East and Central Buttress.

On the main buttresses the quartzite is divided into two layers, the lower half having a more pronounced bedding plane than the upper. At their junction is a less pronounced terrace which marks the line of the *Upper Girdle Traverse* (T. W. Patey and C. J. S. Bonington, 1960)—a first rate expedition with minimum scrambling, at least half a dozen pitches of Severe standard and some remarkable exposure. The fault line is obvious across the entire face and for most of the way this is the only practicable route. The climb starts near the foot of Far East Gully. The first segment of the traverse across the Eastern Ramparts is continuously difficult and exposed for 182m. From East Buttress right along to West Central Gully, the climbing is easier, apart from a single awkward pitch on the east face of Central Buttress. The east face of West Buttress is perhaps the most impressive section of the circuit, with three serious pitches.

The right aspect of each buttress is well-broken but the left profiles rise sheer. That of East Buttress merges with the Eastern Ramparts, a 152m vertical face which stretches back for almost 400m to Far East Gully. The cliffs continue, slightly less formidable, but equally steep—The Far East Wall—to merge onto the col on the ridge leading to Ruadh-stac Mor. It should be noted that in the previous editions of this guide Far East Wall was known as the Northern Ramparts. To the right of the West Buttress is Far West Gully. This is strewn with the wreckage of an aircraft which crashed here in 1952. Beyond this lies Far-West Buttress which is much shorter and less clearly defined. The three main buttresses are separated by East-Central and West-Central Gullies.

Since the first climb here by Dr Norman Collie and his party, by way of West-Central Gully on to Central Buttress, Coire Mhic Fhearchair has attracted an ever-increasing influx of climbing parties and its main rock features have given a wide variety of fine routes.

The Far East Wall holds seven routes. *Sidewinder*—90m Severe (A. Fyffe and P. Williams, 16th October, 1966)—is to the left of the steep central section of the 120m quartzite wall; the start is some 6m to the left of the left-hand end of the low grass terrace. *Sting*—90m Very Severe (J. Ingram and G. Strange, 5th May, 1974)—follows a line on the left hand section of the crag between Sidewinder and the impressive grey wall. The start is at a cairn on the upper ledge. *Sundance*—120m Very Severe (R. Archbold and G. Cohen, 5th May, 1974)—takes the first prominent feature to the right of the grey wall—a line of steep corner cracks. *Colgarra*—105m Hard Very Severe (R. Archbold and G. Cohen, August, 1976)—is a very steep route which starts centrally at a deep slit cave between Sundance and Kami-Kazi. *Kami-Kazi*—105m Very Severe (J. Brumfitt and B. Sproul, 30th May, 1966), follows the line of the left-hand edge of the big pillar at the right-hand end of the cliff. The start is 30m to the left of the deep-slit cave at a large, damp over-hung recess. *Birth of the Cool*—105m Very Severe (R. Archbold and G. Cohen, June, 1974)—to the right of Kami-Kazi. At the right-hand side of the crag is a steep grey pillar cleft by an obvious chimney line in the lower part. The finish is to the left of *Groovin' High*—Hard Very Severe (R. Archbold, J. Ingram and G. S. Strange, July, 1973). This route takes a line of grooves near the centre of the very steep pillar right of Kami-Kazi route. *Far East Gully* gives some 60m of Difficult climbing, a straightforward route on good holds.

The distinctive and extensive left-hand face of the East Buttress forms what is known as the *Eastern Ramparts*. There are nine main routes here, the standard varying from Severe to Extremely Severe. The rock is quartzite and the face is split horizontally at just less than half height by the line of the Upper Girdle. A pale dièdre near the middle of the upper layer marks the line of *Boggle* 135m Very Severe (R. Smith and A. Wightman, October, 1961). The start of this route is on the little grassy ledge which starts at the centre of the face and runs to the right as a shelf just above the top of the scree slope. This is now known as Bottom Shelf. Slanting leftwards from its start 5m to the left of the end of Bottom Shelf, is *Rampart Wall*—120m Very Severe (J. A. Austin and D. G. Roberts, 27th May, 1969). This same party also climbed *Cornice Groove*—60m Very Severe—the slim, V-groove with an overhang at 27m, which is found just round the corner where the Eastern Ramparts fall back to Far East Gully. *Gnome Wall*—150m Hard Severe (T. W. Patey, 16th August, 1959) is an obvious line of weakness near the right-hand end of the Ramparts. The route escapes onto the crest of East Buttress some 30m below the cliff-top, near a projecting gargoyle. The start is from a cairn at the extreme right-hand end of the Bottom Shelf. *Samurai*—120m Very Severe (J. Brumfitt and B. Sproul, 29th May, 1966)—also starts on the Bottom Shelf, 30m to the left of Gnome Wall. It gives a direct line half way between the latter route and Boggle. In 1954, Lovat and Weir attempted a line somewhat to the right of Gnome Wall, starting from the main corrie floor. After six hours of Very Severe climbing, they were forced to retreat from a point 30m below the gargoyle. *Shanghigh*—132m Very Severe (R. Archbold and G. Cohen, August, 1976)—starts 12m right of Samurai, right of a detached pillar. A feature of this route is the prominent chimney between the upper reaches of Samurai and Gnome Wall. Between Boggle and Samuri lies *Rampage*—120m Very Severe (N. Muir and A. Paul, August 1977). The route starts 6m to the right of Boggle at prominent steep crack; a feature of the route is a pale coloured wall in its upper half, just right of a prominent square cut roof at mid-height. *Forge*—120m Very Severe (N. Muir and A. Paul, August 1977)—starts at the foot of a large, pale corner with a rock slab on top some 30m left of Rampart. At the left end of the Eastern Ramparts there is a 'vague pillar', bounded on the left by an obvious corner and, on the right, by a steep, straight crack. This latter is the line of *Heavy Flake*—96m Extremely Severe (G. Cohen and M. Hamilton, July, 1978).

The *East Buttress* gives seven routes. Climbing on the sandstone is found to be more difficult than on the quartzite of the upper tier. A prominent wet chimney near the right-hand end of the buttress is a conspicuous feature of the lower, sandstone tier. This gives 75m of climbing—*The Chimney,* Very Difficult. *Easy Route* starts to the left of The Chimney, to the left of the second grassy bay. The standard of climbing varies from Moderate to Very Difficult according to how far left one goes, traversing left being the answer to any difficulties encountered. *The Gash* 60m Severe (T. W. Patey and A. G. Nicol; K. A. Grassick and J. M. Taylor, June 1962)—starts on Broad Terrace, and follows a deeply-cut chimney in the lowest tier of quartzite. This runs up left to end on a terrace some 30m to the right of the start of Gnome Wall to which it provides a useful preamble. The original route on the buttress is *Ordinary Route*—210m Difficult (G. M. Gibbs, E. Backhouse and W. A. Mounsey, 1907). This starts on Broad Terrace some 10m from the extreme right-hand edge and follows the crest of the buttress. The first ascent avoided the first 30m pitch by going up the gully on the right. *Bloodstone Start*—105m Mild Severe

(W. S. McKerran and D. M. Nichols) is a fine line on the sand-stone tier, being both direct and clean. The start is at a cairn midway between East Central Gully and the Direct Chimney—above is a ledge under a sharp, wet, overhanging chimney. Also on the sand-stone tier, *Mango*—75m Very Severe (N. Muir and A. Paul, August, 1977)—starts left of The Chimney at a small overhang and climbs a groove past a loose block. A winter climb here is *Easy Route/Ordinary Route*—Grade III/IV (D. Donaghue and M. Orr, December, 1978).

East Central Gully is basically a winter route, but was climbed in June 1963 by W. Proudfoot, D. MacKenzie, D. Williamson and P. Acock. The standard was Severe, the route stayed close to the gully bed throughout and was very wet, eventually joining the original route on East Buttress.

The north-east facing left flank of the upper section of Central Buttress has become known as Central Wall. It is seen to be triangular in shape, with the apex at the bottom, level with Broad Terrace. It is bounded on the left by East Central Gully, and on the right by the crest of Central Buttress. The lower part of the wall can be described as a Tower about 45m high rising from East Central Gully at the level of Broad Terrace. The top of the tower is a gently-sloping terrace from which most of the climbs here start. There is a choice of approaches to this: up East Central Gully; up the cleft between the Tower and the main part of Central Buttress; climbing the first 36m of the Ordinary Route on East Buttress and then traversing across East Central Gully. *East Central Ribs*—105m Severe (L. S. Lovat and T. Weir, 9th June, 1954)—follows the crest of three prominent quartzite ribs, just west of East Central Gully. They are bordered on the left by the gully and on the right by a narrow cleft. The ribs are steep, narrow and exposed. Immediately right of East Central Ribs is a parallel rib, about 30m high. Right of this again, is a line of slanting and steep, narrow slabs, ending on the right at a prominent corner. *Assegai*—105m Very Severe (P. Baines and D. Nichols, April, 1976)—starts on the broad terrace 30m left of the neck behind The Tower and climbs slabs initially to the Upper Girdle. *East Wall*—100m Severe (L. S. Lovat and T. Weir, 12 June, 1954).—Above the Tower, easy ground leads to the start of the route which is described as going directly up the middle of the face. High above is another tower. The start was described as being from a cairn. This is no longer there and the route has been difficult to trace.

Fulmar Chimneys—90m Very Difficult (J. Hogan and D. Bell, October, 1970) was climbed while searching for the previous route. *Direct Route*—105m Hard Severe (T. W. Patey, 2nd August, 1957) is a steep, direct route up the right-hand side of the face, in the line of the gully between the Tower and Central Buttress. To the right of Direct Route is a prominent, steep chimney crack line which is climbed to the top—*Pelican*—105m Severe (N. Muir and A. Paul, August, 1977). The steep centre face of the Tower gives a pleasant route (Difficult after an awkward start) useful for access to the Central Wall (D. M. Nichols, 1976).

Central Buttress is seen to have a greater area of sandstone than does the East Buttress, and the quartzite is in three distinct tiers. These are uniform in both size and in the standard of climbing found on them. The lower tier is generally Very Difficult; the middle tier is Difficult or less; the upper tier is Mild Severe. The sandstone tier is conveniently ringed by a broad level grass shelf above the lowest rocks. All climbs start from here, and it is easily reached by scrambling up on the right, near West Central Gully. *Piggott's Route* (A. S. Piggott and Morley Wood, 1922) is the original climb here. The start is from the grass shelf, about a third of the way from the west end of the buttress, beside a large, leaning block. The route takes the middle of the face. The 90m on the sandstone tier is Difficult. The 180m section on the quartzite starts from the highest point of the grass on Broad Terrace and continues straight up. The standard is Mild Severe. Starting about 15m to the left of Piggott's Route is *Readymix,* 100m Severe (M. Green and J. R. Sutcliffe, 3rd June, 1968). The line keeps to the middle of the sandstone throughout. Also on the sandstone tier is *Central Corner*—70m Very Severe (A. Nisbet and N. Spinks, September, 1976). The route follows the very prominent dièdre on the left flank of the buttress, left of Readymix. Regarded as easy for its grade—but sustained. *Slab Route*—75m Difficult—starts from the right-hand end of the terrace, taking a rather indirect line upwards to the right.

There are three main lines on the quartzite tiers of Central Buttress. Piggott's Route has already been indicated. *Parker's Route*—180m Very Difficult—starts below the north-east face at the left end of Broad Terrace. It avoids the main face in the first tier for the north-east face and then crosses Piggott's Route higher up to take the line of least resistance up the final steep tower. *Hamilton and Kerr's Route,* Mild Severe, takes the left branch of West Central Gully for 45m

75

then traverses diagonally left across the sandstone to Broad Terrace. On the quartzite the route keeps to the corner near West Central Gully on the right and is very steep. The original route is probably joined on the upper section. An outstanding first winter ascent here was accomplished by J. Rowayne, K. Spence and K. Urquhart—*Hamilton's Route* (300m) Grade V over two days in February, 1971. To start, the party kept to the right of the buttress. On the lower quartzite tier a corner was climbed on the right near West Central Gully; on the upper quartzite tier they kept to the crest. This was considered to be the easiest winter line on the buttress.

The route was climbed on two separate days; on the first day the party climbed up to the final quartzite band, traversed right into West Central Gully, and roped down this. The following day, West Central Gully was climbed, traversing left onto Hamilton's Route and climbing that.

West Central Gully has been climbed in winter (W. Wallace and C. G. M. Slesser, Easter 1968). The summer route—*Collie's Route*—seems only to be used as an escape route from the gully below the big pitch. This was the original route on Triple Buttress.

West Buttress has more sandstone and less quartzite than the others. It is bounded on the right by *Easy Gully,* which slants rightwards from the foot of the buttress to merge near the rocks which form Ceum Grannda—the ugly step on the main ridge. At the bottom of the quartzite East Gully forks—a branch comes in from the left which is Far West Gully. This *West Buttress Ordinary Route*—300m Severe on sandstone and Difficult on quartzite (J. Bower and T. Meldrum, July, 1919)—starts at the extreme right of the buttress near Easy Gully. It keeps to the right on the sandstone which is taken in four Severe pitches. These may be avoided by use of Broad Terrace. The climbing above on the quartzite is easier. The quartzite tier of Ordinary Route has been climbed in winter—Grade III/IV (R. McGregor and A. Nisbet, January, 1979)—on this occasion the sandstone tier was by-passed.

Two other routes here are *Ordinary Route Variation*—60m Mild Severe (C. J. S. Bonington and T. W. Patey, 9th August, 1960) and *Direct Finish*—60m Hard Severe (W. March, May, 1971). *Fuselage Wall*—90m Mild Severe (T. W. Patey and J. M. Taylor, June, 1961) is a short route on excellent rock on the upper tier of quartzite overlooking the upper part of Far West Gully. It may be included in an ascent of West Buttress by walking round right below the steep, upper section, or may be climbed from the bed of Far West Gully.

Left of the centre of the sandstone tier on West Buttress is a large, obvious corner. Left of this are two grooves; one on the left-hand side of the buttress overlooking *West Central Gully* and the other midway between the central corner and the left edge of the buttress. The following three routes follow the top grooves and the corner and are described from left to right. A fourth route is described last. *Sideshow*—70m Very Severe (B. J. Chislett and R. A. McHardy, August, 1976)—on left-hand side of buttress overlooking *West Central Gully* an obvious groove runs almost to top of the tier. Start below and left of an obvious spike. *Junior*—90m Hard Very Severe (R. A. McHardy and J. McLean, August, 1976)—the groove midway between the central corner and the left edge of the buttress. The lower section is usually wet. *Senior*—120m Hard Very Severe (D. M. Jenkins and P. F. Macdonald, August, 1976)—the central corner. Start from grass terrace and climb direct throughout, taking the right-hand of two cracks at mid-height. Finish straight up quartz wall. The fourth route lies about 15m right of Junior. This is *Relayer*—90m Very Severe (B. J. Chislett and R. A. McHardy, August, 1976).

The east face of West Buttress holds two routes. *Twilight Zone*—180m Very Severe (N. Muir and A. Paul, August, 1976)—this is on the quartzite tier and climbs the centre of the steep east face, passing the large roofs near the top on the left. Start in West Central Gully at the centre of a small buttress where quartzite begins (arrow). *Mistral*—120m Very Severe (B. J. Chislett and R. A. McHardy, August, 1976)—the main feature is an obvious v-corner at the top right of the wall. The route leads fairly directly towards this, starting from the grass terrace at the foot of the wall at an obvious groove (arrow).

Far West Gully—Easy—provides a suitable means of descent to Coire Mhic Fhearchair. *Far West Buttress*—60m Mild Severe (L. S. Lovat and T. Weir, June, 1954)—lies across Far West Gully from West Buttress. The climb starts at the corner left of centre. The upper part steepens and is open to variation.

The steep, broken cliffs of Sail Mhor, which form the south containing spur of Coire Mhic Fhearchair, are not of the same quality as those of the Triple Buttress. They are described as having all the worst features of Torridonian sandstone—wet, occasionally overhanging bands of cliff separated by steep grass ledges girdling the crag—all rock when seen from below and all grass from above. Three deep-cut, easy-angled gullies were the scene of early pioneering and there has been a certain amount of subsequent exploration.

No. 1 Gully (Morrison's Gully) is the most westerly; the first on the north face of Sail Mhor, just outside the corrie. It gives 300m of easy climbing. *No. 2 Gully* was tackled by the original party to climb here—Messrs. Lawson, Ling and Glover in April, 1899. A steep scree fan is seen to issue from the foot of the gully towards the lochan. The first section is easy-angled and the party diverged to the right at the upper section to gain the ridge. This narrows and swings left, giving varied scrambling on rock steps and pinnacles to the summit. The route is scenic and interesting. A more recent route is found on the steep, left-hand wall of the gully. *Overkill*—225m Very Severe (A. MacHardy, P. Nunn and C. Rowland, June, 1968)—starts from the foot of the gully where a prominent groove cuts up in the general line of the rounded rib above. *No. 3 Gully (White's Gully)* has both summer and winter routes. This is the broad gully running up from the head of the lochan, joined by a narrow gully just below mid-height. The line follows this easily until the final, narrow 30m chimney just before the junction. Climbed direct, the gully has few difficulties.

The most recent 'find' on this north side of Beinn Eighe, is the fine quartzite crag lying on the eastern flank of Ruadh-stac Mor. This is Creag Mhor, Coire Ruadh-staca—N.G. 952611. From most directions the crag is difficult to see. It can be approached by descending some 161m from the col at the south end of the ridge of Ruadh-stac Mor. From here, contour the east side of the ridge for 800m along a good stalking path. The crag lies to the top side of this.

The main cliff is described as a jumble of towers, 120m high, continuing to the right as a steep, continuous 60m cliff. Its prominent features are: a gully, consisting of a single deep cave, and the two ridges of the main cliffs which come further down the side of the hill than do the rest.

A number of routes have now been climbed here. *Midge Ridge*—60m Very Difficult (C. S. Rose and S. Peterson, September, 1971), is the ridge some 15m to the right of the gully—Chockstone Gully. *Thin Man's Ridge*—105m (and 45m scrambling) Hard Severe (D. Howard, C. S. Rose and R. W. L. Turnbull, 12th July, 1971)—starts at the lowest point of the right-hand of the two main ridges. *Spog aig Giomach*—105m Severe (C. S. Rose and R. W. L. Turnbull)—is the left-hand of the two ridges. *Sidestep*—75m Very Difficult—is the tower to the previous route. *The Independent*

Pineapple—135m Severe (C. S. Rose and D. Howard, July, 1972)—is a fine natural line starting at a right-angled corner some 90m from the start of Thin Man's Ridge, and 20m left of Chockstone Gully. *The Pineapple Chimney*—105m Very Severe (Miss B. Clough, A. Nisbet and M. Thorp, October, 1977)—climb the chimney formed by the monolith known as The Independent Pineapple. Only the final pitch is Very Severe. Follow the chockstone gully until a narrow traverse ledge leads left to the foot of the chimney.

At the eastern end of the cliff are three chimneys, the right-hand one having a deep cave at its foot. The two left-hand chimneys are separated by a rib which becomes well defined at a platform some 15m up. *Autumn Rib*—90m Severe (S. Ackerly and A. Nisbet, October, 1977).

There are two possible approaches to this north side of Beinn Eighe, both of which take about two hours of steady walking. The track from Grudie Bridge, 7½km north of Kinlochewe, on Loch Maree-side, leads up Glen Grudie for almost half the way, to a height of 270m. The more popular approach, sometimes considered to be more laborious, is the one from Glen Torridon. Leave the road at the bridge over the Allt a'Choire Dhuibh Mhoir, some 9km from Kinlochewe. There is a ruined house just off the roadside and a parking place. The S.M.C. Ling Hut is located nearby on the south side of the road, across Lochan an Iasgaich. A sign-post marks the start of the track, which passes upwards between Liathach and Beinn Eighe into Coire Dubh. The main track is left shortly after it reaches its highest point, one mile past the stepping stones, and a right fork contours round the slopes of Sail Mhor of Beinn Eighe. The line is cairned and the path is easily traced leading upwards into Coire Mhic Fhearchair, where it peters out at the loch-side. A third possibility is the track leading between Meall Ghuibhais and Ruadh-stac Beag from the roadside north of Kinlochewe, just opposite the entrance to the Nature Conservancy field station at Anancaun. Rough ground is eventually encountered and the approach by this route is considerably longer.

The traverse of the Beinn Eighe range makes a long and arduous expedition. Escape routes are plentiful, however, and a useful half-way approach can be made from Loch Bharranch, just over 8km along Glen Torridon from Kinlochewe. A stalker's track leaves from close to a conveniently sited quarry-hole and leads northwards into Coir' an Laoigh. An easy line is taken to the crest of the conspicuous spur on the west side of the corrie. This is followed on to the main ridge of the mountain, 180m west of Spidean Coire nan Clach. If used in the descent from the ridge, a cairn can be found marking the way from the spur in Coir'an Laoigh.

The most usual starting point is from Cromasag, 1.6km south of Kinlochewe on the Torridon road. This follows the course of the Allt a'Chuirn to a height of almost 457m. A steep grass slope continues on to the summit of Creag Dubh (929m) lying to the north-west of Coire Domhainn. 1:50.000. Moving westwards between this latter top and Sgurr an Fhir Dhuibh (963m), unnamed on the map, it is necessary to negotiate a series of shattered pinnacles. These are the Fhir Dhuibh or Bodach Dubh—better known as the Black Carls of Beinn Eighe. To the inexperienced these may cause difficulty and they can only be by-passed by making a long descent and a tiring traverse.

The climbing possibilities here on the north-west face of Sgurr an Fhir Dhuibh were explored by T. W. Patey in August, 1957. The quartzite cliffs are between 90m and 120m in height and take the form of a series of crazy pinnacles and aretes. The ledges dip outwards, the rock is very shattered, and the large number of rickety, loose blocks are a potential hazard. A climb was conveniently included in a west to east traverse of the main ridge, by moving horizontally from the col between Sgurr an Fhir Dhuibh and Sgurr Ban. Patey traversed below the first promising arête, which was very steep in the lower section, and selected the next arête along. This was characterised by a patch of red rock at mid-height, marking a recent rockfall. The narrow arête of 105m was found to be Difficult and needs no description, finishing a few yards west from the summit cairn. The route is not recommended.

This entire pinnacled section of the ridge can be eliminated by climbing onto Beinn Eighe by way of the south-east spur of Sgurr an Fhir Dhuibh from the south side of the Allt a'Chuirn. The ridge dips westwards for 122m before rising over the summit of Sgurr Ban (1002m) whence the going is relatively easy onto Spidean Coire nan Clach (981m). This is the half-way point on the ridge which was mentioned previously.

From Spidean Coire nan Clach to Coinneach Mhor (966m) the way remains good. From here, the west top of the ridge, Sail Mhor (980m) is reached after some easy scrambling to the intervening col. The gully is an alternative starting place for the traverse of the main ridge if one approaches from Coire Mhic Fhearchair at the west end.

From Coinneach Mhor, the way on to the highest point on the ridge, Ruadh-stac Mor (1009m) crosses a narrow col involving a drop and a re-ascent of some 135m. The scree gully on the west side of this gives an easy descent into Coire Mhic Fearchair.

Ruadh-stac Beag (868m) is not usually included in the traverse of the ridge. It is separated from Spidean Coire nan Clach by a dip over 210m. To the north of this again lies the remaining outrider, Meall Ghuibhais (878m) which involves a further descent to 360m. Meal Ghuibhais has a 90m quartzite cliff on its south-west flank which gives a large number of short climbing routes on good rock.

This main section of Beinn Eighe with its seven principal tops gives a superlative ridge walk of around 11km. In winter it is a major expedition, only to be attempted by the experienced and well-equipped.

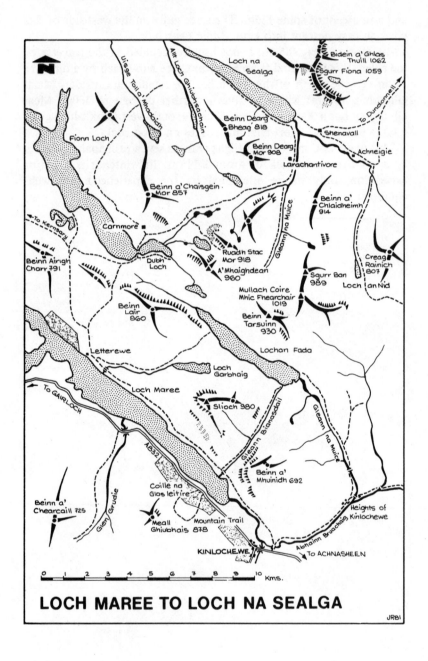

LOCH MAREE TO LOCH NA SEALGA

Loch Maree to Loch Broom

(1) **Slioch** (980m) N.H. 004691
(2) **Beinn a'Mhuinidh** (692m) N.H. 032661
(3) **Beinn Lair** (860m) N.G. 982733
(4) **Meall Mheinnidh** (720m) N.G. 954748
(5) **Beinn Airigh Charr** (791m) N.G. 930762
(6) **Beinn a'Chaisgein Mor** (857m) N.G. 983785
(7) **A'Mhaighdean** (960m) N.H. 007748
(8) **Ruadh Stac-Mor** (918m) N.H. 018756
(9) **Beinn Tarsuinn** (930m) N.H. 039727
(10) **Mullach Coire Mhic Fhearchair** (1019m) N.H. 052735
(11) **Sgurr Ban** (989m) N.H. 055745
(12) **Beinn a'Chlaidheimh** (914m) N.H. 061775
(13) **Beinn Dearg Mhor** (908m) N.H. 032799
(14) **Beinn Dearg Beag** (818m) N.H. 020811
(15) **An Teallach** (1062m) N.H. 069843
(16) **Beinn Ghobhlach** (635m) N.H. 055944

MAPS: O.S. 1:50.000 (2nd Series). Sheet No. 19 Gairloch and Ullapool. Sheet No. 20 Beinn Dearg.

The area between Loch Maree and Little Loch Broom contains the complex group of mountains which lie within the Letterewe, Fisherfield and Strathnasheallag deer forests. To the north-west, the area is bounded by Loch Ewe and Gruinard Bay, with the intervening peninsula of Rubha Mor. To the south-east lie the mountains of the Fannich group. The area is circled on three sides by good motor roads; from Dundonnell at the head of Little Loch Broom, right around the coast line and along the west shore of Loch Maree to Kinlochewe; but the principal means of communication within the uninhabited maze of mountains in the central portion, is by the numerous hill-tracks which lead into and across it.

The most populated centres are to be found around the western coastline. This part suffered little during the Clearances of the 19th century and, from Gairloch right along through Poolewe to Aultbea, the surrounding lowland belt is the scene of thriving crofting and fishing activities. The Mackenzie lairds hereabouts subsidised early experiments in fishing in the early 1800s and Gairloch is now one of the busiest white-fish and herring ports on the west. The sheltered bay of Loch Ewe is climatically ideal for agriculture and the surrounding croftland is probably the most favourable found anywhere in the Northern Highlands. The tropical garden at Inverewe, created in the 1860s by Osgood Mackenzie, is an attraction which draws thousands of visitors each year. It is now administered by the National Trust for Scotland.

Accommodation in the interior is scant. This is estate country, given over wholly to stalking and fishing, and even suitable bothies are in short supply. There are youth hostels at Carn Dearg, west of Gairloch, and at Aultbea. The hostel at Dundonnell is no longer open but the Junior Mountaineering Club of Scotland, Edinburgh Section, have established premises here in The Old Smiddy—now the Clarkson Memorial Hut. The most useful bothy accommodation can be found at Shenavall, in the north of the area, at the end of Loch na Sealga, and at Carnmore in the south, at the end of Fionn Loch. Both lie on the main transverse track. The cottage at Shenavall is in fairly constant use and, apart from during the stalking season, there appears to be little restriction. The use of Carnmore is mentioned later in the text. For the rest of the area, it is best to set up a base camp within the mountains themselves. For most of the year the choice of sites is fairly unrestricted.

Shenavall is approached by leaving the Dundonnel road 2½km before reaching Dundonnell Hotel at the head of Little Loch Broom. This is the 'Destitution Road' built during the potato famine of the 1840s to provide work for the local inhabitants. An obvious land-rover track leaves the south side of the road and follows the Allt Gleann Chaorachain through a birch wood before opening out onto the open moorland on the south-east lower slopes of An Teallach. The way rises steeply over the 375m contour, then drops down into Strath na Sealga to join a narrower track seen bending northwestwards along the north bank of the Abhainn Strath na Sealga past the locked cottage of Achnegie. Shenavall lies less than 2km along the track on this side. The river opens into Loch na Sealga 1.6km further on. The rather tedious bend leading down to Achnegie can now be cut out by means of a right-hand branch of the main track which cuts down towards the river across the rough shoulder from the highest point of the path. This branch track is well-trodden and easily followed, giving a welcome saving of distance. By the main track from the Dundonnell road, the distance to Shenavall is 11km.

It should be noted that the road seen marked as reaching the north end of Loch na Sealga from Gruinard Bay is an established right of way, but visitors are discouraged. Motor access is barred by a locked gate.

From Shenavall the way across the end of the loch to join the track to Carnmore, involves a rough, pathless walk towards the Abhainn Gleann na Muice. The building seen on the far side of the stream is Larachantivore, usually kept locked. A wire bridge framework is found a short way upstream from here, but the footplanks are usually absent and the river has to be forded. The path continues for a mile along Gleann na Muice before rising westwards up Gleann na Muice Beag along the lower south slopes of Beinn Dearg Mhor. The prominent rock face at the junction of the glens is *Junction Buttress*—this affords some rock-climbing. The head of Gleann na Muice Beag is exceptionally steep and this section requires steady going, but once over the top, the way eases off and is straightforward for the next kilometre or so to Lochan Feith Mhic 'Illeen. From here the path slants downwards along the south-eastern slopes of Beinn a'Chaisgein Mor to Carnmore. The total distance from Shenavall is almost 11km.

The Lodge at Carnmore lies above the south-east end of the Fionn Loch, and bothy accommodation is usually obtainable in the barn when it is not required for estate purposes. Camping on the pasture area below the house is discouraged—the estate considers that this particular piece of land provides valuable early grazing for deer. The whole of the surrounding area lies within the Fisherfield Forest and should be avoided when the stalking season is in progress.

Carnmore can also be reached from Poolewe, thus forming an important through route from north-east to south-west. The approach is by way of Kernsary, leaving the main road at the bridge over the River Ewe, near Poolewe Hotel. Permission can be obtained to take a car as far as Inveran, the march boundary; past this point the road is deemed entirely impractical for cars and no vehicles are allowed. The estate stalker lives at Kernsary, some 3km from Inveran, an invaluable contact locally. From Kernsary there is another 13km of rough going to Carnmore, much of which is over stalker's tracks, but parts of which are indistinct. The track past the farm follows the left bank of the stream upwards onto the shoulder at its head and the small plateau is crossed pathless. Descend to pick up a broken track leading down to Loch Doire Chrionaich and this is followed on the north side until a good track is joined. After this the way is straighforward.

There is a direct path to Carnmore from Letterewe which is reached by private ferry from the road on the west side of Loch Maree. Use of this cannot be guaranteed and is largely up to individual negotiation.

From Kinlochewe, a useful track leads around the south-east end of Loch Maree, passing through Gleann Bianasdail to the south end of Loch Fada. This gives good access to both Slioch and Beinn a'Mhuinidh and, by branching upwards over the shoulder of Meall Riabhach, just past the entrance to Gleann Bianasdail, one can follow another main track to Letterewe.

The mountains can also be approached from the east by track along Loch a'Bhraoin to Lochivraon Bothy. From here a good track swings northwards by way of Loch an Nid to connect with the Shenaval track at Achnegie. Alternatively, the cross-country walker can reach the south end of Loch Fada over the Bealach na Croise.

Slioch (980m)

Slioch is the most impressive of the mountains which stands immediately to the north of Loch Maree and its summit can easily be reached from the Gleann Bianasdail track. The upper part of the mountain is of Torridonian sandstone, the lower plinth being of Lewisian gneiss. The summit lies on the western end above the steep cliffs which form the north-west face. Sgurr an Tuill Bhain (931m), the subsidiary summit, lies 1.2km to the east and can be reached without much re-ascent along the connecting ridge. A south-east ridge from the summit terminates at Meall Each and, with the eastern ridge, contains the big east-facing corrie of the mountain—Coire Tuill Bhain.

The steep north-west face of Slioch is reached from the path over the shoulder of Meall Riabhach to Letterewe. The path crosses a stream 1.5km beyond the end of the glen and this is followed to its source—marked by a cairned boulder; the buttress immediately above, difficult in its lower 30m was climbed in 1949. The Main Buttress forms the skyline on the left. Stepped Ridge is beyond it and entirely hidden. The pinnacle which is prominent on the skyline in the view of Slioch from Slattadale or Loch Maree Hotel, is on a broken buttress lying well to the north of Stepped Ridge. There appears to

DONALD BENNET

12.   *On the Central Buttress of Coire Mhic Fhearchair, Beinn Eighe*

DONALD BENNET

13.   *Beinn Eighe from Loch Coulin*

14.   *Beinn Eighe from the east*

15.   *Liathach, main peak from east*

TOM WEIR

16. *The north face of Liathach showing Coire na Caime*

17.   Coire Mhic Fhearchair, Beinn Eighe

DONALD BENNET

18.   *Looking north-west from Liathach to Beinn Dearg and Baosbheinn*

have been some confusion about the identification of these features in the past.

Stepped Ridge gives a 240m rock route graded Very Difficult (McDougall, Cram and Blackwood, 1933). The route is flanked on the right by a slabby, forked gully but escaped as often as possible on the left. The *Main Buttress* gives a climb of 240m, Severe (A. Parker, 1952).

Beinn a'Mhuinidh (692m)

Beinn a'Mhuinidh lies on the east side of Gleann Bianasdail and, like Slioch, it is most easily approached from Kinlochewe. The normal sequence of rock formation on Beinn a'Mhuinidh—Lewisian, Torridonian and Cambrian—is further capped with Lewisian gneiss marking the line of the thrust zone. The summit itself is un-noteworthy, but the crags along the south-west and north-west sides are of interest to the rock climber. The band of quartzite running for most of the length of these sides produces the most interesting features and, at the corner of the glen, has its best and largest of exposure of rock in the **Bonnaidh Donn Buttress.** The buttress on the south-west slope, marked by the 90m waterfall, is *Waterfall Buttress.* This gave one of the original routes on the cliff, first climbed by G. T. Glover and Dr. Inglis Clark in 1899. It can be one of the most rewarding of the many routes now recorded here and is remarkable for its standard and conception at that time. For historical interest, the original description is retained. The original route, the *West Climb,* here starts 45m left of the fall at a grassy chimney, at about 180m above sea-level, and is steep and exposed throughout (Severe). "A precariously perched tree 12m up is reached from the right of the chimney; the second pitch, slightly shorter, leads to the first of the prominent ledges; the next 10m to the higher ledge is the hardest part of the climb by reason of a nasty left traverse just below the upper ledge. From here a line slightly right is taken to an over-hanging cave, which is passed on its left to a reasonable shelf stance. Above, a short chimney and a smooth wall give way to easier ground to the top". It will give some indication of the continuous difficulty of this short route when it is remembered that the original party took six hours over it, though that time included much "gardening". The full spray of the fall enables the vegetation to renew itself quickly so an equal amount of "gardening" is to be expected. The rock is of quartzite.

When seen from Loch Maree, the mountains lying to the north-west of Slioch appear singularly unremarkable, but on their north-eastern side they form an almost continuous line of steep cliffs of hornblende schist which offers a wealth of fine rock-climbing. The summits can be reached with little difficulty from Poolewe, by use of the Kernsary track already described, with a choice of any of the cross-tracks leading from it to Letterewe.

On the way from Gairloch to Poolewe, a right-hand detour for just over a mile along a surfaced road marked "Tollie Bay", leads to the old pier at the west end of Loch Maree. Ths gives ready access to the **Creag Mhor Thollaidh**—or **Tollie Crags**. These crags have become increasingly popular; the rock is of unusually smooth gneiss and the standard of climbing is almost universally 'Very Severe'.

There are four main crags: *Loch Maree Crag,* N.G. 880768—lies about 1.6km east from Tollie Bay. It is reached by following a path from the bay through and beyond the huge lochside boulders. Two large crags—*Upper and Lower Tollie Crags*—rise above Tollie Bay. High up on the right is *Gully Crag*—N.G. 864778

Permission to camp can be obtained at Tollie Farm, and it is in the interest of subsequent parties that permission is sought. The landlord has already taken a friendly interest in climbing activities here.

The crags on this east side of Letterewe—Beinn a'Mhuinidh and Creag Mhor Thollaidh—now hold such a diversity of routes that anything less than a complete description would be inadequate. In addition, this would largely duplicate the text of the existing Climbers Guide. The area is now fully covered in Volume I of the Climbers Guide to the Northern Highlands by I. G. Rowe.

Beinn Airigh Charr (791m)

Beinn Airigh Charr is the most accessible of the group of mountains lying on this north side of Loch Maree and, has extensive cliffs culminating in the north top, known as Martha's Peak. This rises as a huge rock tower above Loch an Doire Chrionaich, just over 3.2km along the track from Kernsary. Martha was a legendary local lass who took her herds to graze on these mountains and is credited with the first and only traverse of the tower. Unfortunately, she dropped her crook, and fell to her death in an effort to recover it. *Staircase Gully*—basically a scree gully with occasional rock pitches—separates Martha's Peak from the rest of the crags, which diminish in height towards the east. East of the gully is a 122m wall of overhanging rock

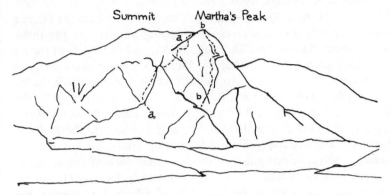

(a) original route South Buttress. (b) original route Main Tower.

Fig. 2. Beinn Airigh Charr: Martha's Peak.

rising from steep slabs and, further on still, a lesser face containing Square Buttress.

The *Eastern Buttress* of Martha's Peak was first climbed in 1909 by G. T. Glover and W. N. Ling. The *Original Route* on the main tower, which gave 330m of Difficult climbing, was made in 1910 by G. T. Glover, H. Walker, R. Corry and W. N. Ling. This route follows a line almost straight up from the broadest part of Loch an Doire Chrionaich to the top of the tower, starting up the easy area between the two lower arms of rock, then threading ledges until directly below the steep, clean, upper face, which is climbed to the right of the steepest section. From the platform half way up the upper crags, there is a choice of routes to the top of the peak. The original party followed the well-defined chimney, which is grassy and steep and scant in holds.

The lower part of Martha's Peak is split in two by a wide grassy scoop. The right branch does not seem to afford any great prospect for climbing, but the left branch was explored by C. G. M. Slesser and party in 1951. This gives *Lower Buttress Direct,* 150m, Severe, starting at the lowest rocks just above the east end of Loch an Doire Chrionaich. The line trends leftwards up a gentle flake, and the first 25m are loose and flaky. It would seem possible to combine the climb with the Original Route to give over 450m of climbing. *Staircase Gully,* which separates the main tower of Martha's Peak from the

89

lower cliffs to the east, gives a long route—360m Severe (P. N. L. Tranter and N. Travers, 1964). The climb starts up the left wall from the bottom of the gully, and has much easy scree between the pitches. Except for the crux pitch—an overhanging chimney in the upper part—the standard is Very Difficult. Below, and to the left of the big overhanging wall east of Staircase Gully, is a steep arête which is climbed with deviations on to the left wall—*The Beanstalk,* 105m, Very Severe (D. Bathgate and P. F. Macdonald, October, 1971). *The Roc*—80m, Very Severe (M. Boysen, P. Braithwaites, P. Nunn, April, 1974)—climbs the centre of the slabby face on the right flank of The Beanstalk arête, starting 23m right and up from this latter route. *Square Buttress* is contained in the last small face of Beinn Airigh Charr, to the south-west of a small, unnamed lochan—N.G. 938765. It gives one route—*Square Buttress,* 120m Difficult (J. C. Stewart and S. MacPherson, W. D. Brooker and J. W. Morgan, 1951)—the difficulties here lie mainly in the lower half.

Meall Mheinnidh (720m)

Meall Mheinnidh stands south-east of Beinn Airigh Charr, with an intervening dip to 350m—Strathan Buidhe—which carries one of the crosstracks to Letterewe. On the south-east again, a drop of 487m separates Meall Mheinnidh from Beinn Lair. The Bealach Mheinnidh, which lies between them, carries the track from Letterewe Ferry to Carnmore Lodge.

There is one route on the mountain—*Glasgow Ridge* 150m Difficult (W. D. Blackwood, D. Parlane and B. Wright, 1947). This goes up the central rise skirting below an obvious terrace, the climbing being generally indefinite.

Beinn Lair (860m)

The cliffs on the north side of Beinn Lair, overlooking the Allt Gleann Tulacha, are comprised, like those of Beinn Airigh Charr, of hornblende schist. The rock slopes steeply into the hill, giving a profusion of incut holds, and is sounder and less vegetated than one might expect. Belays are scarce however and, when wet, the rock needs special care. The face contains more than twenty buttresses, ridges or ribs, each containing deep-cut gullies, the height varying from 120m to 420m. The crags were first attempted in 1909 by G. T. Glover and W. N. Ling but were neglected until 1951. From that time there has been considerably more activity here and there is a profusion of rock-climbing routes of all standards of difficulty. The winter possibilities in the many gullies have still been little explored, partly because of their wetness and partly because of their general inaccessibility. Only two winter routes are recorded to date. *Easachan*—300m Grade III (Q. T. Crichton and G. N. Hunter, 26th February, 1969), is at the east end of main crag. The gully is on the right of a rounded slabby buttress which borders a deep-cut bealach. *Geodha Ban*—360m Grade IV (by the same party) stands some 200m left of a large prominent standing block halfway along the main crag. Looking up, there are two obvious deeply-cut parallel snow gullies. The left-hand one of these is taken.

The cliffs of Beinn Lair normally fall into two main sub-divisions—the Fionn Loch cliffs, at the north-west end of the escarpment, and the Loch Fada cliffs at the south-east end. The principal features and routes are described from north-west to south-east.

Fionn Loch Cliffs

Excalibur Buttress is the obvious clean-looking mass of rock to the right of the crags. There is a deep-cut gully on the left and a buttress beset with overhangs on its right. *Excalibur*—120m Very Difficult (E. A. Wrangham and A. Clegg, 1952) starts at the side of the gully. It is Moderate at first, becoming steeper. *West Chimney Route*—180m Very Difficult (C. G. M. Slesser, G. Dutton and J. Wight, 1951), starts 30m left of the most westerly of the large buttresses. The climb lies on the west side of the buttress which lies west of The Tooth. *The Tooth*—195m Difficult (D. C. Hutchison, B. S. Smith, Miss A. Hood

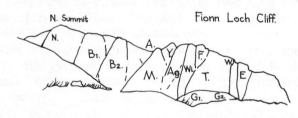

N. North Summit Buttress.	Ag. Angel Buttress.	E. Excalibur.
B. Butterfly Buttress.	Wi. Wisdom Buttress.	
A. Amphitheatre.	F. The Fang.	Creig na Gaorach.
M. Molar Buttress.	T. The Tooth.	G1. Zebra Slabs
Y. Y Buttress.	W. West Chimney.	G2. Jealousy

Fig. 3. Beinn Lair; the Fionn Loch Cliffs.

and J. S. Orr, 1951)—starts towards the middle of the buttress to the right of Cavity Chimney. From mid-height, where the route joins the left-hand edge of the buttress, there is a delightful series of short, exposed pitches to the top. *Cavity Chimney and Wisdom Wall*—210m Very Difficult (D. C. Hutchison and B. S. Smith, 1951)—starts at the base of the chimney to the left of The Tooth. *Wisdom Buttress*—210m Very Difficult (J. Smith, Miss A. Hood and J. S. Orr, 1951) is a magnificent climb, exposed, sustained and of continuous interest. It starts at the bottom, right corner of the buttress, which is a conspicuous object on account of its slender, cigar-shaped aspect.

Between Wisdom Buttress and the next buttress on the left, Angel Buttress, is another fine route, *Bat's Gash*—210m Very Difficult (B. S. Smith and D. C. Hutchison, 1951). This climb starts at the foot of the deep-cut chimney immediately left of Wisdom Buttress. The middle section has magnificent cave scenery.

Angel Buttress is the buttress to the left of Bat's Gash. In the upper half there is an obvious bar of overhangs, split towards the right by a deep chimney. This is continued below as a minor gully, splitting the lower part of the buttress into two separate noses. There are four recorded climbs on the buttress, of which *Pilgrim's Progress*—240m Severe (J. S. Orr and Miss A. Hood, 1951) is the best route. It starts from a scoop in the scree at the lowest point of the rocks, up a large triangle of slab which gives access to the main, slabby face of the right-hand part of the buttress. The other three routes are all Difficult.

Molar Buttress is the broad buttress to the left of Angel Buttress, and right of the Amphitheatre. It has five routes, and another runs up the right-hand gully, then up the minor buttress—Y-Buttress—which lies between the upper parts of Molar and Angel Buttresses. From left to right, the climbs are: *Y-Buttress*—120m Difficult (E. A. Wrangham and F. Adams, 1951)—a rather messy and vegetatious climb. Between the branches of Y-Gully and west of Molar Buttress, *Right-Hand Route*—210m Very Difficult (E. A. Wrangham and F. Adams, 1951)—The climb starts up a stretch of easy-angled, usually wet slabs at the right hand side of the buttress, and uses the most right-hand of the conspicuous breaks through the band of steep rock which crosses the whole buttress at two-thirds of its height. *Damocles Crack*—210m was climbed by a pre-1953 Oxford party. It starts at the lowest rocks and continues straight up the middle of the buttress. *Left-hand Route*—195m Difficult (F. Adams and E. A. Wrangham, 1951) starts at the foot of the buttress, just left of a conspicuous, short, black chimney and follows the left-hand edge of the buttress all the way. *Route I*—240m Very Difficult (D. C. Hutchison and B. S. Smith, 1951) starts up an obvious gully toward the left of the buttress. *Rose Route*—210m Moderate (J. Smith and N. A. Todd, 1951) starts well to the left of the buttress and follows the left wall of the buttress not far from the gully on the left. This gully—*The Amphitheatre*—is suitable for descent.

The large mass of rock, to the left of the Amphitheatre and right of the great bulk of the North Summit Buttress, is Butterfly Buttress. It is in fact composed of four separate buttresses, the two outside ones running the full height of the cliff; the two smaller ones, inserted between them at top and bottom. There are two routes here so far—*Right Wing*—300m Very Difficult (E. A. Wrangham and D. St J. R. Wagstaff, 1953) and *Left Wing*—300m Moderate (I. G. Rowe, 1967) starting at the foot of a wall to the right of a prominent crack at the lowest point.

Two recent winter lines here are: *Cabbage White*—300m Grade III/IV (R. A. McHardy and A. Nisbet, February, 1978). This takes the first gully left of the amphitheatre running the full length of the cliff. Near the top the right hand of two branches was taken. The gully held snow but little ice, giving awkward rock moves.

Butterfly Gully—360m Grade II (D. Dinwoodie and R. Renshaw, April, 1978)—It forks about 150m below the plateau and the more interesting left fork was taken.

Immediately left of Butterfly Buttress, the prominent cone-shaped buttress of enormous bulk which falls from the north summit of Beinn Lair to the upper reaches of Gleann Tulacha, is *North Summit Buttress*. This gives a 420m Moderate route (Miss M. Langmuir and Mr. J . O'Hara, 1957) starting at the bottom left-hand corner of the rocks at the point where a stream emerges from the left-hand bounding gully. The route is recommended as a pleasant way onto the summit of the mountain from Gleann Tulacha, rather than as a rock climb. Under winter conditions, *North Summit Buttress* gives an excellent route—Grade III—(J. Anderson, R. McHardy, A. Nisbet and J. Unwin, February, 1978). After a start up an ice runnel, the route trended left. Much of the enjoyment here is in route finding.

Between the Fionn Loch and the Loch Fada cliffs, rather nearer to the western end, is Marathon Ridge. It is the first on the left of two very prominent buttresses to the south-east of the spur, forming the highest part of the cliffs, and in a straight line between the summit of

Beinn Lair and that of Beinn Tarsuinn Chaol. *Marathon Ridge*—
380m Difficult (W. D. Brooker, S. McPherson, J. W. Morgan and
J. C. Stewart, 1951) has probably an unavoidable pitch situated at
about 240m above the base, which is ". . . more than Difficult".
Loch Fada Cliffs.

The thin buttress on the immediate left of Marathon Ridge gives
one route—*Olympus,* 150m Difficult (E. A. Wrangham and D. St J.
R. Wagstaff, 1953). This is straightforward, keeping as near to the left
edge as possible.

The highest buttress visible from the head of the loch, distinguished
by a large, steep ridge in its upper section, is *Stag Buttress.* This gives a
240m climb, Severe (J. D. Foster and D. Leaver, 1951). The same

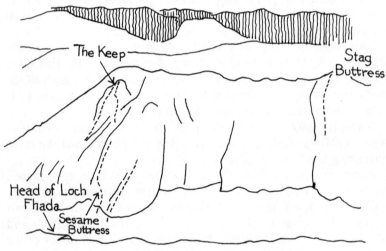

Fig. 4. Beinn Lair; the Fada Cliffs.

party climbed two routes on the two clean-looking buttresses which
come low down near the head of Loch Fada. *Falstaff*—120m Very
Severe—starts at the lowest points of the rocks on the right-hand
buttress and *Sesame Buttress*—135m Severe—on the left-hand
buttress.

The highly distinctive rock tower, high up on the slopes above the
upper part of Loch Fada, is known as The Keep. It appears as a very
steep-sided wedge of clean looking rock. The west face is smaller, but
cleaner and more continuous, and contains *Rainbow Wall*—120m

Severe. *Central Route*—195m Severe—starts at the lowest point of the buttress and goes straight up the nose, with easier variations possible.

Enjoyable climbing on excellent rock is found on Creig na Gaorach—N.G. 972747—below the Fionn Loch cliff of Beinn Lair. It is reached by following the stream south-eastwards from the junction of the paths at the south-west corner of Fionn Loch. There are two obvious buttresses, with a smaller buttress between them, and just below the col there is a second small buttress. West Buttress, the first buttress approaching from this direction, has one climb—*Jealousy*, 200m Very Difficult (M. J. O'Hara and Miss M. Langmuir, 1957). The route starts at the lowest part of the rocks, a few feet above the point where the stream washes against the foot of the rock. The East Buttress, Nannygoat Buttress, has two climbs. *Zebra Slabs*—140m Very Difficult (M. J. O'Hara and Miss M. Langmuir, 1957)—starts from the centre of the buttress behind five large fallen blocks, just left of a small sapling, and right of a water trickle. *Rainbow's End*—140m Very Severe (P. J. Sugden and J. R. Sutcliffe, 1976)—follows an obvious rib which forms the left-hand edge of the buttress. After the first two pitches, the standard is Very Difficult. *Denizin*—140m Very Severe (R. A. Croft and J. R. Sutcliffe, May, 1978)—starts below the centre of the buttress and takes the only obvious breaks through the steep section to finish up pleasant slabs.

The small buttress just below the col, left of Nanny Goat Buttress, has one route, *Sliver*—70m Very Difficult (D. J. McLennan and D. C. Forrest, 1967). Little Crag, above the path junction at the south-west corner of Fionn Loch—N.G. 970753—gives two routes. *Temerity*, 85m Very Severe (D. Ashton and P. C. Machen, 1957), starts left of the nose to the right of the central groove of the crag. The rib at the right end is 75m Very Difficult (E. A. Wrangham and P. E. Evans, 1958).

The Ghost Slabs, to the east of the causeway between Dubh Loch and Fionn Loch—N.G. 977756—is seen to have two main masses with a grassy escarpment separating them. The left-hand side of the right mass gives three routes, all Very Severe. *Doodle*—210m (R. Carrington and M. Shaw, 1967); *Leviathan*—270m (J. R. Jackson and I. Fulton, 1967); *Necrophile*—210m Very Severe (D. Dunwoodie and R. Renshaw, April, 1978)—climb the right-hand section of the right-hand slabs, starting at the lowest point just down and left from an isolated tree. The left hand mass gives two 360m lines—Hard Severe to Mild Very Severe.

Beinn a'Chasgein Mor (857m)

Beinn a'Chasgein Mor is a flat-topped mountain lying on the east side of the Fionn Loch, immediately above Carnmore Lodge. It falls away gradually towards the north and east, and a round-about route on to the summit can be made either by way of the track north along the Fionn Loch or from the track towards Shenavall. Its main importance is in the existence of the extremely fine exposures of Carnmore Crag—N.G. 980773—and of Torr na h'Iolaire—N.G. 984773—both of which overlook the east end of the loch. Between them, these now give more than fifty climbing routes of a wide variety both in standard and in character.

Carnmore Crag, the most westerly of the two, lies above the barn at Carnmore and, from here, is seen to comprise of an upper and a lower wall, with a central bay. The great central nose of the crag is a prominent feature. This is Fionn Buttress, which gives what is considered to be one of the finest climbs in Scotland—*Fionn Buttress*—225m Very Severe (M. J. O'Hara and W. D. Blackwood, April, 1957). The route is steep and exposed. The rock is perfect and the interest sustained. The start is from a turf ledge at the foot of a great chimney, at a prominent pale patch.

To the left of the Great Chimney is the Left Wing of the crag, which contains four routes of varying quality. The Lower Wall of the crag is the extensive mass of rock which forms the wall of the crag below the Central Bay and below Grey Wall. It includes all the rock to the right of Fionn Buttress. The main features are a curving red scar in the rocks on the left, isolating between it and Fionn Buttress route a scimitar-like sweep of very steep, smooth slabs with minor ribs. The First Rib rises from the foot of the crag as a well-formed nose of rock but merges back into the general angle at half height of the Lower Wall, where the Red Scar swings across. To the right of this is a deep scoop, bounded on its right by the Second Rib. This rib also merges with the wall after 75m but is topped by slabs in the Central Bay. At the right of its base is a conspicuous yellow scar. The broad area of steep vegetated slab is Botanist's Boulevard. Finally, a big overhanging mass with slabs to its right.

The Upper Wall is the very steep bar of rock above the Central Bay. On the left it is bounded by the out-thrust nose of Fionn Buttress; to the right its height diminishes. The main features from left to right are an easy-angled grey slab at the bottom left, bounded by the wall of the Fionn Buttress on the left, and above by a bulging overhang topped by a 45m vertical wall. In the top left-hand corner there is prospect of escape by a slanting crack. *Green Corner*—90m Very Severe (A. Cram, R. Schipper and W. Young, 1967). The top right-hand corner of the slab leads to the foot of a wall which is slightly less than vertical. Slanting from top left towards bottom right across this very steep wall is an overhang. Above this is another very steep wall whose height increases towards the right where it forms the left retaining wall of Carnmore Corner, a prominent feature of the crag. This gives *Carnmore Corner*—65m Very Severe (R. Carrington and J. R. Jackson, 1968), perhaps the hardest route on the crag. This has twin cracks in the back and a vertical right wall coming out into a plumb vertical nose. To the right of this, a steep ramp of slabs leads from the bay to the top of the cliffs. This is the line of *Diagonal*—180m Severe (E. A. Wrangham and A. B. Clegg, 1952)—the original climb on this crag, and reputed to be hard of its standard. The start is in the scoop on the Lower Wall between the first and second ribs, nearer to the latter. Traverse right, out into a line of rightward slanting ribs, continuing the line for 30m. Left onto a slab, and climb it using the corner crack, then go straight up on good crack holds until it is possible to traverse left and up to perched block. Easier climbing leads to the slabs and heather of the Central Bay, under the middle portion of the Upper Wall. From here, traverse up and right to the foot of the ramp of slabs just to the right of Carnmore Corner. Climb the slab to the top of the cliff. This upper section of the route can be avoided up a steep, turfy scoop some yards to the right of the finish of Diagonal Route. This is a possible route of descent into the Central Bay from above.

Another easy approach to the Central Bay is *The Gangway,* which gives 30m of Moderate climbing, starting at the bottom right of the crag. Climb the minor gully to the right of Needle till an obvious traverse left leads out above a small conspicuous overhang. Continue up and left by turf ledges to the base of the Grey Wall, which is the area to the left of Diagonal. Follow the ledge beneath the overhang till a final traverse along a very narrow shelf above the trees of Botanist's Boulevard leads to the bay. This route also gives good access to the Grey Wall.

The crag has produced a wide variety of routes, described as comparing favourably with any in Britain. One of the finest and most sensational is *Dragon*—100m Hard Very Severe (G. J. Fraser and M. H. O'Hara, 1957). It is a very steep and, in places, overhanging route with great exposure. The rock is perfect throughout and security is good. Highly recommended.

Torr na h'Iolaire is the great rocky tower which falls south and west from the summit of Sgurr na Laocainn, directly above Carnmore Lodge. Seen from there the main features are: The Lower Wall, slanting down from left to right with two prominent red ribs at its left-hand end, below a huge perched block and a small rib below a steep wall with overhangs along its base. Above a perched block is a bar of steep rock about 45m high, composed of numerous coloured sections—Harlequin Wall. Above this is another terrace, with a prominent, sharp-topped pinnacle—The Shark's Tooth. Above this terrace is a very steep wall divided by numerous ribs and corners. This is Carcase Wall. At the far end left is a lozenge of slab above the great gully. Above Carcase Wall is a block of grey slabs—The Lower Summit Buttress. The summit of the hill is composed of a long wall of very steep and clean looking rock. Twin chimneys high on the left form a prominent landmark. To the left of these is the West Face. Well over to the right is a deep-set slab recess.

The crag has excellent rock for climbing, gives fine views and faces the sun. The rock is well-broken by terraces and many of the original routes find their way up several (or all) of the rock tiers thus formed. This makes route description complicated. The many fine climbs here, as with those on Carnmore Crag, are included in the S.M.C. Climbers' Guide to the Northern Highlands area—Volume 1—Letterewe and East Ross by I. G. Rowe.

An excellent introduction to the district is given by *Ipswich Rib*—375m Very Difficult (G. J. Fraser and P. R. Steele, March 1956). This, the longest climb on the crag, is a well-defined route on the Lower Wall, followed by a considerable amount of easier ground to the foot of the Upper Summit Buttress, and then a route on that. The terraced nature of the crag makes possible other similar combinations.

Ipswich Rib starts on the Lower Wall at the foot of the little rib below and at the right-hand end of the wall. From the very lowest point of the rocks, it aims to finish at the foot of the prominent slab recess of the Upper Summit Buttress. On the Upper Summit Buttress the continuation starts at the base which forms the left-hand boundary of the slab recess, and this combination forms a fairly natural line. Climbing is nowhere more than Difficult after the first section, the rock is perfect and the route finishes at the summit of Sgurr na Laocainn, one of the finest viewpoints of the area.

To the east of the Carnmore-Sheneval track lies *Carnan Ban*—645m N.H. 002764. It gives three areas of climbable rock. *Practice Precipice,* the small outcrop above the zig-zags, above Dubh Loch, gives short pleasant routes of Difficult to Very Difficult standard. *Barndance Slabs*—N.G. 997765—gives three routes of 90m to 120m in standard Difficult to Severe. This is the slabby mass of rock on the west slope of Carnan Ban. *Maiden Buttress* lies on the south-west side—N.H. 001762. The climbing is considered to be 'very pleasant and not too serious'. Seven routes are recorded, none over 120m. Most have one or two difficult pitches at the start, then the routes ease off. The rock is clean and good.

A'Mhaighdean (960m) Ruadh Stac-Mor (918m)

A'Mhaighdean lies almost 14.5km equidistant from Kinlochewe, Poolewe and Dundonnell, and is often described as being the most remote of the 'Munro's'. The mountain rises as a graceful crested ridge in a series of rocky steps from the Dubh Loch. The summit lies at the south-eastern end, 3½km from Carnmore. The north-west end gives the most interesting climb onto the summit and this can be reached with little difficulty, from the track leading up from Carnmore to Lochan Feith Mhic-Illean. Alternatively, follow the track to the lochan and then take the branch track leading across the Allt Bruthach an Easain which leads upwards towards the Feur Loch between A'Mhaighdean and Ruadh Stac-Mor (918m). The track is marked as stopping after a mile but in fact continues right up over the saddle between the two mountains and gives good walking throughout. The atmosphere in this secluded corrie is one of utter seclusion, the scenery having a strange beauty. Feur Loch Mor alternates in colour between deep blue and translucent geen, accentuated by the stark contrast of the red cliffs of Ruadh Stac-Mor on one side of the track and the light grey gneiss of A'Mhaighdean on the other. The summit of either mountain can easily be reached from the saddle.

The view from the summit is extremely fine. The mountain lies in the middle of three lochs—Loch Dubh, Gorm Loch Mor and Feur Loch Mor—and to the north-west and south-east the longer waters of Fionn Loch and Loch Fada stretch between the surrounding hills. The great crags on the north side of the mountains of Letterewe can be examined in detail, while to the north and east the ridges of Mullach Coire Mhic Fhearchair and Sgurr Ban lead the eye towards the great range of An Teallach and its neighbour, Beinn Dearg Mhor.

Climbing on A'Mhaighdean is mainly to be found on the cliffs which fall south-westwards from the summit ridge. The mountain is of sandstone and gneiss. The buttresses on the crest of the ridge on the south-west side are of sandstone giving good, clean rock-climbing. The summit is of gneiss, the highest point to which this formation rises in Scotland, and so is Pillar Buttress which falls 150m from under the summit facing south. Below the west face of the Pillar Buttress is the West Gully.

The four sandstone buttresses, numbered from left to right, can best be approached by contouring round from the north-west ridge. There is no climb on the first buttress. The second, Breccia Buttress, gives one route—*Conglomerate Arête*—90m Very Difficult (M. J. O'Hara and Miss M. Langmuir, 1957). This starts from the bottom right-hand corner. The third buttress, the Red Slab, is identified by the single sheet of slab ending in a steep wall on the right. A huge pinnacle lying against the lower left-hand corner of the slab forms a small subsidiary buttress. *Red Slab Route*—90m Difficult (M. J. O'Hara and Miss M. Langmuir, 1957)—begins from the corner between this subsidiary buttress and the slab, at the furthest right accessible point to the slab. *Doe Crack*—85m Very Difficult (J. D. C. Peacock and A. Finlay, 1957)—starts from the same point. The fourth buttress, Gritstone Buttress, has three routes of Severe standard. The buttress has a central chimney which starts as a cave and narrows to a crack, opening out again at the top of the crag. The upper part is climbed by *Compensation* (54m) (R. Isherwood and E. Birch, 1967).

Two longer routes are found to the right of the four buttresses on the left of the West Gully. *Whitbread's Aiguille*—270m Severe (M. J. O'Hara and G. J. Fraser, 1957) starts at the foot of the easy-angled buttress which forms the left-hand side of the West Gully, using the pinnacle at the left-hand corner. To the left of this is *Vole Buttress*—270m Very Difficult (M. J. O'Hara and R. G. Hargreaves, 1957). The route starts at the foot of the prominent V-groove towards the left of the crag. The prominent, long gully left of West Gully, just left of Vole Buttress gives a winter route—*Ermine Gully*—300m Grade III (R. F. Allan and M. G. Geddes, April, 1978).

On the upper of the two bands of coarsely crystalline rock, which slants across the Dubh Loch face under the sandstone cap of the mountain, are the Octave Ribs. *Fahrenheit* is the 4th rib from the left, next to an obvious red rib. This gives a sustained and exposed climb, 57m Mild Severe. The fifth rib has a shorter route—*Soh What,* 33m Very Difficult.

Access to the south-facing *Pillar Buttress* of A'Mhaighdean from the west is awkward. The best approach from Carnmore is to traverse the summit and descend a big, grassy gully near it which leads towards the mouth of Gorm Loch Mor, traversing rightwards on the 150m contour to the foot of the buttress. Alternatively, climb up to the crags from the shores of Gorm Loch Mor. The true nose of the buttress gives 150m of Difficult climbing, finishing at the summit cairn,—a route pioneered by Dr and Mrs. J. H. B. Bell in 1950. The first 25m on easy rocks from the foot of the rib leads to a platform. From here the route continues up slabs and walls right of the true crest of the buttress, climbing on steep slab by parallel cracks. Easy rocks, a difficult crack, then 6m of difficult slab lead to an impasse requiring an awkward traverse to a large chock-stone filled crack.

The 'parallel cracks' pitch is also utilised by the *Alternative Route*—55m Very Difficult (J. D. Foster and D. Leaver, 1950)—which starts to the right of a large crack up a short wall to the right of a cairn. *Baird, Crofton* and *Leslie's Route*—150m Severe (1953) lies close to and is partly the same as this latter one, starting to the right of Pillar Buttress. *The Slot*—180m Mild Severe (R. G. Hargreaves and M. J. O'Hara, 1957) follows a straight natural line which starts a few metres to the right of Pillar Buttress route, at an obvious deep-cut chimney and continues to the left of the true crest of the buttress as a line of chimneys and cracks. The route is similar to the earlier *Triple Cracks Route*—120m Very Difficult, climbed by D. Bennet's party in 1951.

The west face of Pillar Buttress gives two routes, both of Severe standard. *The West Face Route*—240m (C. G. M. Slesser, G. Dutton and J. Wight) and *Eagle Grooves*—110m (M. J. O'Hara and R. G. Hargreaves, 1957).

Beinn Tarsuinn (930m)

This ridge lies 3.2km to the south-east of A'Mhaighdean on the south-eastern side of the head of Gleann na Muice. It can be reached either by following the line of the glen from the bothy at Sheneval partly by way of the Carnmore track, or from the direction of A'Mhaighdean. From the latter direction, the way is rather tedious, involving a considerable drop in height over some awkward sandstone ledges. Several of these attain a respectable height and force the walker westwards. The ridge seen from the south is uninteresting, but once on the crest it is remarkably narrow in places and in certain weather conditions requires good route-selection. To the north it falls in a series of terraced sandstone cliffs which can be reached from the floor of Gleann na Muice with little difficulty.

The mountain is seldom climbed for its own sake, but is usually included in a circuit of the neighbouring tops which form a ridge along the east side of Gleann na Muice. To the east is a little pointed top of 823m and north of this rises Mullach Coire Mhic Fhearchair (1014m), the highest point on this ridge. The western face is of red sandstone seamed with gullies but, above the 914m contour, the summit cone is covered with quartzite blocks giving the usual unpleasant scrambling. The main feature of the mountain is the ridge of gneiss which extends for 1.5km east-south-east and terminates in some fine pinnacles. These are easier to climb over than to by-pass. The mountain can be approached from this side from the bothy at Lochivraon, but the intervening ground below the ridge gives difficult walking through peat bog, and route finding becomes largely a matter for individual choice.

Sgurr Ban (989m)

Sgurr Ban is similar in many respects to Mullach Coire Mhic Fhearchair. It is mainly of sandstone but, if anything, its quartzite capping is even more unpleasant to walk over than is the latter's. The summit lies half a mile to the north of the last. The quartzite on the eastern side of the summit is extremely unpleasant and in wet or icy conditions becomes dangerous. An unusual feature is the broad sheet of this formation which is exposed, completely unbroken, dipping towards Loch Nid. A descent to Achnegie from Sgurr Ban is a long and tedious business and necessitates negotiating the Amhain Loch an Nid at the most feasible point. The track leading down the east side of the river is usually wet and dirty.

Beinn a'Chlaidheimh (914m)

Beinn a'Chlaidheimh lies 3km north of Sgurr Ban and its ascent involves a drop to 610m. Loch a'Bhrisidh, nestling in the hollow of the intervening saddle, is a good navigational guide in bad weather.

The mountain lies at the north extremity of the ridge and a way can easily be found down on that side towards the Shenavall track. From the bothy, the summit is less than 3.2km distance almost due south.

A complete circuit of the ridge and the summits of A'Mhaighdean and Ruadh Stac-Mor from Shenavall makes an excellent hill-walking circuit for a long summer's day. For the 'peak-bagger' it is worth noting that Beinn a'Chlaidheimh and Ruadh Stac-mor have only recently gained the status of Munros.

Beinn Dearg Mhor (908m)

Beinn Dearg Mhor lies 3.2km to the west of Shenavall overlooking Loch na Sealga. Seen from Shenavall it is an extremely fine mountain, its two ridges, curving inwards from north and south, rise onto the cone-shaped summit, enclosing on its north-east side Coire nan Clach with its fine rock buttresses. In winter the graceful outline of the ridge is even finer, and is especially apparent from the heights of the Fannichs. The summit itself can easily be reached by way of the Carnmore track, which, at the head of Gleann na Muice Beag, gives a straightforward climb with very little extra ascent. Alternatively, by way of the north-east ridge or in conjunction with a climb over Beinn Dearg Beag (818m). This lies 1.6km north-west of Beinn Dearg Mhor and has a fine rocky ridge which gives a good winter traverse.

The cliffs of Coire nan Clach were pioneered in 1899 by Messrs Sang and Morrison, whose original route on the South Peak, the left-hand mass of the corrie wall, was of a Moderate scrambling nature. Fifty years were to elapse before any further recorded exploration took place and most of the subsequent climbing has been done in winter conditions.

The narrow gully, first on the left of Coire nan Clach, is *Twisting Gully*. This finishes at a fierce-looking notch in the skyline, well below the South Peak. It was climbed in 1949, as was a Difficult, unnamed gully, further to the right. The whole of this east face of the corrie is somewhat broken and, although impressive from below, the general angle is easy.

South of the east face are broken craggy slopes, leading to a very slender buttress. This is called *Flake Buttress* in the previous edition of the Guide but is also known as *Book-end Buttress*. The buttress is cut on both sides by deep gullies, of which the left-hand one was climbed by D. Wilson and W. Beverdige in May, 1966, giving a loose and vegetated route of Difficult standard. Both the east and west walls of the buttress are vertical and the buttress itself gives one of the best routes on the mountain. *Flake Buttress*—105m Severe (A. Parker and party, 1952), starts up the left corner and maintains its severity throughout. Climb the corner for 3m, then traverse delicately right to the extreme edge. Go up round the corner on the right to a block, then back left and up to a narrow ledge and piton belay (15m). Thence to the right, round corner to side opposite Central Buttress. Traverse 6m onto this flank, then 2m up steep awkward corner and back to the face of buttress and belay (18m). Up platform on the left; a difficult start up wall 2m right by slanting ledge with crack. Round ledge on right, then across and up exposed slab to ledge, then to right and back again to stance and belay below a steep wall (20m). The crux follows. Traverse on left flank of buttress for 6m, then 3m up a short steep groove. A delicate traverse left and up leads to easier ground. Block belay in cave below chimney (12m). Up chimney, then exit on right to a ledge. Up past the ledge to another harder ledge and piton belay (15m). Finally, round to the left at the next ledge, back and up to slab—rather artificial. A scramble leads to the top of the buttress which is connected to the main hill by a narrow ridge with perched block.

The *Central Buttress* of Beinn Dearg, lying to the right of *Flake Buttress,* has been climbed direct—240m Severe. The left wall of the buttress comprises numerous snow fields in winter, separated by short vertical walls. This gives a winter climb. *Left Flank*—240m Grade II (A. McKeith and I. G. Rowe, November, 1966). The buttress is bounded on the right by Trident Gully, almost 300m long, the lower half being steep snow in winter and scree in summer. The gully forks 90m up, the right fork being the main gully, while the left fork is a chimney between the top of Trident Gully wall and a prominent slender buttress—*Tower Buttress*. About 150m up Trident Gully, above the first fork, is the great triple fork which gives the gully its name. All three branches are about equal in size, the summit of the mountain lying between the central and right branches. The *Left Branch* has a pitch at the bottom but above that it is easy. The *Central Branch,* climbed by P. N. L. Tranter and N. Travers, December, 1963, is similar in nature. The *Right Branch* would appear to be harder.

The narrow buttress to the right of Central Buttress was climbed in 1950 by D. Munro, but the broken buttress with a steep west face—*Wedge Buttress*—to the west of this, remains unexplored.

An Teallach

(1) **Glas Mheall Mor** (981m) lies at the north end of the range and is the only top visible from Dundonnell 4.4km west-south-west of Dundonnell Hotel. N.M. 076854.
(2) **Unnamed Top** (914m) N.H. 070850
(3) **Beidean a'Ghlas Thuill** (1062m) N.H. 069843
(4) **Glas Mheall Liath** (950m) N.H. 077841
(5) **Sgurr Creag an Eich** (1000m) N.H. 055838
(6) **Sgurr Fiona** (1059m) N.H. 064837
(7) **Lord Berkeley's Seat** (1047m) A small Pinnacle. N.H. 064834
(8) **Corrag Bhuidhe** (1020m) North top followed by three slightly lower pinnacles. N.H. 065833
(9) **Corrag Bhuidhe South Buttress** (937m) N.H. 066831
(10) **Top above Cadha Ghoblach** (950m) N.H. 068825
(11) **Sail Liath** (954m) N.H. 071824

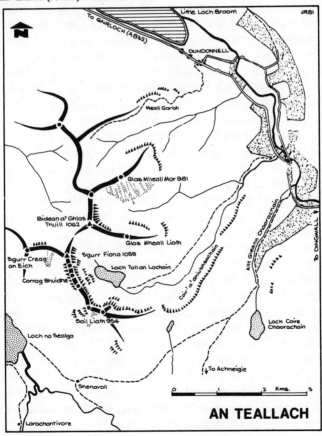

AN TEALLACH

105

An Teallach is the collective name given to the twisting pinnacled ridge of Torridonian sandstone which is the most northerly of the mountains within the area of this chapter. From its position at the head of Inner Loch Broom it is the dominating feature of the surrounding countryside and is clearly seen from most of the neighbouring mountain ridges. It is a magnificent example of Torridonian architecture and ranks amongst the finest mountain ridges in the Scottish Highlands.

It extends roughly north and south for upwards of 5km and forms a crescent-shaped back-bone from which two branch ridges project for about 800m on either side. The slopes to the north and to the west give relatively easy access to the main ridge but, to the east, it drops steeply into the two great corries—A'Ghlas Thuill and Toll an Lochain—and access here is limited in normal conditions to some of the long scree slopes and gullies which lead down into them. In winter these become snow climbing routes and should be recognised as such.

The traverse of An Teallach is a stiff day's expedition and, in winter, one which requires no small amount of mountaineering experience. The approach for the circuit of the tops is usually made from Dundonnell. A well-marked path leaves the road just past the former youth hostel and climbs steeply upwards towards the north-east lower slopes of Glas Mheal Mor ridge and then strike upwards to the main ridge of An Teallach, or climb more or less straight up the north-east slope of the terminal ridge onto the first summit. This is direct, but requires some route selection in the initial stages, through broken rock and wet grassy ledges, which eventually open out onto easier walking to the summit of Glas Mheal Mor. This top is one of the three found to be capped with quartzite.

Once on the ridge at this point, the remainder of the tops can be climbed in order, with little difficulty in normal conditions. Route finding is fairly easy and the whole pattern of the ridge can be seen stretching out in front. In bad conditions a line along a lower level on the west side of the ridge by-passes the 'bad steps'.

The second top is unnamed (914m) and is reached along an easy stretch of ridge. Then follows a climb on to Bidean a'Ghlas Thuill (1062m) the highest point on the range. From here a ridge to the east separating the two great eastern corries leads on to Glas Meall Liath (950m). There are some fine buttresses on the south-west angle of the A'Ghlas Thuill, the most northerly of these, which culminates in two or three pinnacles on the branch ridge. These do not impede progress.

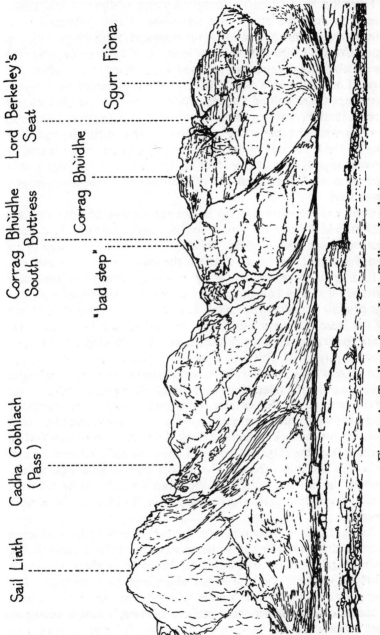

Sail Liath | Cadha Gobhlach (Pass) | Corrag Bhùidhe South Buttress | "bad step" | Corrag Bhùidhe | Lord Berkeley's Seat | Sgurr Fiòna

Fig. 5. An Teallach from Loch Toll an Lochain.

From Bidean A'Ghlas Thuill there is a drop of almost 150m, then a steep rise onto the other main top—*Sgurr Fiona* (1059m)— from whence the north-west branch of the ridge ends after 800m in the top Sgurr Creag an Eich (1000m). The main ridge now narrows over the spectacular rocky pinnacles which add so much to the fine silhouette. First, Lord Berkeley's Seat (1047m), a sharp-pointed peak which overhangs Coire Toll an Lochain; followed by the four pinnacles of Corrag Bhuidhe which gradually decrease from a height of 1020m. In summer these give interesting scrambling, with one difficult stretch of 10m on the south side of the last pinnacle. This can be by-passed by moving slightly out on the Toll an Lochain side. In winter they become more difficult, and all can be by-passed on the west side at a lower level.

Slabs lead down to the dip before the Corrag Bhuidhe Buttress (929m) then follows the top above the Cadha Ghobhlach, a small heather topped peak of 950m. This leads onto the steeper slope to the final flat top of Sail Liath (954m) at the south end of the ridge.

It is usual to return to the dip between the last two tops, and descend into Coire Toll an Lochain to view the cliffs from below, but it is possible to make a reasonable descent from the ridge of Sail Liath by the steep north-east side. A fairly obvious line lies down a big grassy gully some distance past the cairn where the slopes become less continuously rocky. This leads downwards over several small outcrops into Coire a'Ghiubhsachain whence the way towards the Dundonnell road lies along the sides of the Garbh Allt. The upper stretches of the corrie give enjoyable walking over great exposed payments of sandstone which make for quick passage to the road, and more than make up for the lack of marked track. Easy ways down into Toll an Lochain from the ridge can be found down the gully between the two main tops and down those of the Forked Pass or Cadha Ghoblach, between the last two points, on the ridge. Care should be taken by parties descending against dislodging loose boulders in the gullies, however.

Toll an Lochain, the southern of the twin corries of An Teallach is undoubtedly impressive but the tiered sandstone lacks continuity, due to the liberal distribution of wide grass ledges. Its climbing potential is chiefly in winter in the long gullies which drop from the ridge. The long gully running up from a point below the summit of Sgurr Fiona to the base of the upper rocks of Lord Berkeley's Seat is known as Lord's Gully and has produced a fine route for both summer and winter conditions. It is dry even on rainy days, and the rock here is clean and sound. The first summer ascent was in August, 1958, by D. Robertson and F. Old. The first winter ascent was by J. H. B. Bell and E. E. Roberts (Easter, 1923).

The summer route in *Lord's Gully* follows the line of the watercourse over many pitches, one of which, near the top, is severe. From the base of the upper rocks, go right up a steep slab. On the first ascent this was impossible after 45m due to wet mud. A descent was made for 18m then a traverse for 45m across the slabby face below Sgurr Fiona to grass ledges, then up to the main ridge. In dry conditions the direct finish should be possible.

A later winter route—45m Grade II (I. G. Rowe and A. McKeith, November, 1966)—starts directly below the summit of Sgurr Fiona. A narrow gully leads up to the left between the minor rib and the summit buttress of Sgurr Fiona towards Lord Berkeley's Seat. Early in the year there may be a few short pitches, but later they will probably be ironed out. Below Lord Berkeley's Seat, the gully opens out and forks. The direct finishes to both forks are fairly steep; however, a diagonal traverse to the right for 90m out on to the exposed summit buttress leads to a horizontal ledge. It should be possible to reach the col fairly easily by a leftward slanting shelf from this point. However, if the horizontal ledge is followed rightwards for 90m a similar shelf leads to the ridge in a further 90m. A later route here (A. Borthwick and F. Fotheringham, February, 1973) finished by the right branch, which give three pitches—Grade II.

Glover and Ling's route on *Corrag Buidhe South Buttress,* the earliest climb in Toll an Lochain, is of an indeterminate nature whose difficulties can all be avoided. *Constabulary Couloir,* 360m Grade II, is the long shallow couloir on the right of the Corrag Buidhe South Buttress (Top 957m) occupying the angle between the prominent shoulder and the main crags of Corrag Buidhe. It is a snow ribbon throughout most winters and is one of the few consistent winter lines on An Teallach. There are no real pitches, apart from an easy, avoidable lower ice-fall. It is not, however, a descent route.

The 1978 Face Route—450m Grade III/IV (M. Freeman and M. Keir, February, 1978)—is the most recently recorded route on this main face of Corrag Bhuide. It is identified by a snow patch—The Triangle—set above a rock barrier. From the terrace below the rock barrier, which is reached directly from the lochan, access is possible at either base angle of The Triangle or, more directly, access is possible at either base angle of The Triangle or, more directly, by ice-falls, depending from the snowfield. The route then follows a rightward sloping ramp above The Triangle to reach the crest of the buttress which finished to the immediate left of Lord Berkeley's Seat. The technical difficulties are found to be in the final section up the crest to the main ridge.

Lady Gully—Grade II (F. Fotheringham and J. R. R. Fowler, December, 1974)—starts at the apex of The Triangle described in the previous route.

The Sail Liath cliff, though impressive, is too broken to give any worthwhile routes. The small pinnacle just right of Sail Liath and to the left of the left fork of the Cadha Ghoblach, on the main ridge, has been climbed (Mild Severe) but dangerously loose and not recommended.

The south-east corner of Coire a'Ghlas Thuill contains a number of buttresses separated by steep gullies. *Hayfork Gully,* dividing the largest of the buttresses (South Crag on its left and Central Buttress on its right) was the scene of the first climb in the corrie by Messrs. Sang and Morrison in 1910. *Hayfork Gully, Fourth Prong,* has been climbed in winter conditions. The gullies form a set of vertical prongs towards the left of the cliff. This is the fourth from the left and appears to be the steepest. It is just left of Central Buttress, the most defined buttress in the corrie.

Checkmate Gully—210m Grade IV (T. W. Patey and C. J. S. Bonington, March, 1969) gives a fine winter line in A'Ghlas Thuill. It follows the long vertical chimney on the back wall of the corrie, which is in full view during the usual approach from the Dundonnell road. It is the first obvious major line left of the easy slopes at the back of the corrie and is frequently in good condition.

The South Crag of Sgurr Fiona offers two routes *Main Rib*—105m Difficult, lies on the left side, by far the longest buttress in the corrie. Start immediately left of the lowest point of the crags. *Minor Rib* lies to the right of Main Rib and is separated from it by a narrow gully. This gives a climb of 300m which has been done both in summer and in winter conditions.

The dividing gully—*The Alley*—360m Grade II/III (R. Baker and A. McCord, December, 1976)—is well defined in its lower two-thirds and contains four short ice pitches. A rock step and a ramp lead to the ridge.

The shoulder of Glas Mheall Mor has given a winter route—*Little*

19. *Looking across Loch Maree to Glen Bannisdale and the Bonnaidh Donn*

20. *Slioch from the River Grudie*

21. *Beinn Airidgh Charr to Carn Mor Wilderness*

22. *Looking across the Fionn Loch to Beinn Airigh Charr*

DONALD BENNET

23.   *Carnmore Crag with the Lodge Beneath*

24. *Beinn Dearg Mhor and Shenevall Bothy*

Glass Monkey—75m Grade III (D. Wilson and W. Beveridge, 1967). The shoulder ends in a spur with two buttresses divided by a miniature corrie. The northernmost buttress, which is easily reached from the Dundonnell path, is cleft by a Y-shaped gully of which the left fork is taken.

The *Terminal Tower* of Sgurr Ruadh, the westmost bastion of An Teallach, above the west end of Loch na Sealga, gives some climbing of a not-too-serious nature. Starting from the lowest points of the rocks which face north-west, there is much scope for variation.

Coir a'Ghuibhsachain, the west-facing scarp running parallel to, and less than a half km. west of, the Shenavall track, offers a continuous line of clean, steep quartzite of an average height of 60m. It provides an excellent practice crag, readily accessible from the road. The rock is steep and smooth and the holds small but good, with a wide range of possible routes. About 1km N.N.E. of Achnegie and near the short-cut path from Corriehallie to Shenavall, is a quartzite cliff—The Nursery. The central and highest section is composed of three vague buttresses. These give climbs of Very Difficult standard, all done in 1953 by Messrs. Nicol, Wagstaff and Wrangham. On the left is *Freeman*—54m; *Hardy* is in the centre, 66m; *Willis* is on the right, 54m. They form a southern continuation of the Coir a'Ghuibhsachain scarp.

Gruinard Jetty Buttress (N.G. 961927) and *Goat Crag* (N.G. 960920). These two crags lie some 15km from Dundonnell on the road to Aultbea and between them now have some forty or so short climbs (30m) varying in standard from Difficult to Very Severe. A guide to the climbs on Jetty Crag is probaby available on application to the Army Mountain Training Centre at Fort George, Inverness.

Beinn Ghobhlach (635m)

This shapely little mountain is the prominent terminal point of the peninsula between Loch Broom and Little Loch Broom. It can be approached from the east by way of the passenger ferry from Ullapool to Altnaharrie, or from the west by way of Dundonnell. The road from Dundonnell leads to the isolated crofting community of Scoraig and is motorable for almost 8km to Badralloch. Beinn Ghoblach is worth visiting, both for its isolated location and the fine outlook it gives in all directions.

111

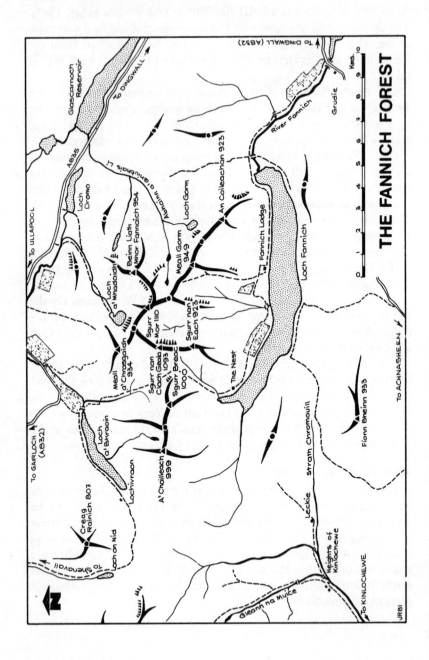

THE FANNICH FOREST

The Fannich Forest

(1) **A'Chailleach** (999m) N.H. 136714
(2) **Toman Coinich** (937m) N.H. 148714 Unnamed on O.S. map, lies between (1) and (3)
(3) **Sgurr Breach** (1000m) N. 158711
(4) **Meall A'Chrasgaidh** (934m) N.H. 184733
(5) **Sgurr Nan Clach Geala (1093m) N.H. 184715**
(6) **Sgurr Nan Each** 923m) N.H. 184697
(7) **Carn Na Criche** (961m) N.H. 196725
(8) **Sgurr Mor** (1110m) N.H. 203718
(9) **Meall Nam Peithirean** (974m) N.H. 207708
(10) **Meall Gorm West Top** (Meallan Rairigidh) (949m) N.H. 222696
(11) **Meall Gorm East Top** (922m) N.H. 232692
(12) **An Coileachan** (923m) N.H. 241680
(13) **Beinn Liath Mhor Fannaich** (954m) N.H. 219724
(14) **Fionn Bheinn** (933m) N.H. 147621. South side of Loch Fannich.

MAPS: O.S. 1:50,000 (2nd Series). Sheet No. 19—Gairloch and Ullapool. Sheet No. 20—Beinn Dearg.

The general area of the mountains of the Fannich group is roughly triangular in shape. The base is formed by the road from Garve to Kinlochewe which is part of the southern boundary of the area of the Northern Highlands and the apex can be taken as the road junction at Braemore. The north-west side is formed firstly by the road from Braemore to Loch a'Bhraoin, then continuing from the south-west end of the loch, along a line across the Bealach na h'Imrich and through Gleann Tanagaidh to Kinlochewe. Apart from some Forestry Commission plantations along the southern boundary, most of the area is deer forest and, once off the main roads, the only habitations are on the north side Loch Fannich. The 11km stretch of water cuts across the centre of the area in a line approximately east to west and, with one exception, the main mountain tops lie to the north side of it. The Fannichs have usually been regarded as a fine high-level walking area with little to offer in the way of summer or winter climbing. This has been disproved by recent exploration of the individual mountains and their true worth is gradually being appreciated. It would be reasonable to claim that it now ranks as one of the finest all-round mountaineering areas in the country, offering fine high-level ridge walks of testing length; climbing routes in both summer and winter; and, like Beinn Dearg and Seana Bhraigh, the chance to combine climbing with ski-touring.

The main mountain group is divided naturally by the hill-pass running approximately due north-south from the east end of Loch a'Bhraoin to the west end of Loch Fannich. A good track follows the pass rising up to 640m contour at the highest point of the bealach and forms the main through route in the area.

From the Braemore-Dundonnell road a rough vehicle track leads down to Locha'Bhraoin in less than 1.5km. This is for foot-travellers only. There is a boat-house and various other outbuildings by the lochside, none of which can be used for accommodation. The bothy at Lochivroan, reached by track along the north side of the loch, is frequently used by climbing parties and others. It must be emphasised that permission to use it should be obtained from the owner—Mr. Robson, Inverbroom Lodge, Loch Broom. Like most bothies, it is unlikely that it can be used during the stalking season—September to mid-October.

A path from the boat-house leads round the east end of the loch, crosses the Abhainn Cuileig by a raised narrow footbridge and continues through the pass. The crossing of the burn 800m from the end of the loch can be awkward, and is largely a matter of personal choice. The south end of the path comes out at the empty house on the west end of Loch Fannich which is known as 'The Nest', then continues along the north shore of the loch to join the Hydro road at Fannich Lodge. The Nest can be used as a bothy when the estate is not using it. The Nest is on Lochrosque Estate but enquiries regarding its use can be made to the stalker at Fannich Lodge.

An unsurfaced vehicle road continues along this north side of Loch Fannich, past the dam and through forestry plantations to reach the main road from Garve at Grudie Bridge, by the head of Loch Luichart—a distance of about 10km.

The gate at the end of this road is often locked but it is possible to obtain a key from Grudie Power Station. During the stalking season, access is restricted for obvious reasons—the road passes through three

114

deer forests. In winter, the road is frequently blocked and consequently should be used with discretion.

A'Chailleach (999m), **Toman Coinich** (967m) and **Sgurr Breac** (972m)

The West Fannich group consists of three main tops— A'Chailleach, Toman Coinich and Sgurr Breac. These run in a line west-north-west to east-south-east equidistant between Loch a'Bhraoin and Loch Fannich. The south-west slopes fall steeply down into the Nest of Fannich, the long U-shaped corrie which opens out on the west end of the loch providing a natural deer sanctuary. A south-easterly curving ridge from the summit of A'Chailleach forms the south leg of the U, terminating at a height of 736m on the top of An Sguman, over-looking the ruin of Cabuie Lodge on the side of Loch Fannich.

On the north side of the main ridge, the walls of the corrie containing Loch Toll an Lochain are formed by the north spur of A'Chailleach, which ends in the rocky bluff of Sron na Coibhre and,the steep-sided, broad-topped ridge leading from the summit of Toman Coinich, which slopes gradually towards the east end of Loch a'Bhraoin. This ridge provides the easiest route on to the summits of all three of the mountains of this western group. From the boat-house at the loch's end, the track into the pass is followed for a short distance and then a steep, grassy climb leads onto the broad, flat, lower slope of Druim Reidh. Easy walking leads upwards to Toman Coinich and from there the other two peaks can be climbed as desired. In summer there is no difficulty but in winter the mountains here take on a different aspect and the summit ridge should be treated with respect. The map does not indicate the true extent of the fall-away of the slopes to the north and south of the main ridge and the edge of the crags can be heavily corniced. The view westward is dominated by Slioch and further to the north the whole splendour of An Teallach is unfolded. The Eastern Fannichs appear as a rolling line of ridges dominated by the peak of Sgurr Mor. To the west, A'Chailleach drops down into the Bealach na h'Imrich which provides a cross-country link by way of Gleann Tanagaidh to Kinlochewe and the mountains of Torridon and Loch Maree. A link track from the Heights of Kinlochewe, 8km from the bealach, leads to the south-east of Loch Fada.

The East Fannich group consists of ten tops of over 914m, seven of which form the spine of a 13km ridge running in a line north-west to south-east from the east end of Loch a'Bhraoin to the dam at the east end of Loch Fannich. From north to south these are in order: Meall a'Chrasgaidh (934m), Carn na Criche (961m), Sgurr Mor (1100m), Meall nam Peithrean (974m), Meallan Rairigidh, the west top of Meall Gorm (949m), the east top of Meall Gorm (922m) and An Coileachan (923m). A secondary ridge swings south from Carn na Criche for 5½km towards the north end of Loch Fannich over the tops of Sgurr nan Clach Geala (1093m) and Sgurr nan Each (923m). The western slopes of this ridge, which fall away into the bealach, are steep but rich in grazing—the top of the broad basin enclosed by the saddle leading on to Sgurr nan Clach Geala from Carn na Criche is aptly named Am Biachdaich—the place of the fattening. The eastern slopes drop precipitously into Choire Mhoir and form the main climbing ground of the Fannichs to date. From Sgurr Mor, a second cross-ridge cuts eastwards for 1.5km to Beinn Liath Mhor Fannaich (954m) from where it falls in broad, rounded slopes towards the roadside by Loch Droma. The south slopes of this ridge terminate in Creag Dubh Fannaich (757m).

A great wedge-shaped glen pierces this eastern side of the Fannichs to the foot of Sgurr Mor, its side formed by the eastern and main ridges. The approach along this is pathless and, although a way can be made along the Abhainn an Torrain Dubh from the road by Loch Glascarnoch, the going is heavy and involves steep climbs from the basins of Loch Li and Loch an Fhuar Thuill Mhoir at the head of the glen. The through-track along Loch Fannich is the key to the traverse of the ridges of this eastern group, giving easy straightforward ascents from three directions. Once on the ridge, the main tops can be climbed in any combination so desired with little difficulty and escape is possible throughout down the grassy western slopes. Visibility in the Fannichs is often impaired by low-cloud and good navigation here is an essential skill. The east faces of Sgurr Mor, Sgurr nan Clach Geala and Sgurr Breac drop sharply from the summit cairns and, at the south-east end of the ridge, the two steep, rocky corries of An Coileachan—Garbh Coire Mhor to the south-east and Coire nan Eun lying north-north-east—should be kept in mind. It is worth noting that the stalker's track marked leading from Fannich Lodge up the south ridge of Meall Gorm is in good condition.

From the north side, the ridge can be approached by three tracks which are worth attention, leading from the road angle around

Braemore Junction. (1) From the road to Dundonnell 4km from the junction, a track leaves the road beside a stone bridge and winds upwards towards Meall a'Chrasgaidh over open moorland. In its upper reaches it tends to be difficult to follow but is useful in that it leads to the foot of the north-east ridge of the mountain. (2) From the first big bend past the junction on the same road a straighter track leads in towards the same feature. On the map it is shown as stopping on the ridge north of Creag Rainich but a line of cairns can be traced and on the ridge south-west of Creag Rainich the path is clearer. A path now leads up on to the saddle betwen Meall a'Chraisgaidh and Carn na Criche to a cairn just below the level of the ridge. (3) Leave the road from Garve at the north end of Loch Droma and follow the hydro road across the dam and along the pipe-line leading to the Allt a'Mhadaidh. A bridge over the burn connects with the stalker's track from the road which leaves the road 1.6km north of the dam beside a tin-roofed stone shed. The track is now followed towards Loch a'Mhadaidh and can be left if desired to climb on to Beinn Liath Mhor Fannaich whose broad slopes and flat summit ridge present no difficulty. The map shows the track as crossing the main stream of the Allt a'Mhadaidh at a junction of the burns, but in fact here it disappears and the crossing is found another 1km on. The path reappears and leads upwards over bad ground to Loch a'Mhadaidh. From here one can ascend the saddle between Sgurr Mor and Carn na Criche with little difficulty. Alternatively, skirt round the south side of the loch and make a direct ascent, giving stiffer going on to Sgurr Mor.

An alternative route into the climbing area on the east side of Sgurr nan Clach Geala is to follow the Allt a'Choire Mhoir over pathless boggy ground from the track past Fannich Lodge to the head of Coire Mhoir.

The Geala Buttresses are not marked on the O.S. map. They lie to the north of the summit of Sgurr nan Clach Geala, rising 240m above the more broken lower crags—N.H. 190715. The six narrow buttresses are of mica-schist and are numbered from 1 to 6 going northwards.

Nos. 1 and 6 should give summer climbs, but Nos. 2 and 3 are probably too broken. No. 4 Buttress is also named *Skyscraper Buttress*—240m Severe (T. W. Patey, J. M. Taylor, J. White and G. K. Annand, 3rd April, 1961). This is the central spire of the crags, with the best climbing in the top 120m. The slabby base of the buttress is by-passed by climbing Gamma Gully to above a narrow, deep-set slot. Grass ledges lead onto the buttress which is climbed from the centre.

The winter route—240m Grade V (R. J. Archbold, M. J. Freeman, J. C. Higham and R. A. Smith, 18th February, 1978)—took eight hours. The summer route was followed throughout.

No. 5 Buttress, or *Sellar's Buttress,* gives a fine introductory rock climb to the crags—180m Very Difficult (T. W. Patey and R. Harper, 16th April, 1961). The start is below a clean rock rib on the left, up the crest of the prominent shoulder, then a shattered rib in direct line to the top for the last 45m. The winter ascent of the Buttress—240m Grade IV (G. S. Strange and D. Stuart, February, 1972)—was described as being 'magnificent'.

No. 2 Butttress—*Sunrise Buttress*—has also been climbed in winter—150m Grade IV (R. Baines and D. M. Nichols, 18th February, 1978). The route follows a line in the middle of the buttress. Starting at the foot of Beta Gully, ice-bulges are climbed for three pitches, then an obvious gully system. An overhang is turned on the left, then the arête followed to the top.

The five deep gullies separating the buttresses offer superb winter climbing. From left to right these are named Alpha, Beta, Gamma, Delta and Epsilon. The approach in winter is awkward, and was described in detail in the C.M.C. Easter Ross Rock and Ice Guide as follows:—

"The approach to the foot of the main cliffs is guarded by a long rock step, and in winter there is a steep apron of snow between it and the foot of the buttresses. The step is breached at only two points. On the very left is a broken section giving access to Buttresses 1 to 4 and Gullies Alpha to Delta, but in any other than snowy conditions, this becomes a 20m ice pitch, and in any case care is needed to locate it from above in event of a forced retreat. On the right is a slanting rake climbing to the right below the feet of Buttresses 5 and 6 and Epsilon Gully. This, (Slanting Gully), links with the Apron about 15m above its only pitch, more or less with the top of the Apron. As the pitch in Slanting Gully can be easily avoided on the north, this approach to the Apron is always easy, so Slanting Gully is recommended as the approach to all climbs."

All five gullies have now been climbed: *Alpha Gully*—240m Grade II (P. Baker and D. S. B. Wright, March, 1965). The gully itself is only 120m but, at the top, a continuation along the crest of No. 2 Buttress is unavoidable and doubles the length of the climb. *Beta*

Gully—270m Grade III. *Centre Fork* (P. F. Macdonald and J. Porteous); *Right Fork*—(I. G. Rowe and W. Sproul, 28th February, 1970). A large ice-fall gives access to the gully, which is straightforward to the trifurcation. Here a short left fork goes out onto No. 2 Buttress; the Centre Fork contains a steep pitch and is rejoined higher up by the Right Fork. *Gamma Gully*—210m Grade IV (P. N. L. Tranter and I. G. Rowe, 6th and 7th March, 1965), gave a superb route and is described as follows:—"The first pitch is on the left of a shallow scoop on ice for 30m, followed by a very narrow, deep-set slot, 30m also. Some 20m above the slot is the crux, a 9m vertical ice wall with overhanging top, held in either side by holdless rock walls. A belay can be had above, followed immediately by a 12m ice pitch. This can also be hard, as it may form a big mushroom growth of ice. The remainder of the gully is easier, steep snow with occasional rock steps and it finally loses itself in the large scoop (often corniced) above Beta Gully." *Delta Gully*—240m Grade IV (D. Dinwoodie and M. Freeman)—was considered a fine gully with impressive rock and ice scenery. *Epsilon Gully*—Grade III/IV (M. Freeman and N. Keir, 16th March, 1974)—after a hard start, was found to be straightforward.

Climbing elsewhere in the Fannichs is still in the process of being developed.

The west face of Beinn Liath Mhor Fannaich has three climbable gullies. The left-most is *Wot Gully*—135m Grade III (R. Graham and R. Warrack, 9th April, 1967). The south corner of the east face of Sgurr Mor has a straightforward snow gully—*Easter Gully*—240m Grade II (B. Brand and O. Bruskeland, 10th April, 1967) *East Face*—300m Grade II (R. Graham and R. Warwick, 11th April, 1967)—climbs a shallow groove in the face winding towards summit. The groove has four pitches, of which the first was the hardest. The most recently recorded route here is *The Resurrection*—450m Grade IV/V (D. Butterfield and J. MacKenzie, 14th March, 1980). It is described as follows:—"Between Easter Gully and East Face Route are a series of icefalls, bordered on the left by a steep gully groove. Follow this to a niche on the right wall at an icefall. Traverse right across a diminishing ledge (peg runner), across a bulge, then weave through bulges to belay shelf (36m). Climb ice above, then traverse left to bulge and up iced slabs to in situ, peg belay on right (45m). Gain steepening snowfield above, heading for icefall in centre (several pitches of 45m). Climb icefall to snow belay at 39m. Go up left to gain steepening shallow scoop then up hard snow or ice steeply to vertical rock headwall (several pitches). A shallow cave behind icicle fringe provides refuge. Now traverse right beneath headwall, round steep rib then up to snow belays above. Traverse up and right again to where headwall suddenly ends and finish up steep snow with cornice finish. A superb but intimidating alpine-like route, with great variety of climbing. Early in the season the snowfields present an avalanche threat, as do the massive cornices in thaw conditions. Despite this, the route is highly recommended.''

Garbh Coire Mhoir of An Coileachan, the most easterly mountain of the Fannichs has certainly been the scene of most activity in recent years. Parties had certainly visited the corrie previously, but details always seem hard to trace. In 1976 C. Rowland and D. Scott climbed *Beta Gully*—210m Grade III—approaching from Fannich Dam, this is the second gully from the left. The first 90m was interesting ice, followed by 120m of easy snow.

A deluge of new routes appeared in the winter of 1979. These are as follows:—

Short Shrift—150m Grade II/III (B. Brown and J. MacKenzie, 27th January, 1979)—on the left (north) wall of the corrie is a prominent, narrow gully which is followed over two ice pitches to its conclusion at 75m. Either finish straight up over snow, or go right and up for a further 150m of mixed ground at Grade II.

Echo Face—360m Grade III/IV (D. McCallum and J. MacKenzie, 13th January, 1979). Between the central gully and the corner on the extreme right of the corrie there is a large slabby face with a thin central line.

Plumline—360m Grade IV (B. Brown and J. MacKenzie, 10th February, 1979). This route climbs the fine corner on the right of the corrie, right of Echo Face.

Prime Buttress—210m Grade III (R. Butler, D. Howard, D. MacCallum and C. Raylance, 11th February, 1979)—climbs the edge of the buttress left of the Central Gully.

Crystal Tripper—210m Grade IV (D. MacCallum and J. MacKenzie, 17th February, 1979)—to the right of the third gully from the left there is an impressive icefall. The start is 30m right of the gully at an inset corner.

Sage Corner—165m Grade II/III (D. Butterfield and J. MacKenzie, 5th May, 1979). About half way up the way easy central gully break out right and head up iced slabs and snow to a prominent icefall bordering a corner. The icefall consists of short, vertical steps and may extend for 90m. The finish is up snow.

There are probably other new routes here still unrecorded.

Fionn Bheinn (933m)

Fionn Behinn lies within the area of the Fannichs but is entirely isolated from the main group of mountains. It must be one of the least inspiring tops in Munro's Tables and can be climbed in under two hours without difficulty, from the road junction at Achnasheen. The top is rounded and grassy and the two wide corries on the north-east side, Toll Mor and Toll Beag, are steep but virtually unbroken. It is possible to approach the mountain by a much more circuitous route along the rough stalker's road to Loch Fannich which leaves the Garve-Achnasheen road at the end of Strathbran Plantation—5km to the east of Achnasheen. This was the road to Cabuie Lodge, which stood at the west end of Loch Fannich until it was dismantled in the 1950's. It is of little interest to the hill walker and not recommended. The one redeeming feature of Fionn Bheinn is the superb view it gives in all directions. The mountain does receive a mention, however, in the prophecies of Kenneth MacKenzie, the Brahan Seer, the famous 17th century sooth-sayer. He predicted that "the day will come when a raven, attired in plaid and bonnet, will drink his fill of human blood on Fionn Bheinn, three times a day, for three successive days". There are no reports to date of this prophecy having been fulfilled.

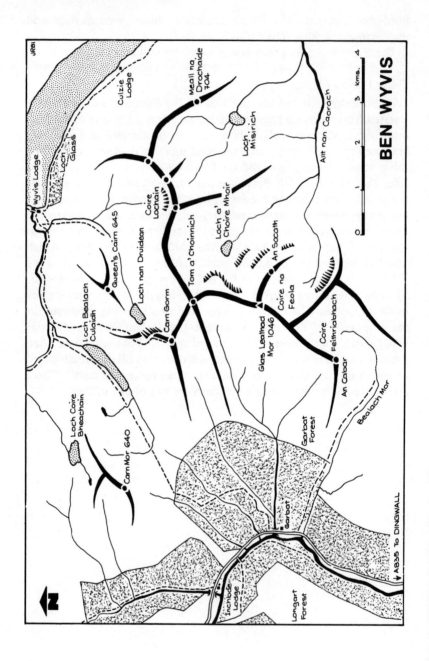

BEN WYVIS

6

Ben Wyvis and Easter Ross

(1) **Glas Leathad Mor** (1046m) N.H. 463684
(2) **An Cabar** (950m) N.H. 450666
(3) **An Socath** (1007m) N.H. 471682
(4) **Tom a'Choinnich** (955m) N.H. 463700
(5) **Glas Leathad Beag** (928m) N.H. 492706

Little Wyvis (764m) N.H. 430645
Carn Chuinneag (838m) N.H. 484833
Beinn a'Chaisteil (787m) N.H. 370801
Meall a'Ghrianan (771m) N.H. 366766

MAPS: O.S. 1:50,000 (2nd Series) Sheet No. 20—Beinn Dearg. Sheet No. 21—Dornoch Firth.

The mountains described in this chapter of the guide book lie on the peninsula of Easter Ross, which is bounded on its north side by the Kyle of Sutherland and the Dornoch Firth, and on its south side by the Cromarty Firth. The western boundary is the line formed by Strath Carron and Strath Vaich.

The eastern part of the area jutting out into the Moray Firth at Tarbet Ness is mainly low-lying farming land. The belt of Old Red Sandstone which occurs all along the north-east coast of the mainland produces rich soil, and the inland moorlands provide good rough grazing for sheep. This part of Easter Ross holds the bulk of the population, and is more like Caithness or the counties of Moray than the mountainous area to the west. The sheltered Cromarty Firth, with its fine natural harbour at Invergordon, has a major role in the development programme for the whole Moray Firth seaboard. The county town of Dingwall at the head of the Firth is one of the main road junctions north of Inverness.

The main road to the north passes through Dingwall and continues around the coastline through Invergordon and Tain to Ardgay at the head of the Dornoch Firth. A road over Struie Hill, which leaves the A9 3km past Evanton and joins the main road again 5km from

Ardgay, is a useful shortcut. This saves about 16km of travel and opens several longish approach routes onto the foothills of the Ben Wyvis range. The road is often blocked in winter but adequate warning is given at either end in the form of A.A. signposts.

From Dingwall the main road to the west branches at Garve, the right-hand fork passing onwards to Ullapool by way of the "Dirrie More" and Loch Broom. At Garbat, 6.5km past Garve, the road passes immediately below the main ridge of Ben Wyvis. There is no continuous road across the western boundary but motor access is possible from either end for the greater part of the way.

On the north, a side road from Ardgay goes up Strath Carron for 14.5km to the bridge at The Craigs. A landrover track branches past Amat Forest, then up Gleann Mhor as far as Deannich Lodge. There is a locked gate near Alladale Lodge and enquiries should be made at the Benmore Estate office at Ardgay.

From the Garve-Ullapool road a side-road from the Black Bridge, 2.5km before Altguish Inn, goes northwards up Strath Vaich towards Loch Vaich. Just below Strath Vaich Lodge, a hydro-road, not marked on older editions of the O.S. map, now continues up the east side of the loch to the head of the glen and over the watershed to Gleann Mhor, above Deannich Lodge. It goes still further up Gleann Beag to finish at a barrage about a mile below the bothy of Glenbeg. There is a locked gate at the start, but the previous estate proprietor, Commander Williams of Strathvaich, courteously indicated his willingness to co-operate if application is made to him for permission and sporting rights recognised. The road is passable for cars and gives 18km of easy access to the interior. The estate has now changed ownership but enquiries can be made at the stalker's house, some 5km up the glen near Strathvaich Lodge—Telephone No. Aultguish 226.

Ben Wyvis (1046m)

The mountain mass of Ben Wyvis is made up of seven tops over 914m. These form a ridge running for more than 6.5km in a south-west to north-east direction, from Garbat to Loch Glass. seen from most directions it shows little indication of any great distinguishing feature. The north-western flanks fall in steep, unbroken slopes to the road by Garbat and its south-eastern face is largely hidden by its own foothills, which stretch down towards the shores of the Cromarty Firth. This eastern side, however, is split by two great corries—Coire

Mor and Coire na Feola—with impressive crags of folded Moine schist. These lie on either side of the eastern spur of Ben Wyvis, An Socach (1007m).

The easiest approach to the mountain is undoubtedly from Garbat, on the road to Ullapool, 24km from Dingwall. A rough track leads off from the road past the farmhouse to the Forestry Commission fence. The gate here is usually unlocked. A boggy land-rover track, definitely unsuitable for any other vehicles, leads through the newly planted forestry ground upwards onto the pass between Ben Wyvis and Little Wyvis—The Bealach Mor. From the pass, a steep heathery slope leads upwards to the summit of An Cabar. The distance from the road is only 3km by this route but involves one in 800m of stiff ascent. Once on the main ridge the traverse of the plateau is easily accomplished and the views in all directions are extensive. On a clear day, seven counties, the North Sea and the Atlantic Ocean can all be seen from the summit. The main top, Glas Leathad Mor (1046m) lies 2.4km N.N.E. of An Cabar along the broad flat plateau, and from here the remainder of the tops can be climbed in any convenient combination. The western slopes obviously take their name from the main top—'the big grey one.' These can easily be descended to the Garbat road at various points but care should be taken in adverse weather conditions when the walking can become treacherous. The circuit from Garbat along the ridge to Tom a'Choinnich and thence back to the start by way of the Carn Gorm shoulder gives a fine 14km hill-walk with very little intermediate ascent.

The mountain can also be approached from the Dingwall-Strathpeffer road by a side road leading to Achterneed which branches north 4.8km west of Dingwall. This is the usual starting place for the annual midnight walk to Ben Wyvis which has long been a local custom, but the 16km route is of no great interest and is not recommended. A longer, but much more rewarding approach from the south-east, is from Evanton, 11km north of Dingwall on the A9. A road, signposted 'Assynt', leaves the main road at the bridge in the centre of the village and leads north-westwards up Glen Glass for almost 8km to the bridge at Eileanach. From here the road continues along the west side of Loch Glass for another 8km or so to the Wyvis Lodge, but the gate at the bridge is locked and permission cannot be obtained to go further.

Between the main road and the Eileanach Bridge, closer exploration of the glen itself is rewarding. The road passes along the north side of the River Glass through extensive forestry plantations of conifers. Leave the road at Assynt house and make a way down through the trees towards the river bed. At first it seems as if the river has gone underground but careful inspection will show that it is running along the foot of a deep, narrow gorge. This is the famous Black Rock of Novar, which is not a solitary rock but a mile long chasm cut through the Old Red Sandstone. The walls drop vertically throughout its length to depths varying from 20m to 40m and, at places, are undercut. The River Glass flows swiftly through the dark gorge, taking with it most of the drainage from the Ben Wyvis range. A local man from Evanton, Donald Macdonald, once jumped across it at a point where it reaches a depth of 30m and, in more recent years a well-equipped party from the Ferranti Mountaineering Club, Messrs. J. C. Cruickshank and D. Macdonald, traversed the gorge at water level.

From Eileanach the way now lies cross-country to the junction of the Allt Coire Mistrich and the Allt nan Caorach. A track follows the Allt nan Caorach for 3km westwards and the choice of route is now open. A good 21km circuit can be completed by ascending the south ridge of Coire na Feola to the summit, then climbing in succession over Tom a'Choinnich and Glas Leathad Beag and descending the broad south-east shoulder of the ridge—Leacann Bhreac—to rejoin the track at Allt nan Caorach. If transport can be made available at the end, the complete traverse from Evanton to Garbat (25km and 1280m of ascent) is a fine expedition.

The approach from Eileanach also opens up the exploration of the two corries on this eastern side of Ben Wyvis. The rock in both of these tends to be vegetated and Coire Feola, the left-most corrie, has given no climbing. Four prominent spurs rise steeply above Coire Mor on its west side. No. 1 is of no interest in summer. An easy gully separates it from Nos. 2 and in winter this gives a fairly steep snow climb with a cornice. No. 2 consists of two buttresses divided by a narrow, easy gully named *Fox Gully*. Both of these offer a climb of about Difficult standard. No. 3 has a vegetated cliff on its lower left and a very large slab on its right at middle height. This has been climbed, taking a diagonal line from lowest right to upper left—125m. Very Difficult (J. MacKenzie, 20th June, 1970). No. 4 consists of a series of short rock steps and grass ledges inconveniently sloping wrongly.

Ben Wyvis in winter garb is a much more impressive mountain, and any expedition increases in difficulty. The snow-fields on the eastern

25.   *Looking south to Sgurr Ban and Beinn a'Chladheimh*

DONALD BENNET

26.   *Toll an Lochan; An Teallach*

DONALD BENNET

27.   *On An Teallach between Corrag Bhuidhe and Sgurr Fiona*

DONALD BENNET

28.   *On Wisdom Buttress, Beinn Lair*

side have become increasingly popular with skiers and the development of a winter sports area for the north is a real possibility.

As has been described in the introduction to this guide book, the best of the corries is the south-east corrie of the main ridge—Coire na Feith Riabhach (or Coire na Fearaich)—unnamed on the O.S. Map. At present, access from Garbat is facilitated by the use of suitably tracked vehicles and conditions for skiing last for a considerable part of the winter. Snow can still be found in patches on the summit ridge even in mid-summer, which no doubt made it easy for the Mackenzie Earls of Cromarty who held this area in the past to pay their rent. Their estates were held from the Crown on condition that they could produce a snow-ball from Ben Wyvis when called to do so throughout the year.

Beinn a'Chaisteall (786m) and Meall a'Ghrianan(771m)

Beinn a'Chaisteall and Meall a'Ghrianan are the highest points on the ridge which rises up from the east side of Loch Vaich, 1.3km north-west of Ben Wyvis. They are best approached from Aultguish Hotel by the road along Strath Vaich already described. A track rises north-eastwards from the bridge past Lubriach over the saddle between Meall a'Ghrianan and Creag Bhreac Mhor into the neighbouring Strath Rannoch. From the saddle, the long south ridge of Meall a'Ghrianan is easily climbed to the summit. Beinn a'Chaisteall lies another 2.5km N.N.E. along the ridge. This is a fine hill-walking area but it lies in the heart of the deer forest and there are restrictions during the stalking season. Both Beinn an Chaisteall and Carn Chuinneag are listed in Corbett's Tables of 2500 ft. tops.

Carn Chuinneag (838m)

Carn Chuinneag is the highest top on the south side of Glen Diebidale , 13km to the north of Ben Wyvis, and the hills of this area are best approached from Ardgay. Following the road along Strath Carron for 16km by way of The Craigs to Glen Calvie Lodge, Diebidale Lodge lies 4km along Glen Calvie and a track rises steeply from the road past the lodge on to the 762m contour below the summit of the ridge. The ridge forms the south side of Glen Diebidale and on its side is served by several long cross country tracks stretching towards the road over Struie Hill, some 19km distant. Their usefulness, however, is limited and permission to approach from this direction is somewhat restricted, mainly because of poachers.

Carn Chuinneag's twin-topped summit is easily reached by the good stalker's track already mentioned and in winter, ski conditions here are often remarkably good. The wide, north-facing corrie is reminiscent of a miniature Coire Cas.

Alladale and Gleann Beag

The road from Ardgay along Strath Carron also provides access to two relatively newly discovered rock faces—The Alladale Wall and the Gleann Beag Crags. These could equally well be included in the area of the next chapter as they lie north of Strath Vaich and Strath Carron. Both have produced a number of worthwhile rock-routes, largely pioneered by the members of the Corriemulzie Mountaineering Club and the late Dr. T. W. Patey.

The Alladale Wall is a 250m cliff on An Socach, at the head of Glen Alladale. The approach is by way of Strath Carron to the Craigs, then past Amat Lodge to Alladale Lodge, 18km from Ardgay. The surfaced road stops at the turning to Glen Calvie and, beyond this, vehicle tracks generally tend to become rough and require care. The locked gate before Alladale has already been mentioned. Just before the lodge, a rough track goes westwards to Alladale and there is an excellent bothy past the woods which can be used with the permission of the Estate Factor at Ardgay. Enquiries can also be made locally to the stalker at Alladale Lodge. This gives an open view up the glen, through which a track leads to the Alladale Wall. The wall is of steep, smooth-polished, glaciated quartzite and gives delicate balance climbing of exceptionally fine quality. Protection, however, is found to be in short supply.

Gleann Beag lies at the head of Gleann Mhor and is approached by way of Deannich, as already described, or, perhaps more easily, from Strath Vaich. The main crag lies south of Carn Loch Sruban Mhor on the north side of the glen. Also on this side, but 1.6km to the east, lies Niagara Slab and on the south side of the glen beyond the bothy is the only other rock explored, Cottage Slab. The bothy at Glenbeg has frequently been used by parties but is private property. It is advisable to enquire for permission to use it from the stalker, Mr. Cameron, Inverlael, Lochbroom. Neither bothy is available during the stalking season (12th August to 31st January). It has been noted that the boulders below the Main Crag are suitable for bivouac purposes.

The climbing on the Gleann Beag crags is not held to be on the same scale as that at Alladale. Routes in both areas were first detailed in the

C.M.C. *Rock and Ice Guide to Easter Ross.* They are now included in the S.M.C. *Climbers' Guide to the Northern Highlands Area*—Volume 1—Letterewe and Easter Ross.

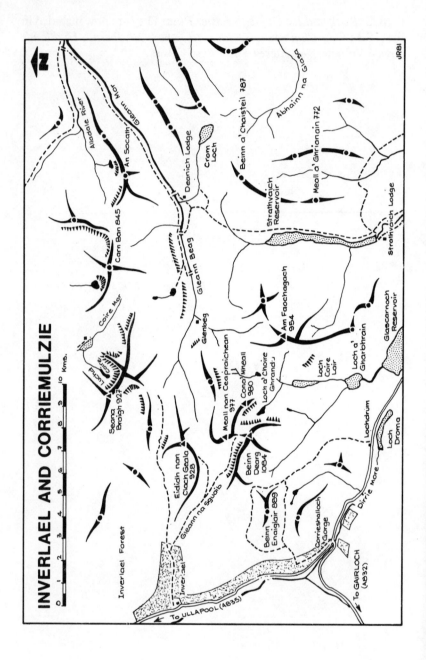

INVERLAEL AND CORRIEMULZIE

Beinn Dearg and Corriemulzie

(1) **Beinn Dearg** (1084m) N.H. 259812
(2) **Cona'Mheall** (980m) N.H. 275816
(3) **Meall Nan Ceapraichean** (977m) N.H. 257825
(4) Ceann Garbh (967m) N.H. 259831
(5) **Eididh Nan Clach Geala** (928m) N.H. 257843
(6) Beinn Enaiglair (889m) N.H. 225805
(7) **Iorguill** (873m) N.H. 239816
(8) Am Faochaghach (954m) N.H. 303793
(9) **Carn Gorm Loch** (910m) N.H. 319801
(10) **Seana Bhraigh** (927m) N.H. 282878
(11) **Carn Ban** (845m) N.H. 338876

MAP: O.S. 1:50,000 (2nd Series) Sheet No. 20—Beinn Dearg. Sheet No. 21—Dornoch Firth.

This exceptionally fine group of mountains lies in the area between Loch Broom and Strath Oykel, to the north-west of Strath Vaich and Strath Carron. In the north, the area is divided from Coigach and Assynt by the road from Ullapool to Ledmore Junction. The main road from Dingwall to Ullapool passes along its west border by way of Garve and Braemore Junction. This is completely reconditioned and now gives a fast passage from the south. The eastern side can be approached by the road from Ardgay to Lochinver which follows the Oykel valley. The road from Ullapool to Ledmore Junction is too distant from the main tops to be of much use and the tracks through Glen Achal and Glen Einig, which form a cross-country link between Ullapool and Oykel Bridge, provide the best access from the north. The approach from the south by way of Strath Vaich and Strath Carron has been described in the previous chapter.

The area is practically all deer forest, but up till now no attempt has been made by the various estate owners to restrict access by walkers or climbers, except during the stalking season. Habitations in the interior are few and far between, being limited largely to shooting lodges and estate workers' houses. Ullapool is the main centre of population on the west side and, on the east, the villages of Ardgay and Bonar Bridge at either side of the head of the Dornoch Firth.

Ullapool is a busy fishing port and one of the most popular holiday resorts in the West. It has now taken the place of Kyle of Lochalsh as the car and passenger ferry terminal for Stornoway and the Island of Lewis. There is a wide choice of hotel, motel, guest-house and bed and breakfast accommodation. In addition, there is a youth hostel on Shore Street and a large camp and caravan site near the pier. Its situation makes it an ideal centre for the exploration of all the mountains within a radius of almost 40km. The present-day port was established as an experiment in 1788 by the British Fisheries Association in the hope that it would become the chief centre for the west coast fishings. Previously, Inverlael, at the head of Broom, had been the main settlement in the immediate locality. Ullapool, however, as the name suggests, must have been in existence still earlier. Pool is a form of the Norse word 'bol' or town and Ullapool was the 'Olave's Town' of the early Viking raiders who must have been attracted by the great, natural harbour, stretching from Annat Bay, at the head of Loch Broom, and the easy pickings to be had from the rich grazing land along its sheltered sides. There is access by sea to the Summer Isles, off-shore from Coigach in outer Loch Broom, and a ferry runs to Alltnaharrie on the west side of Loch Broom, connecting by track across the headland to Dundonnell at the head of Little Loch Broom. This provides a circuitous approach to An Teallach and the mountains of the Fisherfield Forest but the ferry only operates when sea conditions are suitable and does not take cars.

Ardgay is the gateway from the east coast. This little village lies on the main rail-line to the north, on the Ross-shire side of the Dornoch Firth. It connects by road bridge with Bonar Bridge, its counterpart on the Sutherland side of the Firth, 1,6km to the north. Here converge all roads leading from the whole of the north-west. There is a wealth of accommodation in both villages but neither is a really good centre for exploration. They are important rather as a junction. Farming, crofting, forestry and estate work form the main occupations and salmon are netted in season across the mouth of the Kyle at Bonar Bridge, the meeting place of the renowned fishing rivers from Strath Carron and Strath Oykel. It should be noted that there is no through road to the west coast from Ardgay itself. The road which leads up

Strath Carron has already been described in conjunction with the path to Gleann Beag. A more north-westerly branch of this passes along Strath Cuileannach for 8km but, again, the connection with Strath Mulzie is by track. A third road follows the south side of the Oykel valley past the youth hostel at Carbisdale Castle and continues for 21km to Inveroykel Lodge Hotel.

There is now a road bridge across the river, just below the hotel. This provides a long-awaited link between the north and south sides of Strath Oykel. It should be noted, however, that in the event of wet weather the valley of the River Oykel is liable to flood—when it does the bridge becomes impassable. About a mile further up-river, the Oykel can be crossed by foot-bridge.

Strath Carron and Strath Oykel figure prominently in the chronicles of the Highland Clearances of the 19th century and, from the introduction of the Cheviot sheep to the area in 1792—known for long as 'Bliadhna nan Caorach', 'The Year of the Sheep'—the surrounding glens were the scene of many of the more violent and pitiful episodes of the whole affair. In Glen Calvie, the names of those who sheltered in the churchyard after they had been evicted can still be seen scratched on the window glass of the old church at Croick. The sheep-walks were mostly turned over to the deer in the latter half of the century and the roads behind Ardgay now serve a multitude of shooting lodges. Many of these are only used for a part of the year and are attended by estate workers for the remainder of the time.

Nearly all of the mountains in this group are most easily approached from the west side; the exceptions being those which lie at the head of Strath Mulzie. This, however, only applies for parties who have only one day to spend and, in the event of a longer stay in the area, expeditions from either side are made feasible by the use of conveniently placed bothies and the wide choice of camp-sites.

The main group of Munro Tops (914m) lie in a great crescent around the upper part of Gleann Sguaib, which opens westwards to the head of Loch Broom, 10km south of Ullapool. Leave the main road just past the post office at Inverlael by a forestry road, which is motorable for 3km as far as the gate in the deer fence on the north side of the River Lael. The road passes through dense conifers which stretch up the steep sides of the glen's entrance to a height of 225m. Permission for motor use is not guaranteed.

Above the tree-line on the south end of the glen, rises a conspicuous gneiss outcrop—*Strone Nea*. This can be reached by a branch of the forestry road, or directly from the main road, in about twenty minutes. There are several routes here, all between 60m and 90m, first climbed in 1962 by T. W. Patey. The most obvious line is on the steep pillar on the left of the main face—*The Shaft,* 75m Very Difficult—if climbed by the crest direct. Minor evasions reduce the standard to Difficult. The Shaft, *West Face,* is 120m, Difficult, following an obvious scoop through brush vegetation. *Summit Slabs,* 60m Very Difficult, lie on the main crag to the right of the Shaft. They are reached by an intervening gully and give a pleasant climb. *Nick-Nack Wall,* 90m Severe, is on the main crag opposite the foot of the Shaft. *Ivy Chimney,* 90m Severe, gives a fine natural line on the right wall of the main crag. *Glen Lael Buttress,* 120m Very Difficult, is the next buttress up the glen. The crag is well worth visiting but pioneering here requires caution.

From the limit of the forest a well-marked track now leads steeply upwards along the glen, but in its early stages this gives little indication of the mountains. After 2.5km, it forks above the waterfall of Eas Fionn and from here onwards the main features of the great range around the head of the glen can be studied more clearly. The left-hand fork continues to rise steadily for 3.6km onto the 750m pass between *Eididh nan Clach Geala* (928m) and *Meall nan Ceapraichean* (977m). From here the ascent of either top can be made without difficulty. *Eididh nan Clach Geala* has a certain amount of broken rock on its south face above the path at Lochan a'Chnapaich but there is no worthwhile cliff. It gets its name, 'the hill of the white stone', from the quartzite boulders which sprinkle its summit slopes. The view to the north and west is fine but, to the east, the rolling slopes leading across to Seana Bhraigh are rather uninspiring from this direction.

Meall nan Ceapraichean has a subsidiary north top, **Cean Garbh** (967m), which is unnamed on the 1:50,000 map. This sends a long shoulder eastwards in *Cnap Coire Loch Tuath* (875m), whose south slope drops steeply down into the head of Coire Lair. The east ridge of Cnap Coire Loch Tuath can be descended to the bothy at the head of Gleann Beag. From the summit of Meall nan Ceapraichean, easy slopes lead south-eastwards down into the Bealach Coire Ghranda which separates it from Beinn Dearg, to meet the south fork of the path from Eas Fionn. The climb from the bealach to the summit of **Beinn Dearg** is steep and rough but route finding is made easy by following the dry stone dyke which runs straight upwards on to the plateau to a height of 1036m. This does not reach the actual summit cairn which lies 270m south of the angle made by the wall before it runs sharply right down the line of the south side of the glen towards Inverlael.

For 5km from the Eas Fionn junction to the Bealach Coire Ghranda, the south fork of the track passes below the main rock features of this side of Beinn Dearg. This south side of Glen Sguaib is formed by the long sloping shoulder of Beinn Dearg, Diollaid a'Mhill Bhric, fringed for most of its way by precipitous cliffs. These hold six well-defined gullies, all of which have given winter climbs. The first gully on the right as one ascends Glen Lael gives a 120m Grade I climb—*WhatawaytospendEaster*. The second gully is *Rev. Ian Paisley Memorial Gully,* 120m Grade I. Both routes were recorded by B. Sproul and A. McKeith, 25th March, 1967.

Immediately right of Number 2 Gully is a diagonal snow slope, joining the gully at 100m. *Bonus*—210m Grade III (A. McHardy and C. Rowland, January, 1976)—climbs the snow slope for 60m, then moves diagonally right to gain and climb a narrow gully.

The third gully is *Orangeman's Gully*—150m Grade III (T. W. Patey, 10th March, 1968). The first ascent took thirty minutes. *Pickwick*—180m Grade II/III (M. Freeman and G. Stephen, 31st January, 1976)—follows the obvious rightward trending groove system, starting 12m right of Orangeman's Gully. Continue rightwards when the line becomes indefinite, then swing back left into a large snow bay. Choice of finishing routes. *Emerald Gully*—150m Grade III/IV (B. Fuller, P. Nunn and A. Riley)—was first climbed in heavy snow conditions, giving two big ice-pitches. It was thought that earlier in the season or in a 'lean' season, the route would be much harder. *Fenian Gully*—150m Grade III/IV (T. W. Patey, 11th March, 1968), has continuous high-angled ice climbing in its initial 105m and has been compared to Green Gully, Ben Nevis. *Wee Freeze Gully*—240m Grade IV (D. M. Jenkins and P. F. Macdonald, 1st February, 1976). The rightward slanting gully roughly midway between Emerald and Fenian Gullies. From below it appears to fade out at half-height but, in fact, it continues further. From its termination a direct line is taken to the top. The sixth gully is the deepest—*Papists' Passage*—180m Grade III (T. W. Patey, 10th March, 1968). The main obstacle here is a huge chockstone in a cave, 75m up the gully; this was climbed by the right-hand corner.

The cliff-line terminates in 'an imposing corner tower' on the right of a wide scree gully. This is the principal feature of the cliffs and gives a fine route on good rock, the best on Beinn Dearg—*Tower of Babel,* 135m Very Difficult (T. W. Patey, 1962). The climbing was found to be 'airy and pleasantly varied'. The start is cairned.

The wide scree gully to the left of the Tower of Babel is known as the Cadha Amadan, or Fools Pass. It can be a useful way off the mountain but one which requires caution in winter. Beyond this lies the massive West Buttress of Beinn Dearg.

The north-west face, immediately to the left of Cadha Amadan, gives two gully climbs—*Inverlael Gully,* 240m Grade II (J. M. Taylor, A. G. Nicol and T. W. Patey, January, 1963). This deep-cut gully is an obvious feature of the face, looking straight down the glen. The shallow gully to the immediate left, entered by a rightward traverse from Cadha Amadan, is *Gastronomes'Gully,* 360m Grade I (A. W. Ewing, J. Brumfitt, I. G. Rowe and W. Sproul, 14th January, 1967).

The North Face contains *West Buttress*—390m Difficult (T. W. Patey, April, 1962). Seen from the Glensguaib approach the aspect is uninviting, the true corner of the buttress being mainly steep vegetation. However, facing north-north-east and above the small loch, is an extensive exposure of slabs bounded on the left by a shallow ill-defined gully coursing down the full height of the buttress. Immediately to the right of the gully and forming the left wall of the slabs is a poorly defined columnar rib offering the best line, the cleanest rock and a sporting line to the top of Beinn Dearg. Though vegetated in the lower reaches, it improves with height. The climb had numerous cairns left en route, but not at the start.

The furthermost gully in the left-hand side of the West Buttress, left of the poorly-defined rib followed by the previously described route, is *Penguin Gully*—360m Grade III (T. W. Patey,W. H. Murray and N. S. Tennent, 29th March, 1964). Concealed from view from the Glen Lael approach, it is the largest gully on this side of Beinn Dearg; probably one of the few ice routes where consistent conditions prevail from January to April. The steep twisting gully to the left of Penguin Gully gives sustained and interesting route-finding in the lower section—*Vanishing Shelf*—300m Grade IV (J. Bower and D. W. Duncan, 26th March, 1969). The gully proper ends in a chimney cul-de-sac and the natural line continues by a spiralling shelf on the left. *Eigerwanderer*—300m Grade III (T. W. Patey and J. Cleare, 18th March, 1969) starts up a V-shaped gully 15m to the right of the lowest ice-fall of Penguin Gully. It follows a more or less direct line, with a tendency to edge away rightwards from the ribs of West Buttress route.

To the right of the previous route is *The Silken Ladder*—300m Grade III (T. W. Patey, 11th March, 1969). This starts in a large slabby area with a central ice ribbon formed by a water course originating at a prominent ice cascade 210m up in the ill-defined spur dividing the North and North-West Faces. The climb follows the right side of the slabby area and continues by the right edge of the ice-cascade to finish up the dividing spur. Numerous variations would seem to be possible on both of the previous routes, which were highly commended. They would appear to be frequently in good winter condition; the crag is perhaps the most consistent and certainly one of the most accessible in the region.

An alternative route on to the Beinn Dearg range from this side begins at Braemore Junction, 8km further south of Inverlael. Just before the junction the impressive Corrieshalloch Gorge (now the property of the National Trust for Scotland) can be reached in minutes by a path from the roadside. The 120m gorge is bridged by a suspension bridge and there are spectacular views of the Falls of Measach, which fall nearly 80m in their main cascade.

The subsidiary gorge from the south-west, which carries the Abhainn Cuileig into the Abhainn Droma 1.6km below Measach, is seldom visited and hardly known. In many ways it equals the more famous Corrieshalloch Gorge and a detour is worth making. The road to Dundonnell from Braemore Junction passes within 30m of the gorge, which can be crossed with care by a semi-derelict, rusty footbridge. The view down into the 45m chasm is both unexpected and spectacular. It is possible with care to descend to the river bed and traverse the foot of the gorge. At a higher level a path leads back to the Ullapool road about 2.5km from Braemore Junction.

From Braemore Junction, take the road through the gates beside the keeper's house. Permission to use it can usually be obtained here. The road leads back along towards Loch Broom at a higher level along beautiful wooded slopes and in 1.6km reaches the flat site of what was once Braemore Lodge. Looking westwards from here, the view across the Fannichs, especialy in winter, is one of the finest in the Northern Highlands.

A stalker's track now leads north-eastwards across open ground past the Home Loch, and splits after 800m, sending a branch round either side of Beinn Enaiglair (889m). These join again on the saddle between the latter and Iorguill (872m) at a height of 675m. Beinn Enaiglair tends to be overlooked by climbers on their way to the 'Munro' tops of the Beinn Dearg range. It is well worth ascending for the extensive views it gives and it is easily climbed from either of the two branch tracks. The way on to Beinn Dearg now crosses the summit of Iorguill and on to meet the dry-stone dyke already described. The dyke passes the top of the Cadha Amadan and stretches steeply upwards on to the summit plateau. Its line along the edge of the cliffs which drop along this south side of Glen Sguaib make it an invaluable aid in the event of bad visibility. The north-western end, nearest Inverlael, terminates abruptly against a huge, conspicuous boulder which is a useful landmark for the hill-walker.

Cona'Mheall (980m)

Cona'Mheall is the fourth top over 914m in this great range of mountains and is easily reached from the Bealach Coire Ghranda. The summit is at the northern end of the almost level ridge and is marked by a cairn. The western cliffs of the narrow, south-east ridge of Cona'Mheall form, with the easten cliffs of Beinn Dearg, the walls of Coire Ghranda (The Gloomy Corrie), which contains all the rock features of interest on this side of the range. The ridge itself ends in a steep, rocky bluff, overlooking Glen Lair and, with care, it is possible to find a way down southwards to the foot of Coire Ghranda.

Coire Ghranda can be approached equally well by either of two paths which leave the roadside from the north-west and south-east end of Loch Droma, 5km from Braemore Junction towards Garve. The north path leaves the road near Lochdrum—a useful bothy for both Beinn Dearg and the Fannichs—and climbs up on to the long sloping south-easterly tail of Beinn Enaiglair. 1.5km from the road the track forks; the main branch continues along the ridge for another 5km on to the saddle already mentioned between Enaiglair and Iorguil. The branch track leads down into the Long Corrie and crosses the Allt a'Gharbhrain by stepping stones. In wet weather this burn has been known to flood very suddenly and can provide an unexpected hazard to the walker. The way now leads up into the lower corrie on the north-east side—The Princess Corrie; this contains a little lochan—Loch nan Eilean.

The wild and rugged cliffs of the upper corrie—Coire Ghranda of Beinn Dearg and Cona'Mheall—can now be seen clearly. Those of Beinn Dearg rise almost directly from the west side of the loch on the corrie floor and are in two groups. The Lower Crag, rising from the lochside, is steep and slabby with the slabs overlapping the wrong way, like roof tiles. The top section is steeper and is broken by a number of grooves and chimneys. At the south end is seen a deep, black gully which is blocked by a great chockstone in its uppper section, *Yon Spoot,* 255m Grade III (D. W. Duncan and M. Rennie, 2nd March, 1969).

The first route fully described on the crag is *Bell's Route* which starts up the rocks close to their lowest point, above the largest of the two peninsulas on the south side of the loch. The line continues directly above the peninsula throughout and has the best exposure of rock on the crag, but is spoilt rather at the top pitch by vegetation. It gives 150m of climbing, graded Severe, and was first climbed in 1946 by Dr and Mrs J. H. B. Bell. The Upper Crag extends above the Lower Crag further up the corrie towards the Bealach Coire Ghranda, rising to a height of 120m. The steep, dripping walls are frequently overhung and abound in vegetation, and the outlook for rock-climbing on this forbidding crag is very slim. The crags on the Cona'Mheall side are drier and more feasible for climbing but offer little continuity. Most of the routes explored on the series of ribs and faces can be graded about Difficult. There are winter climbing possibilities in the larger gullies however. The twisting gully seen from the summit of Beinn Dearg gives a 240m Grade I route, *Spaghetti Gully* (J. Butson and party, 1967).

The second of the two tracks from Loch Droma leaves the road 1.6km further south and crosses the Long Corrie past Loch a'Gharbhrain. It can easily be used to ascend into Coire Ghranda by way of Loch nan Eilean but also provides the best approach to Am Faochagach (951m) and Carn Gorm Loch (908m) on the east side of Glen Lair.

Continue up the glen to the south end of Loch Coire Lair. The ground is flat but boggy and the river from the loch has to be forded. A steep shoulder rises from the loch, which can be climbed on to the rounded dome-like summit plateau. The climb is stiff and the final steep boulder slope below the summit is distinctly unpleasant and awkward when wet. The summit cairn lies to the west side of the plateau and offers a grand view across into Coire Ghranda. Carn Gorm-Loch lies 1.6km north-east and can be reached by descending 180m into the intervening saddle from which the Allt Glas Toll Beag flows down into Loch Vaich. A track from the lochside follows the burn throughout and this provides an alternative route from Strath Vaich. To the south-east, Am Faochageach sends long grassy ridges down towards the head of Strath Vaich. On the west, the lower slopes are steeper but it is possible to traverse around the head of Coire Lair by way of Loch Prille and include the main 914m tops of Beinn Dearg range in a single long day. This necessitates descending to Inverlael and requires organisation of transport.

In winter months the use of skis helps to cut out the tedium of the Glen Sguaib track and it is possible to traverse up both sides of the glen on to the summits. Snow conditions can be remarkably good here and the ski-mountaineer would find the area of particular interest.

Seana Bhraigh (926m)

Seana Bhraigh is the most northerly of the mountains described in this chapter and is the highest point in the plateau which lies at the head of Strath Mulzie. From the south this is seen as an unbroken heathery mass but, on the north side, it drops in a series of steep rocky corries. Luchd Coire, the most westerly, falls 396m sheer from the summit of the mountain. Feich Coire, separated from the latter by the outstanding feature of Seana Bhraigh, the peak of An Sgurr (899m) which juts out northwards immediately above Loch A'Choire Mhoir. The most easterly is Coir Mor, from which the Allt Coire A'Choire Mhoir feeds down into the loch.

The easiest approach is from the north-east, leaving the Lochinver road at Oykel Bridge. Follow the motor track for 6.5km to Duag Bridge along the south side of the River Einig. The road here passes an old corrugated iron building which was once a school. It is now a hay shed, with some open outbuildings which could be used as a bothy. The motor track stops at Corriemulzie Lodge, 3km further on. The lodge is uninhabited during the winter but a shepherd lives nearby and permission can often be obtained to use one of the outbuildings. The path marked on the map leading up Strath Mulzie runs out after about 3km but the going is easy for the remaining 4km to Loch a'Choire Mhoir. There is a ruined bothy on the north-east side of the loch which is partially roofed and barely usable, but there are plenty of camp-sites to choose from in the vicinity for a long stay. The bothy is not available during the stalking season (1st September-26th October).

The approach from the west is longer. About 1km north of Ullapool a motor track leads along the River Ullapool to the west end of Loch Achall, crossing a dubious wooden bridge. A right-of-way for pedestrians continues along the loch into Glen Achall but permission can usually be obtained from Major Scobie, at Rhidorroch Lodge, to take in a vehicle. The road continues for 8km to Rhidorroch Old Lodge, which lies on the opposite side of the river and is reached by a wooden suspension bridge. A rough road rises steeply onwards for 2.5km past the Lodge, but is unsuitable for cars for any appreciable distance, and the rest of the journey is on foot. At the second prominent track junction, take the right-hand fork leading down towards Loch an Daimh. The way now leads up the side of the Allt nan Caorach, pathless for part of its way, between the south-east end of the cleft of the river and the head of Strathmulzie.

A combination of these two routes, through Glen Einig and Glen Achall, gives a magnificent east-west walk of almost 20km, which is highly recommended. From Duag bridge, leave the Corriemulzie track by a footpath leading north-westwards along the River Poiblidh to Loch an Daimh. The path tends to be heavy in wet weather and, at one point, the River Poiblidh has to be forded. Some 8km from Duag, at the east end of the loch, is Knockdamph bothy. This is in excellent condition and is frequently used by climbers and walkers. Permission to use it is not normally required but it is unavailable during the stalking season (20th September-26th October). The track continues along the north side of Loch Damph but it is advisable to take the north fork, the south one follows the edge of the loch and is partially under water. This path links with the route from Rhidorroch already described. From the west path-junction there is a fine view of An Sgurr on Seana Bhraigh, jutting out beyond the summit ridge. The walk along Loch Achall is especially fine, the way passing beneath the great crags of Creag Ruadh and Creag Grianach towards Rhidorroch Lodge. Once over the motor bridge at the end of the loch, the walk into Ullapool along the deep-cut river gorge is most impressive and, in the evening, becomes almost eerie. For those who appreciate a long walk in peace and solitude, the route is perfection.

A third possible route to Seana Bhraigh is from Gleann Beag by path up to Loch Sruban Mora to cross the plateau and descend into the head of Coire Mhor. The distance from Gleann Beag to Loch a'Choire Mhoir by this way is only 6½km but the going is stiff and the descent into the corrie is awkward, especially carrying a heavy load.

The summit of Seana Bhraigh is easily reached by way of the grassy north shoulder and from there the plateau can be traversed with little difficulty for 5.6km to take in the top of Carn Ban (845m). This rises as a rounded top to the east above the head of Coire Mor. As has been observed previously it is possible to descend the head of the corrie and make back to Loch a'Choire Mhoir. The impressive central spur of Seana Bhraigh is named Creag an Duine on the O.S. map—it is more usually known as An Sgurr. At closer quarters the steep ridge on to An Sgurr becomes less forbidding and it is possible to ascend from the mouth of Luchd Coire on the north-west aspect. The only unavoidable difficulties occur on the last 45m from the summit tower to the plateau, here a rope may be required as a safeguard to the less experienced scrambler.

Seana Bhraigh has no great potential as a rock-climbing area. The rock here is mainly schist and the broken crags are highly vegetated in summer. Like Beinn Dearg, however, it has extensive winter possibilities, discovered only comparatively recently. Despite its low-altitude, snow conditions are better than one might expect and the gullies of Luchd Coire have produced some fine long routes. The pioneer work here was done by members of the Corriemulzie Mountaineering Club during the period 1962-65 and details of routes were first published in the Club's *Rock and Ice Guide to Easter Ross,* 1966. These and subsequent routes are covered in the S.M.C. *Climbers' Guide to the Northern Highlands Area*—Volume I— Letterewe and Easter Ross.

The main features of Luchd Coire, which has given all the climbing so far, are seen to be as follows: The West Wall of An Sgurr is bounded on the south by a gentle, slanting gully. The wall falls further back in a face containing *Bealach Gully*—90m—no grade given. The broad gully seen running down from the plateau at the back of the small inner corrie is *The Chute*—300m Grade I descending. The 90m high cliffs on the right face of the inner corrie contain *Query Cleft*—105m Grade III. Below these, easy ground slants up to the right to meet the plateau—this gives an easy descent route. Continuing to the right, one comes to the Central Massif. This has two parallel posts, *Sunday Post*—300m Grade III—and *Monday Post*—300m Grade II. These share a common start with *Press-on Gully*—300m Grade I—which slants to the right from the bottom of the central rib. The right boundary of the Central Massif is *Pomegranate Gully*—300m Grade II—the most prominent gully on the face. *Flowerpot Buttress*—270m Grade III (P. Devlin and D. Dinwoodie, 16th February, 1978)—climbs the broad buttress between Press-On and Pomegranate Gullies. It took a good natural line near the well

29.   Hay-fork Gully on An Teallach

30. *The Fannichs from Strathban across Loch Fannich*

31.   On the Fannichs looking towards Meall a'Chrasgaidh; An Teallach Behind

32. *Cornices on Sgurr Mor Fannich*

33. *Meall Gorm in cloud with Lochan Fhuar Thuill Mhoir beneath; from Sgurr Mor*

defined right edge. The route crosses a big raking terrace at three-quarter's height, then a direct continuation to the top.

To the right of Pomegranate Gully lies Diamond Buttress. *The Rough Diamond*—270m Grade IV (P. F. MacDonald and I. G. Rowe, 2nd January, 1971)—starts at the left-hand side of the steep, frontal face of Diamond Buttress, in a small snow recess at the foot on Pomegranate Gully. The climb goes straight up this flank of the buttress following a line of weakness with a steep chimney near the top, to finish close to the top of the unclimbed tributary of Pomegranate Gully.

Diamond Edge—250m Grade III/IV (D. Dinwoodie, R. Robb and R. A. Smith, 15th April, 1978)—follows the frontal crest of the buttress, starting left of the crest, up the higher of two obvious right-slanting ramps. The finish was up the big, obvious dièdre clearing the upper nose. This is right of Rough Diamond. It was found to be 'an elegant line with fine situations'.

Pineapple Gully—195m Grade III (P. F. MacDonald, C. and S. Rowland, 21st January, 1978)—is the gully on the left flank of Diamond Buttress. It is entered by climbing the right wall of Pomegranate Gully, starting a short distance below the first pitch of that gully.

On the right of the buttress is Diamond Dièdre, 240m Grade II/III. *Pelican Gully,* 240m, Grade II, lies to the right of *Pelican Rib* and is bounded on the right by the Summit Buttress of Seana Bhraigh. *Sham Gully,* 180m, Grade I, slants up to the right, between the Summit Buttress and *Far West Buttress,* 180m Grade II.

The north shoulders of Seana Bhraigh often give a superb ski-run, from the summit to the floor of Strath Mulzie. The upper section is boulder strewn and requires a fair snow cover, but the lower sections are excellent. A ski approach to the mountain is quite often feasible.

Bodach Mor (819m). The large north-west facing quartzite cliff of Bodach Mor, Am Bodach, 3km north-west of Carn Ban, is still another climbing possibility here. The summit is separated from Carn Ban by a 152m dip leading up over Bodach Beag, but access to the foot of the crags is difficult from any direction and is trackless for a greater part of the way. The steep gully which separates the two main masses of Am Bodach has been explored—*Solomon's Gully*—180m Moderate (P. N. L. Tranter, 1963). It was found to be moist but interesting. Winter prospects here are probably more hopeful.

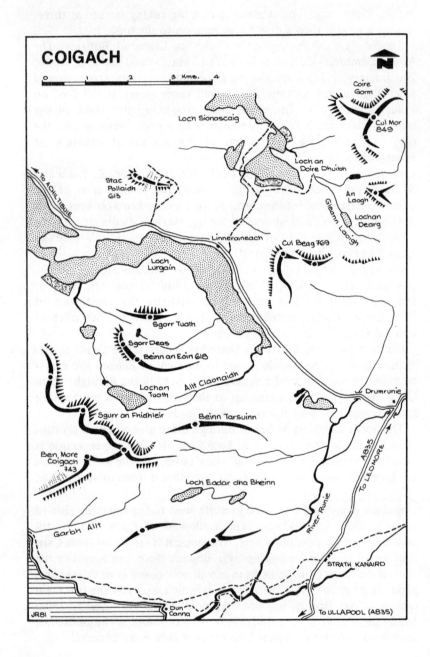

8

Coigach

(1) **Ben More Coigach** (743m) N.C. 094043
(2) **Sgurr an Fhidhleir** (703m) N.C. 094054
(3) **Beinn an Eoin**
    (a) **Sgorr Deas** (618m) N.C. 105064
    (b) **Sgorr Tuath** (549m) N.C. 110075
(4) **Cul Mor**
    (a) **Sron Gharbh** (849m) N.C. 162119
    (b) **Creag nan Calman** (786m) N.C. 159114
(5) **Cul Beag** (769m) N.C. 140088
(6) **Stac Pollaidh** (613m) N.C. 108106

MAP: O.S. 1:50,000 (Second Series) Sheet No. 15—Loch Assynt.

The Parish of Coigach lies in the extreme north-westerly tip of the former county of Ross and Cromarty. The name—Coigach—means the 'fifth-part'. The old celtic custom was to divide land into five parts, and Coigach is the Coigach of Ross—the fifth part of the Cromarties. Its north-east boundary, formed by the River Kirkaig, the Fionn Loch and Loch Veyatie, was the county march with Sutherland, separating Coigach from the neighbouring parish of Assynt. Access from the south is by way of the A835 from Ullalpool, the nearest centre of population. This road has been reconstructed and widened within the past few years and now provides fast, easy passage from Ullapool to Ledmore Junction and beyond that northwards towards Lochinver and Kylesku Ferry. From Drumrunie Junction (16km) north of Ullapool, a secondary road, single-tracked with infrequent passing places, cuts north-westwards to the isolated crofting community of Achiltibuie and the Summer Isles, following the line of well known fishing waters formed by Loch Lurgainn, Loch Bad a'Ghaill and Loch Oscaig. This road conveniently divides the Coigach mountains into two distinct groups and is a useful means of access to both.

One other motorable road cuts off from the Achiltibuie road at Badagyle, on the west end of Loch Bad a'Ghaill, winding its way through a maze of woodland and picturesque lochans to Inverkirkaig and the fishing port of Lochinver, the main township in the parish of Assynt. Scenically, the road is to be recommended, but passing places often occur on awkward corners and drivers should take care.

The area as a whole is sparsely settled, the bulk of the population being concentrated along the seaboard north and south of Achiltibuie. Coigach suffered from the Clearances of the last century; its wealth of hill-grazing was a readily marketable commodity to the landowner, giving bigger and swifter monetary returns than the people who 'were altogether unable to occupy benefically the large extent of hill pasture attached to their little allotments of land'. Despite resistance, the people went, leaving the hills to the sheep and the indigenous red deer. The pattern was similar to that which developed throughout most of the vast estates of the Northern Highlands and now only a dwindling population remain along the perimeter of the area. The present population supplement crofting on a small scale with fishing and the passing tourist trade. Unfortunately, it tends to be an ageing population, as the sadly reduced school rolls bear testimony, and an infusion of new incentive is urgently needed if the young people who are still there are to be encouraged to remain. Security of Tenure of croftland is now ensured but new legislation has been overdue to allow the linking of crofts into more viable working units if crofting as a way of life is to continue in even its present limited form.

The northern half of Coigach forms the Inverpolly Nature Reserve and includes the peaks of Cul Mor, Cul Beag and Stac Pollaidh, all over 610m. The main parts of the 27,000 acre reserve, Drumrunie, Inverpolly and Eisg-Brachaidh, were declared in 1961 under agreement between the Nature Consevancy and the Inverpolly Estates. A further 36 acres were purchased in 1962 to include Knockan Cliff on the reserve's eastern boundary. The Reserve is second only in size to the Cairngorm Reserve and contains a wide range of natural habitats.

The wide range of mammals, representative of the mountains and woodlands of the North-West Highlands, tend to be scattered and not immediately apparent. They include Red Deer, Wild Cat, Otter and Fox. Pine Martins have been observed in the area around Kirkaig. Bird life includes the Black-throated Diver, Red-breasted Merganiser, Ptarmigan, Raven, Buzzard, Golden Plover, Ring Ouzel, Cuckoo, Common Sand-piper, Stone-chat and Tree-creeper. The Red Grouse are not present in great numbers but Woodcock are common in winter in the woods. Some Arctic Terns breed along the coast and Geese and Ducks visit the lochs in winter and on migration.

There is a wide range of plant habitats from the sea-coast to a summit of nearly 914m but the most interesting vegetation of the reserve is its woodlands. This consists mainly of Birch, Hazel, Rowan, Bird Cherry, Aspen, Alder and Holly and is a relic of a northern type of scrub once covering this region but now greatly reduced by heavy grazing and periodic burning. Because of the high rainfall and the impervious underlying acid rock and glacial clay, large expanses of the reserve are covered with peat, bearing a species-poor moorland vegetation. The peat moorland of the lower reserve stops at the limestone outcrop of Knockan Cliff and here can be found some of reserve's richest Flora—Mountain Avens, Rock Sedge, Fairy Flax, Green Spleenwort and Moss Campion. The sandstone cliffs and summits have a much poorer vegetation but there are a number of arctic and alpine species, including Alpine Lady's Mantle, Black Bearberry, Bearberry, Mountain Everlasting, Cloudberry and Dwarf Juniper.

Access to the reserve is not normally restricted but permission to visit Drumrunie should be obtained from the Assynt Estate Office (Lochinver 203) between 15th July and 15th October, and for visits by parties of more than six at any time of the year. The Conservancy require that visitors to the reserve do not collect plants or animal specimens or disturb nesting birds. Requests to carry out scientific work on the reserve should be addressed to the Regional Officer for North Scotland, The Nature Conservancy, 12 Hope Terrace, Edinburgh 9. The Reserve Warden can be contacted at 'Strath-Polly' near Inverpolly Lodge (Lochinver 204) or at Knockan Cottage (Elphin 234).

The structure of the southern part of Coigach is predominantly Torridonian but, as one moves northwards, one comes across some of the oldest rocks in Britain, occurring in an area which escaped the severity of the Caledonian mountain building movements. The oldest rocks, Lewisian gneiss, underlie the north-west half of the Inverpolly Reserve, from Loch Sionascaig to Enard Bay. At some period a series of parallel north-west-south-east dykes (ranging from granites to more basic dolerites and serpentines) intruded the gneiss and erosion of these produced a topography of ridges and troughs on which the latter deposits of Torridonian sandstone were laid down. The more recent removal of the sandstone in this area has re-exposed part of the ancient surface—a fossil landscape modified by ice and river erosion at a later stage.

Torridonian rocks form the south-east half of the reserve, including most of Cul Mor, Cul Beag and Stac Pollaidh. Despite their great age, these rocks have been little affected by Earth movements and are tilted only slightly eastwards.

After submergence and erosion of the sandstone, the marine deposits were laid down which now form the lowest layers of the Cambrian system. These rocks were tilted eastwards so that the layers now outcrop in strips along the east boundary of the reserve. The oldest layer, the Basal Quartzite, outcrops along the east slopes of Cul Beag, with an extension to the summit of Cul Mor. It is followed eastwards by successively younger strata, sandstone, shales and finally the Durness limestone, which all outcrop in the lower part of Knockan Cliff. Half-way up the cliff, however, the normal Cambrian succession is broken by the Moine Thrust Plane, one of the great structural lines of North-West Europe. Above this thrust occur the Moine schists, highly altered rocks which were pushed westwards over the younger, relatively unaltered Cambrian strata by the force of the Caledonian mountain-building movements 400 million years ago. The line of the Thrust extends the full length of the north-western seaboard but its fine exposure at Knockan Cliff has played an important part in the development of Geological Science.

During the past few million years, erosion of these different rocks by ice, rivers, frost and wind has produced some of Scotland's most spectacular scenery. The lowland gneiss in north-west Coigach was heavily glaciated during the Ice Age. Ice scoured the rocky knolls and excavated deep rock basins which now contain lochs or pockets of drift with deep peat. This complex of lochs and bogs lies at a height of between 91m-150m, and above it are the isolated relic masses of Torridonian sandstone which form the mountains of the area. Prolonged weathering of the nearly horizontal strata has produced impressive escarpments on these mountains. Erosion is most advanced on the ridge of Stac Polly where the vertical joints of the sandstone have been sculptured into weird rock pinnacles and chimneys.

The main catchment area for the reserve is Loch Sionascaig, 60m deep and the largest of the multitude of lochs which abound in the region. Sionascaig has a short outlet to the sea via the River Polly.

Ben More Coigach (743m). Seen from Ardmair Bay, 9.5km north of Ullapool, Ben More Coigach appears as a continuous line of gully-seamed sandstone cliffs, stretching over 3km in length from Speicein

Coinich in the east to Garbh Choireachan at its western end.

Approaching from this direction, the easiest route onto Ben More starts 2.5km north of Strathkanaird, leaving the A835 at the top of the rise just before it drops down towards Drumrunie. Cross the River Runie at a ruined bridge—N.G. 149036—whence an easy-angled shoulder leads upwards over firm ground to the foot of Speicein Coinich, by-passing Loch a'Chlaiginn en route. The summit ridge can be reached at a point west of the rocky outcrops, or by contouring round on to the north side and climbing a steep, grassy slope to the top. This slope usually holds a good snow cover in winter. The ridge is wide and fairly flat at this eastern end and the summit cairn is reached with little further ascent. From the road the distance is 6.5km.

From the cairn, the ridge narrows westwards for 1km towards Garbh Choireachan, but presents no problems for the hill walker. The succession of small rocky towers towards the west end can easily be by-passed on the north side and the outlook from the ridge is superb. The mainland hills curve in a great arc from north to south-west and seawards across the lovely Summer Isles in Badentarbat Bay, one can see Lewis and the Western Islands.

Looking down from Garbh Choireachan, one gets a birdseye view of the Holy Isle of St. Martin standing guard at the mouth of Ardmair Bay. St. Columba ministered here at one time but there is some doubt as to whether the island derives its name from the famous St. Martin of Iona or from the cleric who built his tiny chapel on the island, having been banished as a student from Iona until such time as he could give proof to St. Columba that he had changed to a more tasteful way of life. Whatever the case, he died on the island and the ruins of his chapel are to be found near the west corner, with the graves of his followers close by.

There is no great difficulty in finding a route down through the rocky outcrops of Garbh Choireachan to Culnacraig, a scattering of croft houses lying 6.5km south of Achiltibuie at the end of the motorable road. A foot-track leads from Culnacraig in a south-easterly direction, skirting the top of the sea-cliffs overlooking Isle Martin and Ardmair. The track crosses the River Runie near Blughasary where it joins a rough road back to Strathkanaird. From Culnacraig to Strathkanaird the distance is 9km and the track is in reasonable condition.

A fine walking circuit of the Ben More Coigach tops begins at the Allt a'Choire Reidh where it crosses the road to Culnacraig—N.G.

149

137067—29km by road from Drumrunie Junction. The route follows the right hand side of the burn up a 4km firm, grassy slope to the summit of Sgurr an Fhidhleir. Looking northwards from the cairn, which stands on the lip of the 305m cliff, the hills of Coigach and West Assynt can be picked out in succession stretching as far as Quinag, by Kylesku.

The way now drops down for 152m in a southerly direction, following the line of the crags and passing the head of a prominent earthy gully—N.G. 095050—before rising steeply for 213m up the north-east slope leading to the summit cairn of Ben More Coigach. The ridge can then be followed westwards to Garbh Choireachan before descending to the road at Culnacraig.

Sgurr an Fhidhleir (697m)

Seen from Drumrunie, the steep, tooth-shaped peak of Sgurr an Fhidhleir is the most impressive feature of this western group of the Coigach hills.

The 4km approach route largely follows the winding course of the Allt Claonnaidh from the Feur Loch at the south-east end of Loch Lurgainn. Leaving the road 4km from Drumrunie Junction, ford the burn leading into the loch and rise steadily westwards between the two long, rocky-ended spurs flung out by Beinn an Eoin and Ben More Coigach. These are respectively Cloch Beinn an Eoin and Beinn Tarsuinn. Sgurr an Fhidhleir is seen for most of the approach, sharply rising up above Lochan Tuath. There is an excellent camp site here, with sheltered sandy beaches. A good shelter stone for a small party can be found at the top of a boulder field on the north-east side of the lochan.

The prominent gully mentioned previously, follows the south side of the rock face and provides a straightforward, but dirty, access to the saddle between Sgurr an Fhidhleir and Ben More Coigach. The rocks on the north side of the crag are broken and loose.

The first direct ascent of the 305m North Buttress of Sgurr an Fhidhleir—*The Fiddler, Direct Nose Route*—300m Very Severe (N. Drasdo and C. M. Dixon, April, 1962)—was the climax to a series of attempts spread over the last century, and a milestone in the development of climbing in the North-West Highlands. A remarkable early attempt was that made by Messrs. Ling and Sang, subsequent visits confirming the difficulties overcome by these early pioneers.

There is only one true direct line on The Fiddler, that which continues unerringly up the central spur above the Pale Slabs. Earlier parties, credited with the first ascent, did ultimately succeed in reaching the top of the Buttress by following circuitous routes far to the right of the true line. These routes are now of historical interest only and are highly dangerous on account of loose rock and friable vegetation.

The Pale Slabs, the key feature of the direct route up The Fiddler, cannot be seen during the approach or even from Lochan Tuath, as they lie just beyond the skyline edge at about mid-height on the buttress. They quickly come into view as one continues along the side of the small subsidiary lochan beyond Lochan Tuath. The Slabs, which appear to lie at an easy angle, are cut by three hair-line terraces and composed of a lighter coloured rock than their surroundings. They mark the limit of the earlier attempts. Above the Slabs, the buttress rears steeply for a further 91m to the Upper Shoulder, where serious climbing gives way to steep scrambling for the final 91m. Although the climbing, as far as the Pale Slabs at the start of the major difficulties is known to be unpleasantly vegetated, from this point upwards the rock is clean and superbly exposed. The difficulties are prolonged and serious. Dry conditions are recommended though a cross-wind on the exposed upper section could be intimidating. Pegs were twice used for belays and the first party took between five and six hours to complete the climb. The details of the route are as follows: 'Starting at the lowest rocks of the buttress follow cracks and corners (numerous lines) to gain the long grassy groove (an obvious feature) which twists up the centre of the buttress, passing two flat-topped overhangs en route (these are best passed on the right). The groove finally leads to a sweep of slabs (the Pale Slabs) which are not seen from below if approaching the buttress from the left (east) but are obvious when viewed from the screes to the right of and below the buttress. These slabs form the key to the steep upper portion of the buttress.

From a grassy bay below the slabs, climb the first slab centrally (Hard Severe)—or more easily, climb a grassy groove in the right corner and then traverse easily leftwards along a level grass terrace—to reach the upper left corner of the slab. A large block belay, or a rusty peg (sign of ealier attempts) may be used. Turn the second slab above by climbing a steep, right-angled, grassy groove on the left. Hard finish (Hard Severe or Very Severe) on to another good ledge below the third and largest slab. Limit of previous attempts.

151

This could be climbed centrally but the left-hand edge was used on this ascent. A hard step on to the undercut slab just right of the slab edge leads up and back, leftwards, for a few feet to a position where a nasty step can be made on to a large loose-looking block in a groove to the left (Hard). Continue straight up, following the slab or the corner to another good ledge and various belays overlooking the steep left edge of the buttress. Continue up steeply on the right of the belays, moving slightly left, and then straight up a steep, little wall with few holds to the top (Very Severe). From here easier climbing leads to the crest of the buttress and the top of the peak.

The most recently recorded route on Sgurr an Fhidhleir adds an extremely severe finish to the original Nose Route. *Nose Direct, Tower Finish*—90m Extremely Severe (E2) (D. Gilbert and J. Mackenzie, 10th June, 1979). From the ledge immediately above the loose groove of the third slab of the original Direct Route, climb a wall then traverse across a bald slab, up and right via thin grass steps (no protection) to exposed central nook, poor belays. The top vertical wall now looms directly above. Climb up and slightly rightwards past fixed wire runner to overhang. Overcome this on right, then climb wall above to gain groove with steep slab on right. Climb crack in slab to fixed peg. Using this for foothold, step right, and mantelshelf into groove (crux). Step right again into small nook stance with great exposure (45m). Climb crack above to ledge, traverse left into groove and follow this to gain secure chimney stance and belays behind detached tower (7m). Climb chimney onto tower, then groove above, to belays. Easier rocks lead to junction with *Direct Route*.

The north-east face of Sgurr an Fhidhleir, which confronts Loch an Tuath, is a formidable sweep of high angled slabs. There is a theoretical line of weakness, if such it may be called, a short distance to the left of the established line of the crest. *The Magic Bow*—270m Very Severe (M. Boysen and T. W. Patey, 1st June, 1967), lies well to the left of the Direct Route. A huge bow-shaped groove is the main feature of the face which is far steeper than it appears from the road. The route aims for the groove, follows it initially, then deviates on to the sea of slabs on the right. In dry conditions, the route is cleaner, harder and more sustained than the direct route. *The Phantom Fiddler*—285m Very Severe (T. W. Patey, 11th June, 1968), is another very hard line on this east face. It follows more or less directly the rib on the left of the bow-shaped groove of the previous route. This is a more serious climb than The Magic Bow. Dry conditions are considered absolutely essential—the climbing is mainly on the slabs, the cracks holding too much vegetation.

Fidelio—270m Very Severe (D. M. Jenkins, P. F. Macdonald and A. McHardy, May, 1975)—follows a prominent line of weakness on the East Face, between the Direct Route and The Magic Bow slabs, taking the main, rightwards slanting overhangs at about their mid-point and finishing at an obvious, slabby corner. The first main feature is a large open corner to the right of a rock beak, about a third of the way up the face. Climb preliminary tiers to lesser overhangs and traverse left into the open corner. Above the corner, follow leftward trending grooves to a break in the main overhangs. Climb through the break and continue by grooves in three excellent pitches to the top. On the final pitch, the slab was climbed direct by a thin crack.

G String—240m Hard Very Severe (R. McHardy and P. Thomas, Summer, 1977)—This climb lies about 75m right of The Magic Bow and starts from a good rock ledge level with the foot of the groove of that route. Gain this ledge by a series of walls and ledges which become more continuous about 60m below the ledge. Above the ledge is a steep rock bounded on the right by a series of right-trending overhangs. Climb to a bulge at about 12m, climb bulge moving right to gain a slab. Go right, then up 5m, go left to a good ledge and belay. Above is a groove going up to the left of a block overhang. Above and left of this is another block overhang; the two separated by a groove. Enter the groove using a flake on the lower overhang and move right on to steep slabs. Move up and right to a small but long ledge, enter groove above from the right and so to good stance and peg belay. Climb straight up to big ledge, move right and round into grass filled corner. Climb thin slab on right to belay. Climb up and right over a bulge, enter a corner, finish by a wide crack on left wall.

West Face—195m Grade III (P. F. Macdonald and C. Rowland, February, 1979)—This route follows a depression line left of centre on the west of this peak. The length given is to the junction with North West Face. Follow the depression, then a choice of groves leading to more open climbing. The route eventually joins North West Face route above the prominent shoulder. The final gully of that route was then followed.

North West Face—300m Grade III (A. Nisbet, 20 January, 1979). This is the ramp/gully to the right of the nose and well seen in the District Guide photograph. A diagonal ramp leads with one pitch of climbing into the long final gully. This could be tedious, and probably dangerous in loose snow conditions. The narrow gully on the slope just left of Sgurr an Fhidhleir was climbed by J. Marmby and B. Sprunt (Grade II).

No routes have been recorded on the southern cliffs of Ben More Coigach but varied scrambling would seem to be possible.

Cona'Mheall (544m)

Lying some 3km to the west of Sgurr an Fhidhleir, Cona'Mheall forms part of the Coigach group. It is distinguished by the prominent pinnacle, known as the Acheninver Pinnacle, which flanks the hill on its left. The original route here was *Acheninver Pinnacle*—150m Very Difficult (D. Niven and G. F. Webster, 1955). It is described as follows:—'From the lowest rocks climb a large right-angled block and follow the right-hand edge of the pinnacle to the top. A wide crack about half-way up was turned by a left traverse. A short ascent from the pinnacle leads to the main top.' A later party here found that the 'wide crack' which was originally avoided, gave a good 'Severe' pitch.

In 1962, T. W. Patey climbed a 75m Severe route on *Middle Crag*—The central slabby face enclosed by the two arms of a Y-shaped gully, and the second rocky buttress to the right of the Acheninver Pinnacle. Starting from the lowest rocks, a more or less direct line finished up a wide shallow chimney which provides a severe straddling pitch.

The triple-towered narrow arête which juts out to the right of the Acheninver Pinnacle gives a more recent route—*Levitation Towers*—120m Hard Very Severe (J. MacKenzie and D. McCallum, November, 1978). Starting from a cairn at the base, this gives a "good and unusual climb", well protected.

Other shorter routes of the 30m variety have been made on the right-most buttress. The buttress is south-facing and accessible; the rock, though sound and rough, is surprisingly scant of holds.

Beinn an Eoin (601m)

This twin-topped hill is the smallest of the Coigach group in height. Sgorr Deas, the south top, is broken and rocky on its south-west side but, on close inspection, the rock is dirty and vegetated and offers little in the way of satisfactory climbing. Sgorr Tuath, the north top, is rocky on its northerly side overlooking Loch Lurgainn and looks promising from the road but, again, closer contact proves otherwise. A tiny lochan lies in the saddle between the two tops which are best approached by following at first the route along the Allt Claonnaidh then traversing easily upwards on to Cloch Beinn an Eoin. The complete circuit covers 5.5km.

Cul Beag (769m)

Cul Beag rises as a long heather-covered dip slope in a north-westerly direction from Drumrunie Junction. The easiest approach to the summit is from this direction, starting at a point past the bridge over the River Runie about 1.5km from the road junction on the way to Achiltibuie. The final slope leading to the summit cairn is steep and boulder-strewn but presents no difficulty to the walker. The distance from the start is about 4km and the view from the summit is extensive.

Cul Beag presents a line of steep gullied cliffs on its north side overlooking Gleann Laoigh, but no climbs have been recorded. To the west, overlooking Loch Lurgainn, the crags stretch gradually higher from Creag Dubh, providing varied scrambling broken by the usual heathery ledges. As one moves westwards, the rock becomes more continuous and holds better possibilities for more serious climbing.

The main west face of Cul Beag is split in its upper reaches by a prominent Y-shaped gully which sends a long scree tail down to the lower slopes. The gully encloses a wedge-shaped buttress with its apex below and is easily identified from the road by Linneraineach. Early descriptions of climbs on or near this face are too vague to be used as a sure means of identification. In 1914, Messrs. Inglis Clark and Ling started from Loch Lurgainn, making for a 'vivid green patch at 420m where a chimney began'. They reached the summit in 2¼ hours. In 1920, L. W. and T. H. Somervell climbed on the buttress up a series of 15m pitches divided by broad heather ledges, finishing up a long gully which gave interesting climbing and led on to a short arête near the summit of the mountain.

Dr. Bell's lucid account in the S.M.C. Journal of 1959 describes a climb named *Lurgainn Edge.* 'The route had a lower section on the lower rocks to the left of Y-Gully, and the upper section was on the right of the shallow upper gully and above the 'Y', where there is a long steep cliff face. Lurgainn Edge, almost a true ridge, separates the easier rocks facing the upper gully from the wall extending south-eastwards. The lower introductory part gave little over 45m of climbing and would be improved greatly by going up a sharp rather holdless arête on the left of Y-Gully. Start up behind a detached flake more to the left, with one or two difficult pitches on steep, good rock

155

followed by scrambling. Above this, cross Y-Gully above the wedge and then to the base of Lurgainn Edge, which gave 60-75m of delightful climbing on good steep rock with fine, airy situations. After 30m is a difficult chimney to a platform. A cairn was left at the big platform about 30m higher. Then there was a really difficult 9m chimney and some roof-tile slabs to the finish at the top of the rocks. From here a little grassy ridge runs up to the subsidiary southern summit of the mountain with another little dip before the top.'

Seen from Linneraineach, the rocks are in two definite tiers. Wedge Buttress is on the upper tier; the following routes are on the lower—

Quelle Delicatesse—50m Very Severe (J. G. Wright and A. Zaluski, May, 1959). Towards the left is a small, pear shaped slab bounded by a short gully on its left and a deep chimney on the right. Climb the small chimney, splitting the slab diagonally, then follow the right edge to the top.

Curving Chimney—65m Very Difficult (J. G. Wright and J. Ryman, May, 1959). This is the curving chimney which splits the slabby wall on the right of lower tier. Steep grass at the base was climbed, then the chimney, until forced out onto the face on the right. Cross to the Pulpit; traverse back to the line of the chimney and follow it to the top. Other routes are possible from the Pulpit.

Lickerish Quarter—90m Severe (R. Gatehouse and C. Smith, July, 1979). Starts at the foot of Curving Chimney. Climb the rib on the right of the chimney for a few moves, then traverse up and across to a corner (15m). The Pulpit is reached either by climbing the corner or slabs on the left, to finish up slabs above.

Kveldro Ridge—200m Very Difficult (R. Gatehouse and C. Smith, July, 1979)—takes the ridge to the left of the amphitheatre formed by Y-Gully. Approaching from below, the route takes the left-hand skyline, which appears as a three-tiered ridge. Start 90m to the left of Y-Gully at the foot of the second tier seen on the ridge. A scramble (45m) leads to a wall which is climbed by a crack (27m). The next wall is climbed by a groove on the right (24m) followed by a scramble to the final tier. This is climbed by a leftward slanting chimney (30m) to finish just below the summit.

Further exploration here could well produce other lines.

Stac Pollaidh (613m)

Although the smallest of the Coigach group, Stac Pollaidh

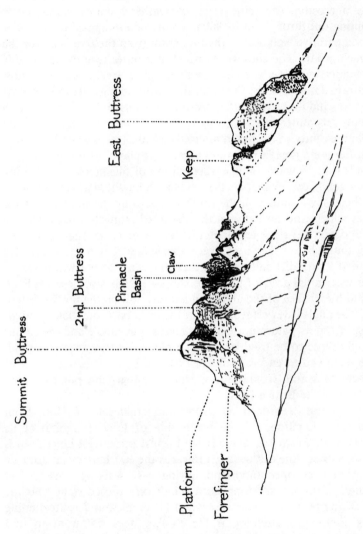

Summit Buttress

2nd. Buttress

East Buttress

Pinnacle
Basin

Claw

Keep

Platform

Forefinger

Fig. 6. Stac Pollaidh from Loch Lurgainn.

undoubtedly holds greater attraction for the mountaineer than any of its neighbours. It is truly a 'mountain in miniature'. The summit ridge rises from an encircling apron of steep talus slopes lying at an angle of 45 degrees and is an outstanding example of sandstone in the final stages of erosion. The weird variety of weathered shapes and pinnacles sprouting out throughout its 800m length gain in appeal by virtue of the comparative isolation of the mountain from the remainder of the Coigach group. The enthusiasm which it arouses is both remarkable and understandable and has resulted in a wealth of enjoyable literature. James Fisher, the naturalist, was amongst its most ardent admirers, and his article in *'Portraits of Mountains'* by E. Molony, is strongly recommended.

The proximity of the mountain to the road along the north shore of Loch Lurgainn greatly facilitates access; the choice of routes onto the summit ridge is wide. In an earlier edition of this guide, W. N. Ling gives a good general introduction to Stac Pollaidh. 'The summit ridge may be easily attained on the north or south by the numerous scree gullies which lead up between the shattered pinnacle ridges. On the east and west the ridge terminates in very steep cliffs, that to the east being somewhat broken up by vegetable ledges. The western cliff has afforded a very difficult and sporting climb, the ascent was made up the true terminal arête of the ridge. An ascent has also been made on the south-east face of the arête and another still on the north-western face. The angle is very steep, but, for the most part, the rock is sound, though from its nature not many hitches are available and the climbs are only those to be tried by a strong party. To traverse the summit ridge from end to end is an interesting and by no means easy bit of rock-climbing and, from the spectacular photographic point of view, is unique in the British Isles.'

The easiest approach is from Linneraineach, 6½km from Drumrunie Junction, on the north side of Loch Lurgainn at its western end. From the obvious lay-by just opposite Linneraineach House, a direct line can be taken towards the east buttress, a distance of 1.6km over open moorland, giving easy walking even in wet weather. A prominent stone cairn stands on exposed slabs near the foot of the buttress. Their succession is complex and route finding needs continuous attention if the climber does not want to find himself in a 'blind alley'. Care should be taken after rain when the ledges can be tricky.

A path leads round the foot of the crag into a steep, dirty chute

HAMISH MACINNES

34.   *Stac Pollaidh across Loch Lurgain*

35.   *From Ben More Coigach to Loch Broom*

TOM WEIR

36.   *Sandstone Pinnacles on Stac Pollaidh*

37.   *Cul Beag from Stac Pollaidh*

38.   Sgurr an Fhidhleir across Lochan Tuath

which leads onto the saddle already mentioned. This is a better exit than a means of ascent. Easier going is found by traversing round from the cairn onto the north side of the east buttress to pick up a track leading steeply up onto the saddle at the same point as the other routes. From the cairn, the distance is 800m.

The most recent approach track rises steeply up from the large, surfaced lay-by just over a 1.6km past Linneraineach. This has been sign-posted at the start by the Nature Conservancy. Although direct, it is too steep and dirty to be recommended, even in dry weather—in bad weather it becomes a quagmire in many places.

Once on the ridge, the tracks along to the west summit, the highest point on Stac Pollaidh, are well defined. These offer countless combinations of walking, scrambling and climbing. Most of the rock problems encountered in the course of the traverse from east to west can be by-passed easily at a lower level if need be, but care should be taken at the west end of the ridge on the step across to the small rock tower that blocks the way to the summit. The holds here are beginning to disintegrate and even the larger blocks need to be tested for security. In addition, the extent of the drop from the connecting col is not immediately apparent from the ridge. In retrospect from the summit cairn it is seen to be quite considerable.

On a clear day, the view from the summit is superb. Looking backwards along the ridge itself, one is amazed how the pinnacles just passed have changed in character seen from a different angle. Every hollow in the surrounding floor of gneiss seems to hold its own lochan, many ringed with little sandy beaches. To the north-east, across Loch Sionascaig with its little wooded islands, the whole length of Suilven dominates the view, while closer at hand the muralled western cliffs of Cul Mor rise steeply above Glen Laoigh. The whole of Coigach is unfolded and, beyond that, the more distant peaks of Sutherland and Wester Ross.

Stac Pollaidh seldom holds much snow but, when it does, the path on the north side should be treated with care. In normal weather conditions routes back down to the road can be found via most of the many gullies on either side of the ridge. A descent down the large gully to the east of the second buttress from the west end leads past some of the mountain's most spectacular pinnacles. Described by Frank Cunningham in an article in the S.M.C.J. (1951) as Pinnacle Basin, three of the pinnacles were seen to resemble the Sphinx, Tam O'Shanter and Madonna and Child. The latter was climbed in 1957 by

I. Clough and D. Pipes of Kinloss Mountain Rescue Team and was called *The Virgin Pinnacle*. It gave 20m of Severe climbing and was described as follows:—'This slender pinnacle, rising almost 30m above the screes in Pinnacle Basin was climbed in continuous drizzle by an obvious crack on its shortest side—nearest the mountain—the ledge below the crack was reached (artificial) and the crack was climbed by artificially inserted chock-stones in the gap between the two summit blocks. The crack was led free (Very Severe) by members of the Cliff Assault Wing of the Royal Marines in May, 1964.'

The arête bounding the bay containing the various pinnacles on the right and leading to the Claw is *Summer Isles Arête*—120m Very Difficult (Mr. and Mrs. J. MacKenzie, July, 1974).

The traverse of the ridge from west to east necessitates rock-climbing and most of the routes on Stac Pollaidh have been concentrated around the West Buttress. The usual route follows the south-west corner of the buttress above the conspicuous rock pinnacle, known either as *The Forefinger* or *Bairds Pinnacle*. The first ascent here was done in 1906 by C. W. Walker and Dr. Inglis Clark. T. W. Patey recorded that the corresponding northerly corner of the west face of the buttress may also be climbed more or less directly by a narrow rib of no great difficulty but of less merit than the south-west corner. This was climbed by him in 1962, and gave 90m of Difficult climbing.

Baird's Pinnacle was first climbed by R.A.F. Kinloss using wooden wedges and a top rope. The crack on the inner wall was climbed free, (Very Severe) involving strenuous finger-jamming, by T. W. Patey, 12th June, 1968.

There are four routes of high standard on the south-east corner of the West Buttress. These can be located by the two long converging dièdres which scar the face. *November Groove*—115m Severe (D. Stewart and G. Cairns, 1953), takes the right-hand one. Start with a rising traverse to a ledge and belay. Climb up to groove. This is grassy at first. Climb up and surmount overhang on the right to belay, then continue up the groove line under an obvious right traverse. Go out to the right and up to the top of the buttress. *Enigma Groove*—105m Very Severe (T. W. Patey and R. W. P. Barclay, 1962) takes the left-hand dièdre. The route looks easier than November Groove but is in fact harder. Climb 30m into the large bay from which both dièdres emanate. The first pitch here is the crux—a 15m inset corner. This has few holds and is often wet. Above, are strenuous chimney moves to the platform below the final crack. An attempt to climb this direct was unsuccessful after 6m. Easier ways are found to the top on either side.

Jack the Ripper—110m Very Severe (M. G. Anderson and G. Mair, 1964), follows the obvious rib between the south-west and the south-east faces. The start is 1½m left of a cairn at the foot of the rib, under an obvious lay-back crack. Climb the wall on the left of the buttress, then the crack, followed by a wider crack trending rightwards to a belay behind a flake (18m). Climb a loose wall on left to twin cracks—the left-hand crack is followed to an amphitheatre and a big flake (20m). Climb right of three ribs above—this is the sustained crux requiring two protective pitons (40m). Go up the crack above the belay for a few feet until an obvious traverse left leads into a chimney gully. This is followed to a large ledge and a poor belay (30m). Do not climb the wall to the top but traverse to the right then take the crack to the top (9m) belay beside the summit cairn.

On the east face of West Buttress is *Felo de Se*—70m Very Severe (R. Carrington and J. MacLean, July, 1969). The route follows the crack-line up the wall to the right of Jack the Ripper for 40m to a good stance. Move up an awkward wide groove to a peg belay below a block overhang (15m) then climb the prominent corner using one nut for aid at mid-height (20m).

Cul Mor (848m)

Cul Mor is the most northerly of the Coigach group, rising steeply from the shore of Loch Veyatie on the Ross-shire-Sutherland border, 3km west of the crofting communities of Knockan and Elphin. Seen from the east, its twin peaks, joined by a smoothly curving saddle and capped with quartzite, form a distinctive landmark. To the west, Cul Mor drops in a line of steep, muralled precipices split by deep gullies, into Gleann Laoigh. This lovely glen separates the mountain from Cul Beag and is by far the most interesting line of approach. Below the main top, Sron Garbh (849m) on the north side of the mountain, lies Coire Gorm—the green corrie—circled by cliffs and hidden from the road. A deep gully formed by a weathered out dyke drops steeply from the north-west shoulder of Cul Mor, and near the point where it meets the ridge is to be seen a distinctive rock pinnacle known as Bod a'Mhiotailt, or 'the Old Man', from its likeness to a human figure when seen in profile. The ascent of this pinnacled ridge affords pleasant scrambling of a Moderate nature, but care should be taken on the pinnacle itself—the top blocks are far from secure. The best line of approach to this north side of the mountain is from Elphin school-house, fording the burn which runs into Loch Veyatie just west of the school and rising upwards along the side of the loch towards Loch na Claise—ref. 162132—a distance of 6.5km over good ground. From here a steep ascent leads round into the foot of the gully bounded by Pinnacle Ridge.

The usual approach to Cul Mor starts at the well-marked stalker's track which leaves the A835 800m north-west of Knockan Rock. This gives good walking for 1.5km and then the broad south-east ridge can be followed to the base of the summit cone of Sron Garbh. A series of steep traverses takes one steadily upwards to the final quartzite boulder field and the summit cairn. This involves 5km of walking from the road.

Descend into the saddle between the two tops and an easy climb leads in 800m onto the south top, Creag nan Calman (786m). The actual summit plateau is broad and flat and affords rough hill grazing for sheep. From Creag nan Calman it is worth detouring on to the west side of the mountain. A small jutting platform gives a spectacular view down into the deep gullies on that side and across to Cul Beag. This can be descended on its west side into Gleann Laoigh with no great difficulty.

The south-west face of Creag nan Calman has one recorded route on its lower tier—*Buffalo Ballet*—127m Very Severe (R. Gatehouse and C. Smith, July, 1979).

Three buttresses can be identified—West, Central and East. East Buttress merges with crags overlooking Loch Dearg a'Chuill Mhor. West Gully is a large amphitheatre separating West and Central Buttress. East Gully slopes diagonally up left between Central and East Buttresses. The route starts at the foot of East Gully on the right wall below a prominent chimney.—'Climb groove, then chimney, traverse right to easy ground. Follow gully to beneath chimney crack. Climb rib on left of gully for 24m to below narrow chimney, climb this, then another chimney, traverse left below overhang to narrow rib. Climb to top of rib, tension right across steep slab to gain top of overhang. Follow chimney to top.'

Gleann Laoigh provides the most rewarding approach to the western crags of Cul Mor and is in itself one of the loveliest walking routes in the whole area. It can be approached either from the A835 at Knockan Rock or from Linneraineach on Loch Lurgainn. From Knockan Rock, the route passes between Loch an Als and Lochan

Fada to skirt the south end of Loch nan Ealachan, and then crosses the Alt an Loin Duibh at the head of the glen. Traverse the lower slopes of An Laogh, the rocky southerly satellite of Cul Mor, to rise gradually past Lochan Dearg. The boulder field at the north end is a good bivouac site.

If the intention is to reach the west crags of Cul Mor, make for the prominent waterfall which drops over the lowest crags and ascend it to Loch Dearg a'Chuill Mhoir which lies at the foot of the main crags. The choice of route to the top is governed by personal ability and there is undoubtedly scope here for climbing routes.

If one continues along the glen, the way leads through woodland and flat meadows to Loch Gainmheich, circled with sandy beaches.

For many years a subsantial shepherd's bothy stood at the north-east end of the loch—for reasons unknown this has now disappeared. The path crosses the narrow neck of water between Loch Gainmheich and Loch Sionascaig by a dubious single-plank bridge and then joins to the well-marked stalker's track which passes over between Cul Beag and Stac Pollaidh to Linneraineach. The distance either way to the foot of the crags is 5km and the route is to be recommended.

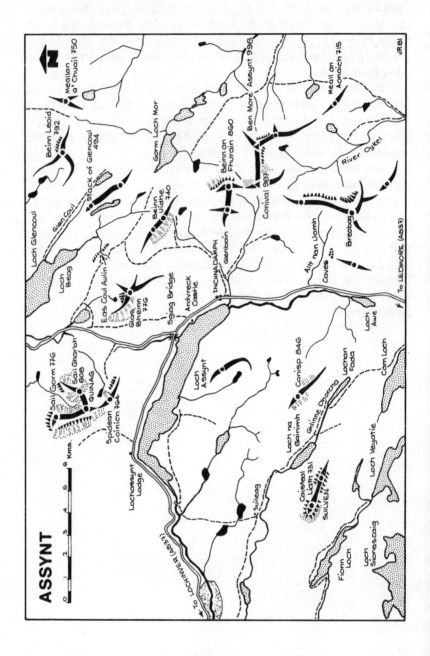

ASSYNT

Assynt

(1) **Suilven** (731m) N.C. 153184
(2) **Canisp** (846m) N.C. 203188
(3) **Quinag** (808m) N.C. 209292
(4) **Glas Bheinn** (776m) N.C. 254265
(5) **Beinn Uidhe** (740m) N.C. 282252
(6) **Beinn an Fhurain** (860m) N.C. 304216
(7) **Conival** (987m) N.C. 303199
(8) **Ben More Assynt** (998m) N.C. 318201
(9) **Breabag** (814m) N.C. 287158
(10) **Beinn Leoid** (792m) N.C. 320295

MAP: O.S. 1:50,000 (2nd Series) Sheet No. 15—Loch Assynt.

Assynt forms the south-west portion of the old county of Sutherland and is separated from Coigach by the boundary line along Loch Veyatie and the River Kirkaig. Sutherland is the 'Sunderland' or 'Southland' of the Norsemen who were the scourge of the northern mainland of Scotland for over 400 years from A.D.800 to A.D.1263. Their influence in Assynt, as in other parts of the Sutherland and Caithness areas which came under their power, it still to be seen in many of the place names—often a corrupted combination of Norse and Ancient Gaelic. The name 'Assynt' itself has been suggested as deriving from the Norse 'A-ssynt—seen from afar, in reference to its mountains. The Norse word 'Ass' means 'rocky'. An alternative meaning of 'Assynt' comes from a vague tradition that at one time there were two brothers—Unt and Ass-Unt—meaning Man of Peace and Man of Discord. In olden days they fought for the mastery of Assynt and Unt was slain, his brother then giving his name to the parish. Equally likely is the contraction of the Gaelic compound—Agur Unt—to As-int—In and Out—which is descriptive of the broken nature of the surface of the area.

On its northern border, Assynt is separated from the neighbouring parish of Eddrachillis by the great sea loch of A'Chairn Bhain

(Anglicised into Cairnbawn), which opens westwards into the broad bay of Eddrachillis, with its host of sandy inlets and low-lying islands. In the past these islands were used as grazing grounds for the mainland, and here sheep and cattle were fattened—the old statistical accounts of the 18th century detail the number of animals which each of the many islands could carry. Oldany Island, lying just off the Assynt shore near the mouth of the bay, is the largest of these and in the days when Assynt swarmed with wolves it was used as a burial ground for the mainland settlements. At its inland end Loch Cairnbawn narrows to less than 400m and a car ferry (now no longer free) operates seven days a week across from Kylesku to Kylestrome on the north side of the channel. In the past, drovers from the north swam their cattle across the narrows and, 19th century prints of the area show a sizeable fleet of herring boats anchored in Unapool Bay, once the centre of a thriving fishing industry.

East of the narrows, Loch Cairnbawn divides, sending two fingers probing inland for almost 6.5km. The northerly inlet is Loch Glendhu; the southerly inlet is Loch Glencoul. This is an area of special attraction to the geologist. Aird da Loch, the headland dividing the two lochs, shows a classic exposure of the Glencoul Thrust Plane, one of the great earth movements which took place in the development of the mountain ranges of the Northern Highlands. Here the displacement of the native gneiss over the sedimentary layer of Cambrian strata can be clearly seen.

The parish boundary on the east side follows the watershed along the ridges of Beinn Uidhe, Conival and Breabag, paradoxically excluding Ben More Assynt, the highest mountain top in Sutherland. To further exclude it from this chapter on the Assynt mountains would be illogical and, for similar geographical reasons, we include here mention of Beinn Leoid. This mountain officially lies in the parish of Eddrachillis (in the Glen Coul—Glen Dhu hinterland).

At the south-eastern corner of Assynt, the Ross-shire border makes a strange, wedge-like invasion northwards into Sutherland as far as Conival and the slopes of Ben More Assynt. The road from the south crosses the border by the fishing hotel at Altnacealgach. A dispute took place here in the past over the demarcation of the county boundaries. When two witnesses were called, they maintained that while walking the boundaries their feet had never left Ross-shire soil. This was true. They had first filled their shoes with Balnagowan earth. Altnacealgach means 'the burn of the cheat'.

Two good motor roads lead into Assynt from the south. The road from Ullapool, with its branch road to Lochinver, has been described in a previous chapter. This links with the Bonar Bridge-Lochinver road (A837) at Ledmore Junction, 3km north-west of Altnacealgach Hotel. The road from Bonar Bridge leaves the A9 at the head of the Kyle of Sutherland and follows the Oykel Valley for most of its way north-westwards. This wide river valley, running roughly north-west to south-east, separates Sutherland and Caithness from the rest of the southern mainland and inspired early geographers to name the area 'Innismor'—'The Great Island'.

The road rises steeply out of the river valley onto the watershed at Craggie, then continues past Ledmore northwards through Inchnadamph and on along Loch Assynt side to Lochinver. Its route conveniently passes through the main mountain mass of Assynt providing easy access to both east and west. 3km north of Inchnadamph, at Skiag Bridge, a branch road leads northwards to Kylesku Ferry and the Reay country, crossing between Quinag and Glas Bheinn at its highest point. A secondary road branches westwards some 3km from the ferry, passing along the coastline and across the neck of the Stoer Peninsula to link the crofting communities of Nedd, Drumbeg, Clashnessie, Culkein and Stoer with Lochinver. The circuit is one of the most picturesque in the area and should not be omitted. The road passes beneath the great northern buttresses of Quinag then winds and switchbacks its way westwards to Stoer, the largest of the villages through which it passes. Stoer lies 11km north of Lochinver and has a good camping site by its broad sandy beach. 1.6km north of the village a side road branches on to the Point of Stoer. A car can be taken as far as Culkein, which is a scattered community of croft houses, but the final 3km to the sea is by peat road and moorland.

From the road south of Stoer one gets a fine panoramic view of the Coigach and Assynt hills rising in all their varied shapes from the surrounding moorland. One can well believe the legend that this is where the Old Norse Gods came when the world was still young and malleable to practice mountain building. They are said to have returned and modelled Norway with more experienced hands.

The country stretches inland for 15km to Loch Assynt and is a maze of fresh water lochs of every shape and size—a paradise for fishermen but difficult to navigate. The roads throughout Assynt pass few inhabited communities. The population is scattered mainly along the coastal areas from Lochinver round to Drumbeg. Here crofting and fishing are the main occupations and most houses will provide overnight accommodation for the tourists. Once away from the coastal strip, Assynt is virtually uninhabited, apart from the scattering of houses around Inchnadamph Hotel at the east end of Loch Assynt; the tiny village of Unapool by Kylesku Ferry; and along the stretch of road between Ledmore Junction and the small crofting townships of Elphin and Knockan.

From Enard Bay in the south, round the peninsula of Rubh a'Stoer to Eddrachillis, the Assynt coastline is indented by numerous sandy-bayed sea lochs; the most important is Loch Inver. The village of Lochinver, which lies at its head, is the main centre of population in the area and has become an important port for the landing of white fish. Its central location at the junction of motor roads from north, south and east make it a popular centre for summer visitors and superb sea-angling ranks high among its many attractions.

The Rubh a'Stoer peninsula culminates in the Point of Stoer, which juts out into the Minch, 12km north-west of Lochinver. The 'Old Man of Stoer'—not to be confused with the 'Old Man of Storr' in Skye—stands 800m south of the Point. This 67m sandstone sea stack was considered 'unclimbable' until it was ascended in 1966 by T. W. Patey, B. Robertson, B. Henderson and P. Nunn. It was found to give a 'fine free climb of Severe standard on the best Torridonian sandstone in Scotland'.

From its slender base, the pinnacle bulges at mid-height, before it begins to taper and, from its appearance, might suggest a more exacting climb than its better known namesake in Skye (which it overtops by about 20m). Huge, rough-grained holds flatter the climber, so that almost anything may be attempted. Puking Fulmars elevate the standard during the nesting season. Scramble down steeply for 90m to the broad shelf opposite the Old Man. To gain the supporting plinth, a deep channel, 8m side at its narrowest point, must be crossed. A 9m ladder, a Tyrolean traverse rope, and swimming offered different solutions on different visits, but tidal currents and underwater seaweed could often hamper swimmers. 4m up the landward face, twin horizontal cracks are followed left round the first corner, then go straight up excellent rock to a large platform on the corner (20m).

Above the platform, climb a steep slab (crux) to a fringe of overhangs. Pass the overhangs by a crack, and step delicately left to reach easy ledges. Continue for 9m to a cave below, above a large chockstone (21m). Traverse round the airy corner to the right on the landward face and veer up rightwards avoiding the first upward break, to reach a small ledge and block belay (12m). Climb the prominent V-chimney above, facing left, to easy ground. Finish up obvious corner crack (15m). Descent by rappel: go straight down the line of the south-east corner to the first belay platform (45m). Move along a thin ledge on the landward face to an abseil piton. Go down to the starting point (18m)—70m. Hard Severe. Few climbers will resist the temptation to visit this classic corner of the north-west coastline when in the Assynt area.

Assynt is the legendary hunting ground of the Thanes of Sutherland and is still almost entirely divided among great sporting estates which are let throughout the season for their fishing and stalking rights. The exception is the limestone area lying east of Inchnadamph Hotel towards the slopes of Ben More Assynt where 3200 acres of Assynt Estate are managed by the Nature Conservancy. Here vegetation changes are being studied and the existing herb-rich pastures maintained by strict control of burning and grazing. Evidence of earlier inhabitants is to be seen close to the roadside from Ledmore to Loch Assynt in the relics of early burial chambers, and in the isolated standing stones in the neighbourhood of Clachtoll, while later ruins of brochs are to be found at Clashnessie and Stoer Bay along the coastline.

During the 12th century the area was continuously pillaged by the Norsemen until eventually passing into the hands of a son of Macleod of Lewis. Macleod received a charter for the land from King David II with the approval of the Thane of Sutherland in 1346, and fourteen successive Macleod lairds ruled Assynt until the end of the 17th century. Ardvreck Castle, the stronghold of the family, was built in 1597 and the ruins still stand out into the waters of Loch Assynt on a narrow, easily-defended peninsula, 2km north-west of Inchnadamph. The devil is reputed to have had a hand in both its building and its ultimate fate.

The downfall of Macleod power began with the part played by Neil Macleod in the betrayal of the Marquis of Montrose in 1650. After his little army of 1200 men had been cut to pieces at Carbisdale by Strachan's cavalry, the wounded Marquis fled westwards with three companions and wandered the hills for two days and nights. Separated from his companions, Montrose was forced to beg food at a herd's shieling on the third day and was captured by Macleod's men. He was imprisoned in a dungeon in Ardvreck castle and then taken to Edinburgh where he was executed on 21st May, 1650. Though Macleod tried to vindicate himself it is recorded that he accepted payment for his service and his fortunes, and those of his family, declined from that time on. A dispute with the Mackenzie lairds of Seaforth came to litigation and was upheld in Mackenzie's favour by the law court. Mackenzie was given permssion to exact the pledge by the force of arms and, after a prolonged siege, Ardvreck Castle fell and the Macleod laird fled, allegedly to Holland. After the Jacobite risings the Mackenzie estates were forfeit to the crown and in 1760 passed back into the hands of the Sutherland family by purchase. The ruined house on the roadside near Ardvreck is Calda House—known locally as The White House—a stronghold built and burned by the Mackenzies, allegedly rather than see it pass into the hands of the Sutherlands.

In 1760, Assynt passed back into the hands of the original Sutherland family by purchase, and on the marriage of Elizabeth, Countess of Sutherland, to Lord Stafford, who was to become the first Duke of Sutherland and the owner of almost the entire county. Like the remainder of his estates, Assynt suffered in his schemes for agricultural improvement and, between 1812 and 1820, large numbers of the inhabitants were 'cleared' to make way for sheep-walks. The major part of the area now forms the Assynt Estate.

The mountains of Assynt fall into two distinct groups—West and East—divided by the road from Ledmore Junction to Kylesku. This is no artificial division. From Ullapool to Kylesku the road follows the boundary of the main thrust planes and one cannot fail to observe the change in rock formation and scenery on either side of it. To the west is the undisturbed Lewisian gneiss and to the east the crystalline schists of the Moine series. The gneiss forms a platform for the western mountains—which are predominantly sandstone monoliths capped in varying degrees with Cambrian quartzite. To the east, the gneiss is found rising to a much greater height as a result of the thrust movements, and on Ben More Assynt (998m) rises close to the summit, the highest occurrence of this formation in Britain.

In the north-west there are four main formation which go to build the mountain slopes. The oldest (oldest in the world) is the Lewisian gneiss. On top of it rests the younger Torridonian sandstone. Next is the Cambrian (certain fossils) which here take the form of white quartzite and a series of limestones. After the Cambrian had been laid down came a series of vast movements which thrust forward great slabs of rock and piled them up, older rocks over-riding on younger rocks upsetting the natural sequence and sometimes causing complete inversion to the confusion of early Geologists. Last and greatest of these thrusts was the Moine Thrust, which brought forward the great series of schists—the Moine schists—over the Lewisian, Torridonian and Cambrian strata. This thrust runs in a sinuous line from Whitten Head on the north coast of Sutherland, (outer Loch Eriboll) to Sleat in Skye—a distance of 192km. The width of the thrust various from 18km in Skye to 1.5km in Sutherland. In Assynt it is 11km wide. It is not known for sure whether the pressure built up from the south-south-east to pile up the schists on the fringe of a stable area of older rocks, or whether the older strata moved from the west-north-west and pushed the schists up over them. The minimum distance through which the Moine schists have been displaced westwards relative to the formation beneath the Moine Thrust Plane is estimated at 16km.

A fuller treatise on these movements and the manner in which they affected the Northern Highlands is to be found in *Basic Regional Geology: Scotland: The Northern Highlands* (2nd Edition) by J. Phemister, H.M.S.O. Publication.

WEST ASSYNT
Suilven

(1) **Casteal Liath** (731m) 8km S.E. of Lochinver
(2) **Meall Mheadhonach** (701m) 800m E. of 1
(3) **Meall Bheag** (610m) 800m E. of 2.

Suilven is the most westerly of the Assynt mountains and dominates the surrounding landscape. It is one of the most remarkable and best known peaks in the British Isles. Viewed from east or west it appears as a solitary peak. This is how the Vikings saw it coming into the Assynt coast from the sea and causing them to name it Sul-Fhal—the Pillar Mountain. To the native Gael, the great rounded western dome became Caisteal Liath—the Grey Castle—a more fitting name for this splendid sculptured sandstone tower than the 'Sugar Loaf'. Seen across the Cam Loch from Elphin, in the south-east, it appears as a sharp cone with only a glimpse of the precipices on Caisteal Liath, the ridge being greatly fore-shortened. Seen from north or south, the whole splendour of its triple-peaked ridge is unfolded, rising in splendid isolation from the surrounding lochan-strewn moorland like a ship riding at anchor.

The ridge extends for 2.5km . The rounded red-flanked tower of Caisteal Liath lies at the western end, the sharp peak of Meall Mheadhonach in the middle and the much smaller peak of Meall Beag, with its sharp drop facing Meall Mheadhonach, at the eastern end. Between Caisteal Liath and Meall Mheadhonach lies the Bealach Mor—a prominent col from which steep stone shoots drop down to north and south. The easy route onto the summit ridge lies up either of those; that on the north side is possibly a little easier but there is nothing to choose between them. The descent should be treated carefully. Loose stone abounds.

Approaching Suilven from the north side, there is a choice of three starting points:

From Little Assynt at the west end of Loch Assynt on the Inchnadamph-Lochinver road (A837) the River Inver is crossed by a footbridge and a stalker's track is followed for 4km to Suileag in Glen Canisp.

The same point can be reached from Lochinver. A private road leads for over 3km to Glencanisp Lodge, owned by Mr. Vestey, the Estate proprietor, and a stalker's track leads to the junction with the Little Assynt track near Suileag. Continue along the north side of Amhainn na Clach Airigh for 2.5km to the bridge at the head of Loch na Gainimh. The main track continues for a good 3km along the north shore of the loch towards Lochan Fada, below Canisp. From the bridge a steep climb over rough ground leads to the foot of the stone shoot leading to the north side of Bealach Mor.

The stone shoot on the south side of the Bealach Mor is reached from Inver Kirkaig, at the bridge over the River Kirkaig, 5km south of Lochinver. A good track follows the river of the Fionn Loch—5km. The track passes the Falls of Kirkaig—20m perpendicular fall—and continues along the north side of the loch for another 1.5km before making a way upwards to the foot of the stone shoot on the south side of the Bealach Mor.

Once on the bealach, an easy climb westwards leads to the summit cairn on Caisteal Liath, passing en route through a gap in the dry stone dyke which, amazingly enough, has been built across the line of the ridge at this point. Retrace the route to the bealach, and a splendid ridge walk with some scrambling leads onto the summit of Meall Mheadhonach, giving spectacular views down either flank. The route drops steeply between Mheall Mheadhonach and Mheall Bheag and the ascent of the latter from the col requires some care. An exposed corner is turned on the north side along a rocky shelf and a way can then be made up to the top of Mheall Bheag, on the same side, by way of a series of terraces. The situation is slightly exposed but affords no great difficulty. A little way down the east ridge, a narrow transverse gap is easily crossed and the difficulties are then over.

A way may be made with care down the south side of the col between Mheall Mheadhonach and Mheall Bheag but this is loose and dirty, and care should be taken in the lower stretches where a steep drop is by-passed by keeping eastwards. The east ridge can be followed down to the head of Cam Loch and from there along the south side of the loch for a little over 1.5km. The loch is indented by a wide bay on this side and a line overland from the southern corner brings one to the waterfall between Cam Loch and Loch Veyatie. The water can be forded at the head of Loch Veyatie, from where a rough road leads up to meet the main Ullapool-Ledmore road in Elphin Village.

The approach to Suilven from this easterly direction is long and arduous. An alternative is to go by canoe along Loch Veyatie for about 4km to an obvious natural harbour on its north shore—Ref. 178141. A direct line north is then taken overland to the end of Loch nan Rac—a distance of just over 2km. A steep, but straight-forward ascent then leads onto the east ridge of the mountain and Mheall Bheag. This makes for a delightful day's expedition.

The traverse of Suilven from west to east, involving the ascent of Caisteal Liath, with its near vertical cliffs, is undoubtedly a classic of its kind. The problem posed by the 250m terraced-sandstone which encircles the north-western end of Suilven already has produced a variety of solutions but the possibilities are by no means exhausted. It can be tackled by way of several of the numerous gullies which breach the walls, but these eventually run out and the climber must be prepared for steep vegetation, exposure and little protection.

The original climbing route on Caisteal Liath lies up the steep open gully on the southern side of the north-west buttress. It has no technical difficulty but is exposed and vegetated, as are many of the subsequently-recorded routes. The first people to climb this way were C. Pilkington and H. Walker in 1892. Almost directly below this south-western angle, to the right of the foot of the gully, another early route—G. Sang, 1914—starts up a deeply-cleft 10m chimney with a

173

difficult, holdless exit over the copestone. Above this the line taken is less definite. The best routes were subsequently found on the middle of the north-west buttress itself. *Gray's Route* begins at an open groove in the middle of the face above the lower tier of slabs. At few points was there great technical difficulty, but there was considerable exposure and it was necessary to accept, and to use with care, whatever holds there were, whether vegetation or quartz pebbles projecting from the sandstone. The route was recorded by Robin Gray in the Rucksack Club Journal 1935.

Portcullis Route—180m Severe (A. Parker and S. Paterson, 1949), starts to the right of Gray's Route. Start from the rock step at bottom of lower wall and climb to the terrace, trending left then right. Here a cairn marks the start shared with two of the other routes. From this point, a short climb is followed by a long, delicate horizontal traverse to the left. A mantelshelf is followed by a short left traverse into a small corner. Exit with a strenuous pull-out to the right and reach a ledge by delicate move and long reach. Continue with slight deviations in a more or less direct line to the top. Portcullis joins Gray's Route two-thirds of the way up the buttress.

Rose Route—140m Mild Severe (A. Smart and A. Mitchell, Through leads, July, 1957) starts at the foot of the north-west buttress, right of the prominent central rib (Portcullis Route), and left of black water-slides. 'From the cairn, climb a steep 2m wall and turn a steeper one to the right, to reach the foot of a fine red slab. Climb obliquely upwards to the right for 6m to the ledge above it—dubious flake belay. Up 2m from the ledge and traverse left round a nose to the foot of two narrow slabs, the right set back from the left. Climb 6m up between them to a larger ledge at the edge of the nearest waterslide. Jammed stone belay. A spectacular and exposed (but not technically hard) traverse left round a corner and along ledges more secure than they look, leads to the broken ledges of the traverse directly below the south edge of the main buttress. The remainder of the climb more or less follows this edge. Start at the obvious corner of the buttress. This corner is taken throughout as being the edge of the buttress, as against a lesser corner further right (cairn). Climb 4m and then over or round a large block. At 8m a small slab leads to a mantelshelf movement onto a large block on the right. Traverse right to the buttress edge and go up 6m further to a notable stalactite belay at the foot of a small chimney (20m). Climb the chimney and by-pass a small wall on the right leading back to a dark corner on the left at 10m. Traverse right,

TOM STRANG

39.   *Stac Pollaidh and Cul Beag from Inverkirkaig*

40.   *Scourie with a back-cloth of peaks from Ben More Assynt to Suilven*

41.   *Cul More from west over Loch Sionascaig*

42.   *Am Buachaille, Sandwood Bay*

ALEX GILLESPIE

43.   *Looking east on the ridge of Suilven*

round a projecting block (hands above, feet beneath) to a good ledge, again near the buttress edge. 10m of easier climbing leads to a broad ledge above which the angle obviously lessens (25m). Three long run-outs over more broken rocks leads in 60m to the top of the climb. Some distance from the top of the buttress the climbing is easier and variations possible. The rock is sound and the climb, which is a good one, is always steep and generally exposed.'

Heatwave—140m Severe (H. MacInnes and M. C. MacInnes, 1968), starts at the same point as Portcullis Route and takes a slightly more direct line to the terrace. From here it takes an almost parallel line to Rose Route and eventually joins it (after numerous short traverses and loose rock) at the top of the buttress. The easiest line on the wall ahead is taken to the top.

Canisp—(846m) 8km N.E. of Ledmore Junction.

In itself Canisp holds little of interest to the climber but its position, some 5km east of Suilven across Glen Canisp, makes it an ideal viewpoint for the latter mountain. Its long south-eastern slope is best approached from the road some 3km north of Ledmore Junction. The River Loanan, which flows out of Loch Awe, can be crossed at the end of the loch by a footbridge and the summit of Canisp is easily reached in just under two hours. The distance from the road is 5.5km. The view across to the ridge of Suilven, especially in winter, is in itself ample reward, but the northern side of Canisp drops unexpectedly in broken quartzite cliffs in its upper reaches and here the golden eagle can often be seen. The derivation of Canisp is doubtful but, in view of its quartzite capping, the old Gaelic word 'can', meaning 'white', may well form part of the name. The rock is too shattered to offer much climbing but in winter the mountain holds snow well and gives an extremely fine ski-expedition. The descent from the summit to Loch Awe can often be unbelievably fine for almost 3km. The return to the road at other times of the year can be made down the side of the attractive Allt Mhic Mhurchaidh Gheir which drops in series of falls and natural bathing pools into Loch Awe.

QUINAG

(1) **Spidean Coinich** (764m) N.C. 205278
(2) **Centre Top** (748m) 1km N.N.W. of 1
(3) **Sail Gharbh** (Main Top on East Ridge) (808m) 800m N.E. of 2
(4) **Sail Ghorm** (776m) 1.6km N.W. of 2

Quinag stands as a mighty sentinel guarding the northern border of

175

Assynt and is the last distinctive 'Mountain' in that chain of Torridonian sandstone which stretches from Applecross along the entire western seaboard of the Northern Highlands. Only around the Cape Wrath peninsula, on the extreme northern tip, does the sandstone again reach a height of any impressive proportions.

Quinag is shaped like a gigantic 'Y'. The main leg is formed by the 2km long dip slope running north-westwards from Loch Assynt onto Spidean Coinich (764m) the southern peak, which stands out boldly like a giant water spout. This peak gives the mountains its name; 'Cuinneag' is Gaelic for a narrow-mouthed bucket. The slope has an overlying cover of white quartzite, widely exposed in many places, giving pleasant walking. The quartzite also appears as an impressive cliff falling from the north-east side of Spidean Coinich. The ridge continues slightly north-westwards for 1.5km to the centre, unnamed-top (748m), dropping on the way into the Bealach a'Chornaidh, the deep saddle which bisects the ridge and provides an easy route across from east to west.

Past the junction top the ridge divides and sends out two broad arms. In their fork is contained the deep corrie out of which flows the Alt a'Bhathaich—the burn of the Byre. The north spur continues in the main line of the ridge and terminates in the rocky buttress of Sail Ghorm (776m). Here on the north face the underlying gneiss rises to a height of 610m. The north-east spur rises to the highest top of Quinag (808m) and terminates in the great sandstone buttress of Sail Gharbh. The main top of Sail Gharbh has a capping of white quartzite; the deeply gullied face of Sail Gharbh is of sandstone, which drops in a series of bold steps, broken here and there by heathery terraces. The western side of Quinag extends for some 3km as a line of well-seamed crags, rising in places to a height of over 200m.

The mountain is easy of access from all sides. The south-east dip slope rises from the junction of the Lochinver and Kylesku roads at Skiag Bridge, some 3km north of Inchnadamph Hotel on the north shore of Loch Assynt. The Kylesku road is followed northwards for 3km and, from any convenient point, the line of the slope can be followed to the summit of Spidean Coinich. Alternatively, a stalkers' track leaves the road nearby at point N.C. 232274—and leads into the north side of Lochan Bealach Chornaidh thence onto the saddle below the centre top Bealach a'Chornaidh. The distance is 4.5km and the track goes in further than is marked on the map. This is a good escape route from the ridge if need be and also gives a fine view of the prominent north cliff of Spidean Coinich. The nearest point of access to the rock faces of Sail Gharbh is from the Kylesku road where it crosses the Unapool burn—2.5km—the way is largely across moorland, but eventually a track is joined which leads to the foot of the rocks.

Other approaches are possible from the Drumbeg road, which branches off from the Kylesku road just 3km before the ferry. The most obvious starting point is from the bridge over Alt a'Ghamhna—3km from the junction.

From Tumore, on the Lochinver road, 5.5km west of Skiag Bridge, a stalkers' track leads through Gleann Leireag to join the Drumbeg road 8km from the junction near Kylesku. This passes along the foot of the western cliffs of Quinag, giving a fine view of the length of the ridge with its succession of subsidiary tops. From Creag na h'Iolaire on the 228m contour, the bealach lies 800m east of the track and to reach it from this point involves only 366m of ascent. Further north the track passes Loch an Leathaid and, from here, one can make a way up the long slope leading on to Sail Ghorm.

The western cliff-line holds a number of features which facilitate the location of climbs—(a) seen from the path the Bealach a'Chornaidh, the lowest col between the Central Top and Spidean Coinnich is easily picked out.

(b) The Junction Top of Quinag—pt. 745
(c) A small col
(d) A square-topped tower, unnamed
(e) A second col
(f) A small col
(g) Pt. 776.

The buttresses on the whole are too heathery to be of interest; the vertical features, however, here give several routes to date. These are described from right to left facing the cliff. *The Family Way,* 60m Severe (B. Dunn and J. R. Houston, 3rd July, 1971), starts at the back right corner of a shallow gully which splits the buttress lying to the left and below the Bealach a'Chornaidh. The route follows a mossy groove, then a horizontal traverse to a steep crack giving access to the crest of the rib. Belay on rock platform on the crest (27m). Continue up the rib, finishing up a steep chimney (33m). The prominent rib seen rising from right to left immediately below the small square-topped tower (d) is *Tenement Ridge* 150m Very Difficult (G. R. Ambler and J. R. Sutcliffe). This rib is separated from the main face of the mountain by a deep gully branching left from the Geodha Rudha; it rises in a series of steep rock steps divided by spacious ledges and can worthily be considered a 'ridge'. The scree gully—Geodha Rudha—is crossed to gain a heather ledge at the base of the rock ridge. The climb starts up a sloping corner with a slab on its left. Minor variations are possible on most pitches. Thread, or block belays were found on all but the third platform, when a piton was used. In the prevailing weather condition of heavy rain, the final steep rock step before the ridge levels out was passed by a short rightward traverse above the gully and the crest regained by a chimney. Easy scrambling along the final section of the ridge before it joins the mountain is interrupted by a steep 5m wall which provides an unavoidable problem to the finish of the climb.

The Pillar of Assynt, 120m, Very Severe (T. W. Patey and H. MacInnes, 12th June, 1968) is a 75m clean-cut column, the best looking feature below the second small col. Between the second and third cols is a wide crag. The most continuous of the rocky ribs in the centre of this is *Ricketty Ridge,* 150m, Very Severe (T. W. Patey, 28th June, 1968). A deep gully below the third col gives one of the few easy descent routes along the cliffline. Beyond this, another extensive and complex buttress on the flank of Pt. 776 remains uninvestigated. The further side of this is cut by two very deep gullies—*The Waste Pipe* and *The Wind Pipe. The Waste Pipe,* 150m, Grade II (T. W. Patey and R. Ford, March, 1965), has exciting scenery but no great difficulties. It is deeply recessed, faces north-west, and as a result is often the only gully on the cliffs to hold snow for any appreciable period. *The Wind Pipe,* 150m Very Severe and Grade II (T. W. Patey and John Cleare, 17th March, 1969), is distinguished by its great chimney ice-pitch which is very technical and overhanging. The upper chimney above this presents no major difficulty.

To the left of the Waste Pipe are three buttresses. *Toby*—150m Very Severe (D. Gardner and A. Paul, 9th July, 1977)—lies on the clean-cut right edge of the third of these. Starting at the lowest rocks, climb to a belay on a grassy ledge, then continue up the ledge turning the nose at 15m on the right. Go on up the ledge to a small stance; step left and climb a cracked wall to roof. Move left; climb bulge and continue to belay—scrambling leads to the top.

The *Barrel Buttress* of Sail Gharbh, which was pioneered in 1907 by Messrs. Raeburn, Mackay and Ling, is undoubtedly the mountain's most impressive rock feature. It is best approached by leaving the

Kylesku road near Loch an Gainmhich and making across the moor past Loch nan Eun whence a sheep track leads to the foot of the buttress. The pioneer route has often proved difficult to identify— the confusion being caused by the fact that the buttress is in two tiers. The upper-tier, which holds all the climbing, is split by two long chimney-faults, and the most worthwhile climbing is to be found on the central 'stave' so formed. The pioneer's route started below the left-hand chimney-fault, made an excursion on to the left-hand flanking heathery face, and finished up the chimney. The standard is Very Difficult. The character of the climbing is preserved in the original description.

'Steep grass and rocks led to the foot of the first chimney. The first portion of this is a narrow crack, overhanging and impossible, and a ledge on the right is taken. This rises sharply and on it are some large blocks of rock which have to be swarmed over and are none too secure. Above this is a small platform from which a shallow chimney leads to another ledge from which one can get back to the chimney. The leader could not get enough purchase off the heather to make the ascent, so stones were passed up to him to enable him to do so. The ledge above is rather wider and enables the party to assemble. This is about 45m from the start. The chimney above this is difficult and is closed by a large jammed block which is difficult to overcome. At the entrance of the next chimney is a large jammed block overhanging, which can only be surmounted, and that with difficulty, from the second's shoulder. The last man has to kick off and be pulled up. After this the climbing is sensational, but the rock is excellent and the holds good. About half an hour from the top of the buttress leads to the summit of Quinag.'

There are two fine steep climbs on the central stave on excellent rough sandstone. These can probably be taken as the first ascents of the true Barrel Buttress. *Mild*—105m Very Severe (T. W. Patey, 1962)—starts up rocks to the right of the left-hand chimney fault. Steep climbing on good rock leads to the crux pitch, about 45m up—twin cracks in a slabby wall. *Bitter*—105m Very Severe (T. W. Patey and A. G. Nicol, Summer, 1963)—starts up the opposite right-hand border of the central stave and climbs the obvious 15m V-shaped depression. A 12m wall was avoided by a detour to the left but could probably be climbed directly. Cross an inset corner to gain the right bounding edge, which is followed to the top.

More recent exploration around the Barrel Buttress has produced

179

several Grade I/II winter routes. *Y-Gully Right Fork*—300m Grade II (J. Barnaby and B. Sprunt); *Y-Gully Left Fork*—300m Grade I/II (J. Anderson and A. Nisbet) (In Descent). This is the deep-cut Y-shaped gully left of Barrell Buttress; both routes were climbed in January, 1979. *Cave Gully*—300m Grade II (J. Anderson and A. Nisbet, January, 1979)—this narrow gully lies on the left side of Barrel Buttress, overlooking the right branch of Y-Gully. The route passes the steep section of the Buttress climb via the cave pitch. *Y-Buttress*—360m Grade II (A. Nisbet and N. Spinks, February, 1979)—this is the buttress bounded by the left and right forks of Y-Gully. The line here is variable. *Cooper Gully*—300m Grade I (B. Clough, J. Elliot and R. MacGregor, 13th February, 1979)—this is the gully to the right of Barrel Buttress. The buttress lying to the east of Barrel Buttress was first tackled by Goggs, Arthur and Young in 1914. The nature of the climbing makes accurate description difficult and the frequent ledges allow for much variation on original lines.

EASTERN ASSYNT

(1) **Glas Bheinn** (776m) N.C. 254265
(2) **Beinn Uidhe** (740m) N.C. 282252
(3) **Beinn An Fhurain** (860m) N.C. 304215
(4) **Conival** (987m) N.C. 303199
(5) **Ben More Assynt** (998m) N.C. 318201
(6) **Ben More South Top** (960m) N.C. 324193
(7) **Carn Nan Conbhairean** (868m) 1.6km S. of 6
(8) **Meall An Aonaich** (715m) 1.6km S. of 7
(9) **Creag Liath Breabag** (814m) N.C. 287158
(10) **Beinn Leoid** (792m) N.C. 320295

The mountains of the eastern part of Assynt form a continuous range stretching more than 17km in a north-west to south-east direction. Throughout its length, the range never drops below 600m, rising upwards from either end to over 914m on the summits of Conival and Ben More Assynt, the highest points in Sutherland. Despite its greater height, Ben More does not stand out as conspicuously in the Assynt landscape as do the isolated sandstone peaks of the western area. Even from Inchnadamph, its summit is hidden by Conival and from most points along the roadside it is almost completely concealed by its own foothills. Only when viewed from a distance is the greater part of the ridge unfolded at one time—from the top of the Oykel watershed just east of Altnacealgach; from Rosehall at the south end of Glen Cassley; from the road along the north side of Loch Shin.

Gneiss and quartzite are the main rock formations in this eastern area and on Ben More Assynt the former extends almost to the summit of the mountain, the highest point it reaches in Scotland. The lower western slopes at the head of Gleann Dubh are of Cambrian Limestone which outcrops in both dark blue and lighter varieties all along the Moine Thrust and along the Traligill Burn is burrowed by underground rivers and caves, as mentioned previously.

The Munro tops are usually climbed from Inchnadamph. The main road is left 180m past the hotel and a rough motor road leads for a mile along the River Traligill to the former shepherd's cottage at Glenbain. The proprietor of Inchnadamph Estate has indicated that the privacy of the road, in respect of passage of cars, should be acknowledged. Likewise, camping along the glen is discouraged. From Glenbain, a faint track continues along Gleann Dubh for half a mile to cross the Traligill at the Nature Conservancy sign. If the track is followed for half a mile south-east, one of the main entrances to the Traligill caves and underground river is easily found at the head of a short limestone gulch (N.C. 276206). Traligill has a Norse derivation—Troll's Gill—meaning Giant's Ravine—the name can be aptly applied to many of the water-sculptured limestone formations in the immediate area. In particular, the fine hollowed-out cavern entered by a gigantic arch, which lies some distance south of the main cave entrance along the obvious dried-out river bed.

For the ascent of Conival and Ben More, leave the track at the signpost already mentioned and keep to the east bank of the Traligill River, traversing upwards for just over 3km on to the saddle between Conival and Beinn an Fhurain. Even in wet conditions the going is firm and the 610m of ascent to the cairn on the saddle requires no great effort. A direct line up the side of the burn which drops down from the saddle further to the west is not recommended. 1.5km and a further 250m of climbing up a steep quartzite ridge leads to the summit cairn of Conival. A narrow ridge now turns eastwards and continues for 1.5km onto the main top of Ben More. The way is rough and requires some mild boulder scrambling in places but presents no difficulty to the climber in dry weather. Extreme care should be taken, however, in winter conditions or in poor visibility. The connecting ridge between Conival and Ben More drops steeply on the south into the head of Glen Oykel and is precipitous in stretches in its initial stage.

From the main top, the view to the east across the deserted central part of Sutherland is broken by Ben Klibreck and, further north, by the mountains of the Reay Forest. The view westwards encompasses, on a clear day, the mountains of the Inverlael Forest and, beyond that, the Fannichs and the peaks of Wester Ross. Given snow conditions the panorama becomes very spectacular.

The south top is reached in just over 600m, involving two or three bad steps across exposed slab. Here the Ben More ridge drops steeply down into Dubh Loch Mor—a good example of a corrie Loch—from which originates the River Oykel, one of the finest fishing rivers in the country. The slopes are of deeply-gullied gneiss, but, with care, a way can be made down into the glen, the slopes becoming progressively easier as one moves southwards. From the loch, a stalkers' path follows the course of the water down into the glen leading to Benmore Lodge, on the shores of Loch Ailsh, and from there to the road. A distance of over 13km. If, however, one wishes to return to Inchnadamph, traverse round from the lochside onto the bealach between Conival and Tarsuinn Breabag, an ascent of just over 60m. There is no well-defined track but this narrow, picturesque defile can easily be followed back to rejoin the outward route. However, in bad weather the going can be decidedly boggy.

The Breabag ridge can also be climbed from the bealach. The route passes from Beinn Tarsuinn (623m) for just under 5km to Creag Liath (813m), the highest point on the ridge. This gives pleasant hill-walking, alternatively over rough hill pasture and broken rocky pavements of gneiss. The ridge is broad and flat for most of its length, but drops unexpectedly in great vertical cliffs into the head of Glen Oykel. These could well afford some climbing.

The traverse of the entire range from north to south is undoubtedly the most worthwhile expedition in this eastern part of Assynt. Start from the stalkers' track 7km north of Inchnadamph, at the highest point on the road to Kylesku, beside Loch na Ghainmhich. The track is followed eastwards for a short distance before climbing directly up the steep slopes onto the flat, grassy, richly-vegetated summit plateau of Glas Bheinn.—2.5km and 550m of ascent. Descend on to the saddle between Glas Bheinn and Beinn Uidhe by way of the steep and narrow east ridge and continue up the long boulder-strewn slope to the summit of Beinn Uidhe. The going here is rather unpleasant for 3km past Mullach an Leathaid Riaghaich, then dip into the saddle above Lochan an Caorach. From here, a long, heavy trudge leads up on to the highest point of Beinn an Fhurain—almost 5km, involving 180m of ascent. On the north, an impressive rock buttress falls steeply down into Coire a'Mhadaidh. The ridge now drops past some rocky outcrops and an attractive little lochan on to the saddle leading up to Conival. From the south top of Ben More the ridge continues in a southerly direction for 1.5km to Carn nan Conbhairean, and becoming progressively broader and less rocky in character. A further 1.5km leads over Meall an Aonaich and Eagle Rock—the south end of the range then down on to the track to Benmore Lodge. The descent to the track and thence to the road—4km south of Altnacealgeach—is a distance of 9.5km.

The main Ben More Assynt ridge is often described as resembling the Aonoach Eagach ridge in Glencoe. While not presenting the same rock problems, it should not be treated lightly; in winter conditions a pleasant ridge route becomes a serious mountaineering exercise. The isolated nature of the area, which is virtually devoid of habitation throughout its one hundred and sixty odd square miles, is a factor which should be kept well in mind in adverse weather conditions.

Creag Liath Breabag (813m) is the highest point of the hills on the west side Glen Oykel. These form the subsidiary branch of the main Ben Assynt range. Tarsuinn Breabag (623m) at the north end of the ridge can easily be climbed from the Bealach Traligill. The approach to the south end of the ridge involves a rather uninteresting moorland walk from Altnacealgeach Hotel. The Breabag mass slopes upwards from the western moorland, forming a broad flat ridge, alternating between rough hill pasture, rich in herbage, to broken rocky pavements. It then drops unexpectedly into the Oykel valley in a line of steep, cleaning cut cliffs which could well provide some worthwhile climbing routes. Five kilometres past Ledmore junction at the Nature Conservancy signpost on the east side of the road, a track strikes inwards towards Breabag along the Allt nan Uamh past the recently established fish hatchery. A prominent limestone cliff 1.5km up the glen on the right-hand side contains the well-known Allt nan Uamh Bone caves. Continuing up the side of the water provides a straightforward and interesting approach into the Breabag ridge.

The most spectacular feature on the Ben More massif is the great waterfall of Eas Coulin, (or Eas Coul Aulin), which leaps over the cliff line of Leiter Dhubh 2km north-west of Glas Bheinn, into the basin of Loch Glencoul. The Eas Coulin rivals the Falls of Glomach in Kintail to be the highest fall in Britain. The claim can only be disputed by difference in interpretation of the continuity of the 153m vertical drop which cascades still further for yet another 45m at the foot of the cliffs.

From the Inchnadamph-Kylesku road there are two ways to the waterfall. The south side of Loch Glencoul can be reached from the bridge over the Unapool burn. The route along the lochside is virtually trackless and at the one point the walker is forced to traverse on steep grass some 60m above the loch. This can be awkward in bad weather. It is also possible to hire a boat from the proprietor of Kylesku Hotel. This lands you at the head of Loch Glencoul at a ruined jetty beside the empty keeper's house. The 5km trip gives magnificent views of the Quinag range and allows close inspection of the geological structure of the area along the Aird da Loch cliffs where the action of the thrust plane is clearly seen. Seals are often seen playing in the secluded expanse of water and the journey culminates in the spectacle of the full drop of Eas Coulin into the head of the glen. It is possible to climb up the side of the waterfall onto the top of the Leiter Dhubh from the floor of the glen with little difficulty.

The had of the falls can also be reached by a track leaving the road 5km past Skiag Bridge along Loch na Gainmich, which rises steeply from the east end of the loch over the 487m Bealach a'Bhuirich—the pass of the roaring. The path gives a fine walk through the geniss scenery of the lower foothills of Glasbheinn and is left 800m beyond the head of the pass. A cairn marks the point where the path crosses a stream beside the fair sized lochan but this can easily be missed. The stream which feeds the fall is followed down past a huge split boulder and the fall can be crossed with care at the lip of the cliff. It is worth continuing along the cliff top for about 90m and descending the series of grassy terraces to get a full side view of the drop. The basin formed by the head of the glen is a gathering place of stages during the rutting season when their roaring, echoing up from the basin at the foot of the waterfall, provides a fitting background to the scene.

Beinn Leoid (792m)

Beinn Leoid is usually climbed from the landing place at the head of Loch Glencoul and continues upwards along the glen to Loch an Eirciol, a distance of 5km involving 304m of ascent. The Stack has a steep western face but has more to offer the geologist than the climber. Like the Aird da Loch, it is a show-piece of the thrust movement and the national rock sequence here has been completely reversed. The gneiss lying on top of the Cambrian strata. From Loch an Eircoll 2.5km leads on to the summit of Beinn Leoid and opens up the view across to the Reay Forest. The return journey can be made north-westwards to the head of Loch Glendhu, where a good track is joined to lead for 8km along the north side of the Loch to Kylestrome and the ferry. This makes a fine day's walking expedition through the far north-west corner of Assynt.

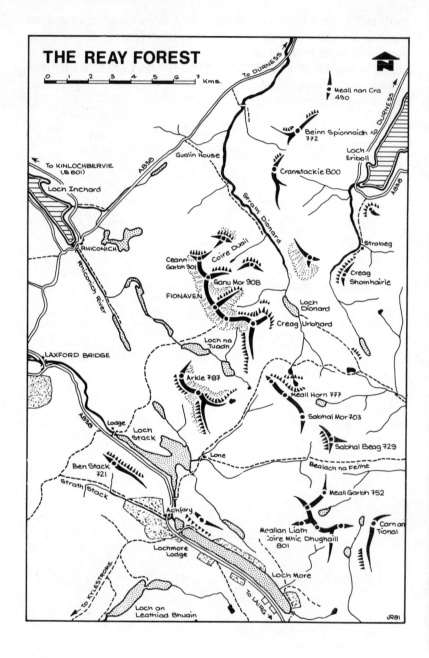

The Reay Forest

FOINAVEN is the name of the range embracing the five following peaks:—

(1) **Ceann Garbh** (901m) N.C. 313515
(2) **Ganu Mor** (908m) 800m south of 1.N.C. 317507
(3) **A'Cheir Ghorm** (807m) 1.2km south of 2.N.C. 319494
(4) **Unnamed Top** (806m) 2km south of 2.N.C. 325487
(5) **Creag Dionard** (778m) 3.2km south-east of 2.N.C. 338484

Arkle (787m) N.C. 303462
Meall Horn (777m) N.C. 353449
Sabhal Mor (703m) N.C. 360441
Sabhal Beg (729m) N.C. 373429
Meallan Liath Coire Mhic Dhughaill (801m) N.C. 357392
Carn Dearg (796m) N.C. 377389
Ben Hee (873m) N.C. 426339
Ben Stack (712m) N.C. 270442
Cranstackie (800m) N.C. 351556
Beinn Spionnaidh (772m) N.C. 362573

MAPS: O.S. 1:50,000 (2nd Series) Sheet No. 9—Cape Wrath. Sheet No. 16—Lairg and Loch Shin.

The mountains of the Reay Forest are situated in the north-west corner of Sutherland, one of the wildest and most remote parts of the Scottish mainland. The area falls into the parishes of Eddrachillis and Durness.

On the north and on the west, the sea forms a natural boundary, the deeply indented coastline stretching from Eddrachillis Bay around Cape Wrath to the eastern shore of Loch Eriboll—measured straight, a distance of sixty or so kilometres, but double that if all the numerous bays and sea lochs are taken into account.

The southern boundary with Assynt can be taken as a line drawn eastwards from the head of Loch Glencoul to the north end of Loch Shin. The main road north from Lairg to Tongue passes through Altnaharra, one of the rare communities of any size left in central Sutherland. A branch road travels north-westwards by way of Glen

Mudale and Strathmore along the side of Loch Hope to meet the north coast road at the mouth of Loch Eriboll. This forms the eastern boundary.

The natural centre of Sutherland and of the whole of the North of Scotland is the market village of Lairg at the south end of Loch Shin and here the majority of roads from north and west converge to meet with those coming from the south. Roads in the north-west follow natural, rather than direct lines from point to point, and are forced by the nature of the country to by-pass obstacles by devious routes. They are mostly single-tracked, twisting and not built for speed. Lairg has a railway station on the main line north from Inverness to Caithness and is the depot for the daily mail bus service which covers the outlying districts of Sutherland.

The A836 by way of Altnaharra has already been mentioned. This leads to the eastern side of the Reay country. 3.2km North of Lairg the road forks and the A838 leads northwestwards to Laxford Bridge following the continuous line of waterway which stretches diagonally across Sutherland from the Dornoch Firth on the North Sea to Loch Laxford on the Atlantic coast. For 25km the road follows the north shore of Loch Shin, the largest freshwater loch in Sutherland, then winds between Loch Ghriama, Loch Merkland, Loch More and Loch Stack to the road junction at Laxford Bridge. From Laxford Bridge the A836 continues north-eastwards by way of the scattered community of Rhiconich to Durness, then follows the coastline around Loch Eriboll to link up with the road through Strathmore. The majority of the mountains of the Reay Forest lie within this circuit.

From Kylesku Ferry the A894, a narrow twisting road, follows the western coastline by way of the crofting village of Scourie to join the Lairg road at Laxford Bridge. This road is currently undergoing major reconstruction.

The Cape Wrath Peninsula is virtually roadless. The only direct route leaves the A836 at Rhiconich and follows the north shore of Loch Inchard to Kinlochbervie. Situated on the isthmus between Loch Inchard and Loch Clash, its natural harbour and up-to-date ice plant make it one of the busiest fishing bases on the west coast. The road continues for another 8km to serve the crofting communities of Oldshore and terminates abruptly at Sheigra. There is one other road on the north coast of the peninsula but this has no motor link with the mainland. A ferry for pedestrians operates over the Kyle of Durness from Keodale, near the Cape Wrath Hotel, and links with the Cape

Wrath Minibus Service to the Cape Wrath Lighthouse. The Ferry runs daily, Sundays included, weather permitting.

The principal mountain ranges of the Reay Forest lie almost wholly to the east of the Lairg-Laxford road. Ben Stack, rising from the west shore of Loch Stack, is the only notable exception. These formed the traditional hunting forests of the Lords of Reay, chiefs of the Clan Mackay, one of the great families who ruled in Sutherland in the past.

A 17th century account of the area by a Sir Robert Gordon gives a full and picturesque account of the variety of wild life to be found here in the days of these early Lords of Reay.

'All these forests and schases are verie profitable for feiding of bestiall and delectable for hunting. They are full of reid-deir and roes, woulffs, foxes, wyld catts, brocks, skuyrells, whittrets, weasels, otters, martrixes, hares and fumarts. In these forests, and in all this province, there is great store of patridges, pluivers, capercalegs, blackwaks, murefowls, heth-hens, swanes, bewters, turtle-doves, herons, dowes, steares or starlings, lairigigh or knag (which is a fould like unto a paroket or parret, which make place for her nest with her beck in the oak trie), duke, draig, widgeon, teale, wild grouse, ringhouse, routs, whaips, shot-whaips, woodcock, larkes, sparrows, snyps, blackburds, or osills, meireis, thrushes, and all other kinds of wild-foule and birds, which are to be had in any pairt of this kingdom.'

In 1829, the area passed into the hands of Lord Stafford, later created first Duke of Sutherland, who, in the course of his great schemes of 'Improvement', swallowed up vast tracts of land in the north and west of Sutherland and was an instigator of the Clearances of the first half of the 19th century. The area is now divided among several smaller estates, but the main mountain mass falls largely into those belonging to the Duchess of Westminster, one of the country's biggest landowners. The estate office is in the village of Achfary, at the head of Loch More.

The area is still preserved for its sporting facilities and is virtually uninhabited. Apart from a few forestry and estate workers' houses, the only habitations are some seasonal shooting lodges and stalkers' bothies. The few centres of population of any size are to be found along the coastline and to the west of the Lairg-Laxford road. Crofting, fishing and tourism are the main means of livelihood.

The western coastline is rich in history and is well worth visiting. For the 400 years from the 9th to 13th centuries A.D., the Vikings raided here, penetrating every inlet, and eventually ruling the whole of the North of Scotland from their Jarldom of Orkney. They have left behind them a legacy of place-names throughout the whole of Sutherland and Caithness, Vik, Ness, Stac, Cleit, Bol, Geo, Sgeir, Tunga, Dal, Fjord, Gil Setr, Ob, Smoo, all indicate the Viking influence in a locality. The five great fjords or sea-lochs which indent the north-west coast bear purely Norse names. Laxford was Lax-fjord—the Salmon Loch—and the name is still apt after all those years. The River Laxford is one of the finest salmon rivers in the country. Inchard was Engi-fjord or Meadow-loch. Durness was the Deer's point. Eriboll was Eyrr-bol or Beach Town. Tongue was Tunga or Tongue of Land. The great sea-cliffs around Cape Wrath, the ultimate point on the mainland, were the 'Hvarf' or Turning Point of the Norsemen. Once around the point, the raiding longships were clear of the treacherous tides and storms of the 'Pettland' or Pentland Firth.

Gneiss is the predominant formation of the southern part of the coastal region, from Kylesku to Rhiconich, and the country here is a maze of hillocks, hollows and lochans.

From Kylestrome, on the north side of the ferry, a stalker's track leads north-eastwards across the moorland to come out at Loch More on the Lairg-Laxford road. A lower branch of the track initially follows the north shore of Loch Glen Dhu, then rejoins the main track by way of the fine waterfall which drops spectacularly into the loch from the Maldie Burn. Another useful cross-country track leaves the road some 3.2km farther north, past the forestry plantation at Duartmore Bridge. This passes across for a little more than 10km to reach the Laxford road on the north side of Ben Stack. A locked shooting bothy is maintained by the estate halfway along it.

The road follows the coast to Scourie, which is the main village in this part. 3km south it passes Badcall Bay, at one time a safe anchorage for cargo vessels, but now unused. Scourie lies 14.5km north of Kylestrome at the head of a wide sandy bay. It was the birthplace of General Hugh Mackay—a famous soldier of the 17th century who saw service in the European campaigns of the times and was the author of a manual on infantry tactics. He commanded the forces which were defeated by Graham of Claverhouse at the Battle of Killiecrankie in 1689. The name is a corruption of Norse and Gaelic. Skoga—copse, and Airigh—shieling, or summer grazing. Crofting is carried on here in the traditional manner and the sheltered sandy

DONALD BENNET

44.   Suilven across Loch Sionascaig

45.   The Old Man of Stoer

PETER MACDONALD

46.   *Tyrolean Traverse onto the Old Man of Stoer*

PETER MACDONALD

47.   *Cape Wrath*

hollow is a favourite with summer visitors. Hotel and other accommodation is available and Scourie is the best centre from which to visit the famous island bird sanctuary of Handa, lying 3km off-shore to the north-west. The island is approached by sea from the tiny clachan of Tarbet, 3km due north of Scourie by track but 8km by road. From here a boat-hire service to the island operates, weather permitting. There are excellent camping facilities at the head of the Bay.

Handa is composed of stratified sandstone, which has been tilted up from east and south-east to the heathery moors rising gradually upwards to Sithean Mor (124m)—The Great Hill of the Fairies—on the north-west corner of the island. The sea-cliffs rise to their highest point here under Sithean Mor and stretch towards the furthest north-west point of the island. On the east side of the point, a geo (Norse—inlet) with walls of almost 100m encloses the Great Stack of Handa, which rises from the sea to almost the same height—a distance of 25m from the shore at its closest, west side. In 1876 a Lewis man, Donald Macdonald, secured a rope over the flat-top of the stack and climbed across the gap, hand over hand. The feat was repeated in 1967 by Dr. T. W. Patey. A climbing rope was carried outwards on either side of the geo until the middle lay across the top of the stack. The ends were anchored, one to rock the other to spikes driven into rock. The shortest rope length across the gap was 45m and this was crossed using sliding clamps. In the light of the second crossing, using modern equipment, the incredible original feat is undoubtedly without parallel in mountaineering as practised at that time, nor is there anything comparable in the present era in Scotland.

The Stack was climbed in July 1969 by G. N . Hunter, D. F. Lang and H. MacInnes. The party timed their attempt opportunely with essential calm sea conditions—the approach is of necessity by boat. The route, *Great Arch* 114m Very Severe, lies on the north face and the landing from the boat is at a steep, green wall. The description of the line taken is as follows: Climb to a ledge and belay (12m). Climb the wall to the right of the belay to a higher belay ledge. From here follow a steep groove above to reach a left traverse line above the Great Arch overhangs. Continue the traverse left (peg runner) into a hidden corner. Surmount the wall and overhang above to peg belays on the Diving Board. A further 45m of easier climbing follows to more broken rocks below the top. Scramble to the summit by a loose chimney. The descent was made by abseiling down the 45m pitch to the Diving Board. The boat was then lined up below for a dramatic free abseil from a jammed nut. The rock is excellent and comparatively bird-free.

The nearby Mini-Stack—Stacan Geodh Bhrisidh—appears to have been sliced off from the cliffside. It lies 360m east of the Great Stack and can easily be reached by a grassy descent from the cliff top. This also has been climbed—*Great Corner,* 60m Very Severe (G. N. Hunter and D. F. Lang, July, 1969), starting at an arrow in the corner on the landward side. From here, traversing left to easier but loose rock led to a peg belay below a great corner crack. The corner was climbed (4 pegs) to a belay on a ledge with piled blocks (20m). Flakes behind the belay were climbed to the crest of the ridge. A rounded ledge was traversed right for 10m. The first groove above is followed to reach the summit cairn (on knife edge). The descent of the north-west face was made by abseiling from a bolt on the summit to a ledge 15m below. From here, a final 45m abseil from a chockstone was made to the base of the stack.

Nine km to the north-west of Scourie is the road junction at Laxford Bridge. Laxford Bridge is not a village, only a junction and an A.A. telephone point. From here the road now continues north-westwards for 8km to Rhiconich, a scattered crofting community with a small hotel and shop. The lonely peninsula of Ardmore lies between Loch Laxford and Loch Inchard on the north-west side of the road. Its broken coastline has more fine harbours and is surrounded by islands. There is no through motorable road onto the peninsula, which in the Gaelic is Ceathramh Garbh—The Rough Quarter.

From Rhiconich, the road leads north to Durness past Gualin Lodge, a distance of 22km. Gualin means 'shoulder' and this point is the summit of the road. When you descend into Strath Dionard towards the Kyle of Durness, the Archaean gneiss gives way to limestone and the scenery changes—this is a region of flat sheep lands, green fields, wide waters and homely hills. The ruins of Brochs line this strath—relics of earlier inhabitants.

Durness is still basically a collection of crofting townships but it has developed in recent years into one of the most popular tourist centres on the north coast. Hotel and guest-house accommodation is readily available and there is a Youth Hostel. West of the village the sandy Kyle of Durness broadens into the bay of Balnakiel. At the head of the bay stands the old church of Balnakeil, built in 1619 on the site of a still older cell associated with the Monastery in Dornoch—Balnakeil means a place of the kirk. Nearby is the house of Balnakeil, once the hunting residence of the Bishops of Caithness and later passing into the hands of the Lords of Reay. In the churchyard is buried Rob Donn (1714-78) the celebrated, unlettered Celtic Bard. His works were handed down by word of mouth through the years until 1829 when the first collection of his poems was published in book form. The former Air Ministry Station, some 800m from Durness, has now been developed as a craft village.

The Durness peninsula is bounded on the east by the great sea-loch of Eriboll, one of the finest natural harbours in Britain. Its potential has so far been neglected. There are rich unworked deposits of Dolomite in the area but the uneconomic process of producing Magnesium and the limited market for the product in the light of new technological development in the field of Carbon-fibres makes their developement unlikely. A major development is visualised here, however, in connection with oil, and it would seem that this hitherto remote wilderness could well be the site of a considerable industrial community—a prospect which mountain lovers must regard with very mixed feelings.

One and a half kilometres west of Durness, at the head of a small bay, is to be found the Smoo Cave. The name is derived from the Norse word—Smjuga—a narrow cleft to creep through. From the sea-shore the cave is entered under an arch, 15m high and 35m wide. An inner cave extends from the right of the waterfall which drops into the main limestone cavern some 25m from the entrance. This was explored as early as 1833.

As one would expect, the cave has numerous legends. The first Lord Reay, like many Scots of his time, served under Gustavus Adolphus in his continental wars in the middle of the 17th century. While abroad he is reputed to have met the Devil and bested him in several battles of wit. The Devil pursued him to Scotland and planned to way-lay him while he was visiting the Smoo Cave which lay within the Reay domain. Lord Reay got into the second cavern, when his dog, which had raced ahead of him, returned howling and hairless. Lord Reay realised what lay ahead but then the cock crowed and the Devil and his three attendant witches were powerless. They blew holes in the roof of the cavern and so escaped, facing Lord Reay in the outer cave. This is the reputed origin of the holes through which the Alt Smoo falls into caverns.

The cave now boasts one rock-route—*The Hole,* 36m Severe (J.

Cunningham and B. March, 21st June, 1971). An abseil is made down the biggest hole south of the road crossing the Smoo Cave to gain a ledge some 3m above the water level. Climb crack to corner for 18m, breaking right over a bulge (peg runner) to exit up the back wall of the cave. Dry weather is desirable for an attempt and, in the event of failure, a retreat is advocated by swimming seaward.

The road from Rhiconich to Durness passes across the neck of the great north-west peninsula which culminates in Cape Wrath. Wrath is purely a map maker's name—a corruption of the Norse 'Hvarf' (turning point). In Gaelic, this becomes Parbh or Parph and in many texts this derivation is the one used. The northernmost of the two roads on to the peninsula passes near the great sandstone sea cliffs of Cleit Dhubh, which runs to a height of 260m—the highest sea cliffs in Britain. For 3km they stretch westwards, falling down towards the sandy bay at Kearaig where there is a solitary croft house. Along their length, at Clo Mor, they attain a height of about 185m and are generally described as both formidable and unfriendly. Difficulties encountered include bad rock, lack of belays, lack of protection and intermittently hostile bird life. The accepted form of gaining the base of the cliffs would appear to be a long, daring abseil. Despite determined investigation, Clo Mor's defences remain unbreached.

The surrounding area is the Parph Moor proper, an awe inspiring, wilderness—where fact and legend draw close together. One can well believe that hereabouts can be met the terrible monster Cu-Saeng whom no one has lived to describe—unlike the 'Grey Man of Ben MacDhui—the Cu-Saeng wanders throughout all the wilder parts of the Scottish Highlands. Once a man hereabouts is reputed to have seen his shadow on the hillside—'it had two heads'.

The Cape Wrath Lighthouse, built in 1828, stands on a 122m cliff of Archaean gneiss veined with pink pegmatite, known as An Dunan—the small fort. This is the end of Scotland—there is no land between here and the North Pole. The Nature Reserve of North Rona can often be seen 70km to the north-west, a breeding ground for the Atlantic Grey Seal and the Stormy Petrel. 10km south, along the coastline, is Sandwood Bay, one of the loveliest and certainly most private in the country. There is no track to Sandwood from Cape Wrath but the possibility of constructing one is currently being explored. One and a half kilometres to the south, two rock stacks rise up from the sea. They are A'Chailleach and Am Bodach—the Old Woman and the Old Man. A prominent sandstone stack guards the entrance to the bay itself on the south side. This is Am Buachaille—The Herdsman—which gives a 60m route (Very Severe) first climbed by T. W. Patey, J. Cleare and I. Clough in 1967. The 8m channel which separates the foot of the stack from the shoreline was crossed at low tide. There is a choice of three methods of accomplishing this—ladders, swimming, or by fixed Tyrolean rope. Swimmers should be careful of seaweed. From low tide mark there are approximately four hours in which to complete the climb before the anchorage on the shore becomes awash. The route is described as follows:

'Start left of centre and climb overhanging rocks up and onto the prow on the right. Continue straight up till impending rocks force a traverse along a horizontal ledge on the left. Climb left edge for 4m to a large ledge and large rusty belay peg (25m). From inset corner of the ledge, make an awkward move up and across retaining wall to ledge on right edge. Continue up to an inset crack of 10m. Climb this on dubious rock to another left traverse and belay on left edge (20m). Return to centre below deep overhanging crack. From the base traverse left below overhangs until mantelshelf can be made up between two large 'soup-plates'. Cross the slab to rejoin the main crack. Pull out awkwardly at the top (20m).

Sandwood (from the Norse—Sand Vat or Sandy Water) lies 6.5km north of Sheigra, the last inhabited community on the road from Rhiconich along the side of Loch Inchard. The Norse fleet anchored near here on 10th August, 1263, on its way to the battle of Largs. Its defeat there ended the Norse domination of the North of Scotland and the Hebrides. Three years later at Perth, these were ceded to Scotland for a payment of 4000 marks down, and a further yearly sum of 100 marks, but Orkney and Shetland remained part of Norway until 1468.

A peat road leaves the motor road between Blairmore and Sheigra leading to Loch a'Mhuillin and then on by track to Sandwood Bay and the fresh water loch behind it. At its widest point the beach stretches about 3km and the shore rocks here are rich in semi-precious stones. Strath Shinary, which stretches south-eastwards from Sandwood Loch, produces a feasible cross-country route to reach the Durness road at Gualin House. The way is trackless, as indeed is the whole of the inland part of the peninsula. Cross-country explorers here should be sound in navigational skills.

For the climber, another comparatively recently explored crag is to be found in this corner of the Parph peninsula. This is Creag

195

Riabhach—N.C. 279638—best approached from the Rhiconich Durness road. Transport can be left about 800m north-east of Gualin House, thence a line, more or less direct, is taken in a north-westerly direction for about 7km through the intervening hills. Creag Riabhach is a modest 486m in height, but the crags on the north-east side are highly recommended—giving universally hard lines—consequently no place for the novice.

Three hard routes are recorded on the crags to date, although probably more has been done here. In the centre of the crag is a vertical and blank section of wall. 30m to the left of this is an overhanging, vegetated groove/crack line. *The Godfather*—175m Hard Very Severe (D. Marshall and C. Rowland, May, 1972)—starts right of the gully at a vegetated steep slab. Climb slab, trending rightwards, to belay in corner under steep left wall (40m). Traverse right to groove and climb to top of pedestal (30m). The first part of the corner above is blank. Climb short overhanging chimney on left wall, exit onto blank slab (extremely difficult), move back right into corner and follow this to stance (40m). Climb steep chimney crack on left (35m). An easy gully leads to top. Left of the Godfather is *Masquerade*—180m Hard Very Severe (T. Howard and A. Maskery, June, 1976). About 45m above the start is a terrace. This is reached by chimneys at the left side of the central scoop taken by The Godfather (45m). Traverse left on the terrace and climb steep red cracks to stance below roof (42m). Traverse left under roof and climb cracks, traverse right using one peg to gain cracks above initial line (35m). Finish in two pitches (60m). *Herod's Evil*—189m Hard Very Severe (B. Griffiths, P. Nunn and R. Toogood, June, 1976). This route climbs the centre of the right-hand mass of the crag, following steep cracks and chimneys through overhanging walls. Start at recess chimney about 75m right of the central scoop. Climb groove, then right fork into steep crack, follow this to terraces with difficult landing and belay on high terrace (45m). Climb right-hand groove and a block-filled chimney to midway ledge (42m). (Several pegs were used to overcome vegetation in the groove but these could be unnecessary at a later date). Continue up chimney to its closure, continue by steep crack to dangerous landing (peg runner), go up to higher belay on steep vegetation (39m). Continue more reasonably in groove until short traverse left leads to ledge right of hanging slab (39m). Climb steep corner right of slab then thin crack on left, loose blocks (24m).

Ben Stack (721m)

Ben Stack is the only summit within the Reay Forest on the west side of the Lairg-Laxford road to reach a height of over 600m. It rises above the road along the side of Loch stack just north of the village of Achfary and its relative isolation bestows on its conical peak a grandeur disproportionate to its size. It can be climbed from all sides with little difficulty. Two tracks, already mentioned leading cross-country to the road from Kylestrome to Scourie, pass along its north and west ends and from either of these a steep direct route can be made onto the summit in just over an hour from the road.

The north-eastern side of the hill above Loch Stack is flanked by two bands of cliffs which provide scope for scrambling and rock-climbing within easy access from the roadside. The higher band starts at about 244m above sea-level and four short routes were climbed on its left end in 1958 by members of Kinloss Mountain Rescue Team—I. Clough, J. M. Alexander, A. Flegg and B. Halpin. The main feature is 'a big, right-angled corner about 30m high, well seen from the road near the south end of Loch Stack'. This gives enjoyable short climbs on good rock. *Cracked Slab*—25m Very Difficult—Climb the big, right-angled corner for 6m and then go up slab—20m. This forms the left wall of the corner, finishing up wall above on good holds. *Eastern Buttress*—30m Very Difficult—goes up the buttress to right of corner. Start 4m right of lowest part of buttress. Up to flake, mantelshelf onto it, and trend right over small overhang to groove. Up short chimney, then diagonally left to top of buttress. *Halpin's Route*—30m Very Difficult. Reach the same stance as on previous route by a difficult crack to the left of that route. Up short chimney, then straight up or slightly right. *The Groove*—25m. An obvious groove with overhangs on left of big corner. Mostly artificial—A.2. Finish up wall as for Cracked Slab.

The main mountain mass of the Reay Forest is contained in an area roughly rectangular in shape, measuring approximately 22km by 11km. the whole being tilted so that the longer sides run in a north-west/south-east direction. Motor roads already described, form the north and west sides of the area. The south and east sides of the rectangle run through the great cross-country glens which converge on Gobernuisgeach Lodge in the south-eastern corner. The eastern side passes through Strath Dionard and Glen Golly but there is no continuous through track.

800m beyond Gaulin House, on the Laxford-Durness road, a well-maintained track leads into Strath Dionard from a stone road bridge. This continues up the Strath along the river side for 6.5km but stops at the Allt Coire Duail. From here the going is bad for the 3km to Loch Dionard. Any attempted direct line is wet and boggy; it is probably best to keep to the river-bank. The path gives one means of access to the relatively new climbing area in the eastern corries of Foinaven.

At the south-eastern end of Glen Golly—a deep rocky glen skirted by birchwood, through which the River Golly drops in a series of small waterfalls—lies Gobernuisgeach Lodge. This is used throughout the stalking season and is inhabited by an estate keeper for the rest of the year. It is reached by private road from a junction with the Altnaharra-Hope road near the ruined bothy at Altnabad, 13.5km from Altnaharra. The road to the lodge has a gate which is sometimes locked but enquiries should be made at the Lodge for access.

The track which passes along Glen Golly north-westwards is one of three which spread out from Gobernuisgeach Lodge through the southern part of the Reay mountains. It rises upwards for 12km onto the saddle between Creagan Meall Horn and Plat Reidh on the lower slopes of Foinaven to a height of 518m, but has no direct link with the Dionard track. The track now continues across south-westwards to connect with another track from Achfary, which will be described later.

The track to the south side of the Reay area passes over the Bealach nan Meirleach—the Robber's pass—which connects the valley of Strathmore with that of Loch More and Loch Shin. It stretches for over 11km from Gobernuisgeach to the north-east of Loch Merkland, reaching (244m) at its highest point. This was an old drove road, and is still the only recognised right-of-way through the Reay Forest. The track is only suitable for landrovers. The gate at the Loch Merkland end is usually unlocked but enquiries can be made at the nearby shepherd's house.

This track separates Ben Hee (873m)—The Fairies' Hill from the main mountain mass. The ascent from the track is straightforward. Follow the track for (1.5km) to the first bridge and an obvious hill path leads upwards along the Allt Coir a'Chruiteir for just over (2.5km) to the (610m) contour. Another (800m) and (260m) of steep, but easy, climbing brings one out onto the summit cairn. The view from here eastwards is across the central Sutherland moors to Klibreck. The ridge can be followed for (1.6km) to the subsidiary top (843m), and the descent to the track by way of the broad shoulder of

Sail Gharbh. The hill has no special features and is more interesting in winter when the Coire Allt a'Ghorm provides some modest snow climbing onto the summit, from the east. From this direction it can be approached by private road from Loch Shin to Fiag Lodge at the south side of Loch Fiag, but this involves a (6.5km) cross-country pathless walk to Loch a'Ghorm-choire.

From the west, the mountains are best approached from Achfary at the head of Loch More on the Lairg-Laxford road. Half a mile north of the village, a motorable branch road turns off across the river to the right, reaching the keeper's house at Airdachuillin in (1.5km). The road continues for another mile to the disused steading a Lone, the junction of two cross-country tracks. This road is private and although the gate is seldom locked, permission should be obtained before using it.

From Lone, the north fork of the track rises along the Allt Horn for nearly (5km) to connect on the saddle with the track to Glen Golly previously described.

This is the easiest approach to the main tops of both Arkle and Foinaven. Continue past Lone for 1.5km then take to the slabby ridge leading onto the saddle overlooking An Garbh Coire, the steep rocky corrie between Arkle and Foinaven. The line now runs up between two burns for about 270m, a distance of 1.5km. The ground to the left may look tempting but the going here is bad. The first cairn on the Arkle ridge (751m) is reached in another 800m.

The ridge of Arkle is sickle-shaped, bending to the north-east and narrowing considerably with steep drops to the east and gentler slopes to the west. The main top is almost 1.5km further on and any difficulty which may be encountered by the three small 'towers' guarding its approach can be easily turned by descending slightly westward in the event of high wind or wintry conditions.

The terminal ridge of Arkle can be descended into the corrie on the north-east side. From here it is possible to follow a track on the north shore of Loch na Taudh, over the shoulder of Sail Mhor towards Lochstack Lodge, a distance of some 8km.

Arkle's western flank is split by several gullies which are prominent from the road past Achfary. The largest of these was climbed by T. Weir and A. D. S. Macpherson in 1951—*Arkle South Rib*. This rib is the right edge of the first gully on the right and makes a pleasant scramble for 180m. By its easiest route it is no more than Moderate and is a pleasant way of gaining height on the peak, but difficulty can be found if required.

The approach route to Foinaven is dictated by the nature of the expedition. The traverse of the complete ridge is best started from Achfary, taking the north track from Lone. 6km of steady going leads onto the summit of Creag Dionard (778m) and from here all the main points on the ridge can be followed without difficulty to Ceann Garbh. A fine rocky pinnacle Lord Reay's Seat guards the ridge just north of the pass of Cadha na Beucaich, but this is easily by-passed on its west side. Immediately north of this is the unnamed top. A detour should be made from here to explore the 1.5km long quartzite spur, A'Cheir Ghorm, which juts out in a north-easterly direction from the main ridge. The view from here is extensive, taking in the steep north face of Creag Dionard and the main summit, Ganu Mor. To the east, across Cranstackie, Ben Hope is a prominent feature in the landscape. It is possible to descend the north slopes of Ceann Garbh and thread a way through a maze of water-filled peat hags to Gualin, on the Durness road. The lower part of Ceann Garbh should be descended with caution, especially if visibility is bad; the way is down steep grass and loose rocky exposures and there is a lower band of short cliffs, hard to see from above, which require to be circum-navigated. The 5km from the foot of the slope to Gualin are rough, wet and boggy and not really pleasant. In adverse weather conditions, or in winter, the narrow summit ridge of Foinaven, with its almost continuously precipitous eastern flanks, should not be attempted by inexperienced parties.

The approach from Gualin has already been described. An alternative route is the north track from Lone, which gives access to Creag Urbhard and the cliffs to the south of it. A third route into the area starts at the head of Loch Eriboll. A track leaves the north coast road to Durness below the crags of Creag na Faoilinn, which is motorable for about 800m inland along Strath Beag. Rough going, it leads for 1.5km from the end of the motor track to Strabeg Cottage. This is locked but the outhouse is open and has been in the past used as a bothy. Its availability, however, cannot be garanteed.

The track continues past Strabeg on the east side of the river beneath the quartzite cliffline of Creag Shomhairle for more than 1.5km. An ill-defined track then continues over the lower Cranstackie foothills by way of the Bealach na h'Imrich to Strath Dionard.

Creag na Faoilinn and Creag Shomhairle both have several

recorded routes. Creag na Faoilinn has a central rib which gives 120m of Difficult-Very Difficult climbing. The standard becomes Severe if the middle of the smooth 24m slab is taken on the second pitch of the climb. *Monkey Gull*—171m Severe (Miss M. Horsburgh and K. Schwartz, 4th August, 1971) goes up left of the obvious smooth right-hand side of the crag. The start is to the right of a tree. *Offside*—114m Very Difficult (C. Stead and Mrs. M. Stead, 23rd August, 1969), starts at the right end of the crag, right of a prominent nose. The earliest route on Creag Shomhairle was *Crescent Chimney*—240m Very Severe (D. H. Haworth and Miss J. Tester, 28th June, 1953). The climb is difficult to locate, but starts up the wall left of a prominent chimney between the Great Slab on the left and the lowest tongue of rock on the right. The general line follows three chimneys. A main feature of the crag is the Great Slab. *The Cage*—210m Very Severe (J. Brumfitt and B. Sproul, 21st May, 1967), follows the line of an obvious corner at the right side which runs directly up the cliff. The climb starts at the lowest slab and crosses into the corner proper which is climbed in three pitches. *Land of the Dancing Dead*—60m Very Severe (C. Jackson and T. Proctor, 21st August, 1971)—follows a thin crack on the right-hand side of a prominent slab. *The Ramp*—105m Very Severe (R. How and J. R. Sutcliffe, 28th May, 1969) follows an obvious diagonal fault, starting about 45m along the terrace from the right-hand edge of the main face. This starts up leftwards as a narrow slab, continuous, apart from one section in the middle. Three routes made here by members of the Caithness Mountaineering Club in 1962 are as follows: *Cat Walk*—180m Very Difficult, follows a shallow gully in the corner at the extreme right of the crag. From a belay on the right in a grassy recess at 30m, traverse left across the slab to an exposed corner and on to a recessed shelf of large blocks. A direct line is continued to the top—mainly scrambling. *The Roost*—60m Severe—is an extremely fine route here. It starts 15m to the left of the previous route on a heather ledge. The line keeps trending leftwards up a strenuous curved crack and on up to a second heather ledge and a holly-tree belay (30m). Up left round an exposed corner, then the straight crack is taken to slabs above. *Windy Corner*—60m Difficult—is the broken corner to the left of The Roost.

Foinaven's climbing potential becomes increasingly apparent from the track through Strath Dionard. When seen from the west, the ridge certainly rises steeply from the surrounding moorlands but there is no hint of the quality or extent of the crags which stretch along its eastern flanks.

From north to south, the principal features of this eastern side of Foinaven are:

1. *Cnoc a'Mhadaidh*—On the north side of the entrance to Coire Duaill. The crag is virtually an extension at a lower level of the north-east shoulder of Ceann Garbh.

There are now certainly six routes on the cliff. *East Slabs*—150m Very Severe (T. Lewis and R. Toogood, June, 1975)—climbs the slabs at the east edge of the main crag, just right of the slit gully. *Pilastre*—175m Very Severe (M. Boysen and P. Nunn alt. leads Whitsun 1973)—just left of the crag centre, a prominent square cut pillar stands out from the surrounding slabs and cuts through the overhangs. The climb takes this pillar, which is reached by scrambling across heather from the gully bottom at the left edge of the main crag. Climb slabs over a bulge to a stance (20m). Up and traverse left to a corner. Move into the corner and climb it in two pitches, the intermediate belay being taken in the centre of the slab on the right. At the top of the upper corner belay on a ledge on the right. Go up the groove and swing left at the bulge. Belay on the edge. Ascend shallow cracks to a vee-groove. Follow the corner to the roof (junction with Quergang) and move left round the crest to a ledge and tree. Pull over a bulge and go up left, then back right to escape (60m). *Star Turn*—175m Very Severe (B. Griffiths, P. Nunn and R. Toogood, June, 1976)—Start at large block left of Pilastre. Climb overlap a little to the left and up slab to ledge under roof (20m). Go up crack left of roof and climb slabs to stance below black slab (35m). Go up slab to overhanging wall, using a nut, gain a hanging ramp and climb to small stance on upper slab (35m). Climb up left, then straight up, finishing up awkward wall at a flat shelf (40m). Finish up groove and slabs, usually wet (40m) *Quergang*—200m Very Severe (P. Nunn and B. Toogood, 2nd June, 1971)—start in the middle of the crag below a large crack splitting the central overhangs. The detailed description of this earliest route on the crag is: 'Climb vegetated slabs to large grass terrace (30m). Take red slab at centre and climb to fault, trending right. Follow it to peg belay in crack descending from the roof crack (39m). Follow cracks to wet bay. Five metres above it, strike out across slabs to left, passing several overlaps and heading for junction of overhangs and steep central area of cliff. Belay at very wet blackledge (45m). Climb wet slab to base of Fisheye Corner—a peculiar overhanging crack. Climb the corner (3-4 pegs in upper reaches, may be avoidable by low exit) to hanging block ledge (peg belay, 27m). Descend (abseil) to grass ledge on left and climb to eyrie belay (peg belay, 15m). Up corner (loose blocks) to ledge (peg belay 12m). Traverse slab left below steep walls into recess and gain rib (peg runner). Step left and move up to ledge (36m). Move up steep chimney on right and continue up easier ground (60m).'

The Great Roof—180m Very Severe and A3 (P. Burke and R. S. Dearman, June, 1975)—The route climbs the lower slabs right of Quergang, then follows the 20m roof crack (using large pegs). Above, the finish is by difficult free climbing. *West Slabs*—180m Very Severe and A2/3 (R. S. Dearman and D. Moorhouse, June, 1976)—Climb the lower slabs towards the right of the crag, then the great roof where a pillar abuts against it. The roof required about seven pegs or other points of aid and was followed by several Very Severe pitches above.

2. *Creag Dubh*—A gneiss cliff on the east face of Ceann Garbh at the head of Coire Duail. The cliffs attain a height of 210m and present an obvious feature to the Gualin-Strath Dionard track and yet, paradoxically, they are the last to have been investigated. The features of the face are well described in the 1969 *Journal* as follows: A broken right wing bounded by a deep gully. Beyond are the Central Slabs. A landmark here is a sizeable corner with a red left wall, halfway up the slabs. Left of the Central Slabs, the tallest part of cliff is a recessed area with an indefinite crack-groove line. Left again is a sweep of steep, overlapping slabs forming the right edge of a line of grooves easily identified by the red rock in their lower part. A pillar bounds the grooves on their left, followed by a recessed corner and more slabs. To the left of the Central Slabs the cliff steadily diminishes in height. The rock is found to be good and five routes have been recorded.

Red Grooves—150m Very Difficult (M. G. Bond and I. Clough, 27th August, 1968). The climb follows a conspicuous line of pink cracks and grooves on the right of the 'sweep of steep and overlapping slabs'. *Coire Duail Grooves*—195m Severe (G. N. Hunter and D. F. Lang, July, 1969)—starts to the left of the Central Slabs and follows a series of obvious grooves for 90m to a flake belay below a dark overhanging corner on the left. This is climbed to a stance and belay, then the corner on the right followed for 45m to a grass ledge. From the highest point of the ledge, a chimney and grooved slabs on the right are followed by 60m of scrambling to the summit. *Gualin Wall*—105m Severe (J. A. Brooder and M. Simpkins. July, 1971) lies on a large grass terrace above the broken lower rocks and directly below an obvious corner in the upper part of the cliff. The slabs are climbed direct, trending right at the top to a belay on the upper grass ledge below a wet crack—45m. This is by-passed by the wall on the left, trending right at the top to a ledge at the foot of corner (30m). Climb the corner, exit on the right wall, and scramble to the top (30m). *Seers Corner*—180m Very Severe (D. Gardner and A. Paul, 11th August, 1977)—in the middle of the Central Slabs is a sizeable corner bounded by a red wall on the left. Climb the light-coloured slab directly below the corner to reach the foot of a white tongue of rock. Continue up this and cross overlap to enter groove leading to spike belay in recess. Continue up the corner in another two pitches, then easier climbing leads to the top. *Sava*—120m Severe—follows the obvious crack and groove system bounding the sweep of overlapping slabs on the left-hand section of the crag. Scramble to start, then cracks and grooves were followed to a large grass ledge. Step left and climb corner and cracks above to large prominent corner which is climbed to belay near top. Continue by groove above and finish directly up by flake cracks. It would seem that several parties have been active here, which has led to some confusion in recording this last route. It is reported that an attempt on the pillar to the left of the grooves petered out after 60m of black slabs—'A delicate traverse below a steep, pink wall led to the groove of Sava below the corner.'

3. *A'Cheir Ghorm*—The long easterly ridge which stretches from the unnamed point on the Foinaven ridge—Point 867m—1.2km south of Ganu Mor. Its sides are steep but mainly of scree. The east buttress, however, is seen to have three converging ridges onto its apparent summit. Each of these has been climbed. The North and South Ridges in 1954 by Messrs T. Weir, L. S. Lovat and A. D. S. MacPherson. The Central Ridge in 1959 by I. G. Cumming and Miss H. Rose. The latter was named *Cave Ridge*—105m Moderate. The ridge is bounded by stone chutes and a small cave is visible from below. *South Ridge*—180m Very Difficult—starts at the lowest rocks where an avoidable lower wall leads to a vertical wall, climbed 18m to easy ground. The rock steepens in another 18m to a vertical rib which is climbed on insecure rock. The crest of the ridge is followed to below the summit cairn. *North Ridge*—165m Difficult—starts at the cairn right of the lowest rocks. Two pitches of insecure rock lead to a belay below a prominent grey overhang (45m). Traverse right round the steep nose and up a steep wall on exposed rock to the foot of a formidable overhanging tower. Start left of its nose and traverse left along a ledge onto the nose. Climb the steep exposed edge of the tower

on good holds to an easier arête. Keep on the crest and finish under the summit cairn.

4. *Lord Reay's Seat*—The prominent peak on the main ridge of Foinaven just to the south of Point 867 and immediately north of Cadha na Beucaich at the head of Coire na Lice (un-named on the O.S. map). The east face is a 210m quartzite cliff of clean rock, continuously steep in its lower half. The *Original Route* here—225m Very Difficult (T. W. Patey, A. Scott-Russell, D. and N. Bull, 28th August, 1964)—is S-shaped and cut vertically by *Fishmonger*—225m Severe (W. D. Fraser and P. N. L. Tranter, 12th September, 1964). The latter route was considered by the pioneers to be the better of the two lines. The obvious chimney to the right of the central nose is the general line of Fishmonger. This was evaded by T. W. Patey's party, who elected to climb the right edge of the buttress for 45m. The crux pitch of Fishmonger was also circumnavigated by following a rib on the left skyline for 30m before returning to finish on the ridge. Fishmonger is a fine, varied climb going straight up the cliff. It is steep in the lower half but, though there is some loose rock, the harder climbing is found to be sound. The route is described as follows: 24m up chimney to small wet overhang. To left is good platform and peg belay. From belay, traverse 3m left, then delicately 6m back right, into the chimney again above the overhang. Then climb up right 15m to a large platform clearly visible from the belay. The line of the chimney now continues straight up a little to the left as a very steep broken wall but' this defeated the original party. Instead, traverse a big ledge 18m right to the foot of the next chimney. Peg belay. Climb this chimney to a scree shelf. Belay to left at 24m. Climb the obvious long Difficult chimney (loose) to belay on grassy ledge 36m. The final tower lies ahead, with an obvious chimney up its centre. Climb holdless, awkward rocks for 9m to foot of chimney. Peg Belay. Traverse 3m right and climb the 8m crack (crux) between a detached pillar and the main cliff. Then traverse 6m horizontally left to regain the line of the chimney to the left of the nose, where belay above is a right-angled corner with a crack. Climb it. Moderate climbing leads from here up the narrow summit arête to an amusing gap in 30m crossed by bridging to belay beyond. Thence, scrambling to the top of Lord Reay's Seat.

Pobble—210m Severe (P. F. Macdonald and R. A. North, 8th May, 1971) is a fine steep route following a line of chimneys to the left of the nose and finishing at the summit of the Seat. The start is near the centre of the face, left of a light-coloured patch of rock, climbing rightwards round an exposed corner to a grassy ledge at the foot of the first chimney (30m). This is climbed for 75m to reach the foot of a grey crinkly slab. Ascend the slab, then trend left to foot of an ill-defined arête. Climb the arête, traverse right above a steep wall, then return left and climb a short corner to easier ground.

Breakaway—150m Very Severe (B. Dunn and A. Paul, 13th August, 1976)—starts just left of Pobble. Climb 6m to ledge at right of white rock scar, continue up leftward slanting groove to large flake belays on ledge (39m). Climb wall above for 12m to small ledge, continue up smooth groove, move rightwards to terrace (45m). Climb groove immediately right of rock scar (36m). Take easier rock to arête, belay below corner (45m). Climb corner to top, as for Pobble (24m). Peg belays used.

5. *The North Face of Creag Dionard*—The cliff is 1.6km long, continuous only at its two ends. The central section would seem to have more climbing potential in winter. There are two routes on this comparatively unexplored face. *Rhino Buttress*—120m Difficult (P. N. L. Tranter and D. B. Martin, 2nd April, 1966)—is the most easterly buttress. The route follows the large central rib and avoids the separate steep wall on the top right. *Cantilever Climb*—150m Difficult (B. Halpin, J. Bradley and I. Clough, 21st June, 1958)—is at the right end of Creag Coire na Lice. The crag is seen to be very steep with a terrace 60m up. The start is near the small lochan by way of a shallow gully.

6. *Creag Urbhard*—The complex mass of quartzite cliff which forms the East Face of Creag Dionard is the dominating feature of this inner sanctum of Strath Dionard. It has been described as having the greatest potential of any cliff north of Carnmore and the majority of the routes climbed on Foinaven are still to be found here. Despite the continuing increase in activity, both in winter and summer, large areas of rock remain untouched and, while most of the main features have been investigated, it is considered unlikely that any two parties would take exactly the same line. Route finding interest, scale, the variable quality of rock and the very remoteness of the crags, all combine to make any climbing here a serious undertaking. The crags range from 200m to 300m in height and stretch for over 1.5km in length. The strata is seen to rise steadily from south to north (left to right) and climbing lies along left-slanting lines of weakness rather than being truly vertical. As has been said, the cliff is highly complex

in its layout but the following distinguishing features are now generally accepted. These are described from south to north.

(a) *The First Waterfall*—This marks the left-hand end of Creag Urbhard and divides it from the loaf-shaped slabby buttress to the south—The First Dionard Buttress.

(b) *The South Ridge*—A long, rising face of clean rock, split by a terrace at mid-height. There are few features on the lower tier but the upper tier is seen to be deeply cut with square dièdres and fissures.

(c) *The Sickle*—towards the centre of the face, a prominent dièdre on the upper tier links with a curved line on the lower tier to form this feature.

(d) *The Second Waterfall*—the right hand end of South Ridge. The waterfall drains a small hanging corrie high up at the back of the crag.

The Central Buttress—To the right of the Second Waterfall the face develops three tiers separated by two wide terraces—The Upper and Lower Pavements. The Lower Pavement can be used as an easy method of descent, the rocks above its rightward end become very broken. The Upper Pavement starts some 120m up the cliff face.

The Third Waterfall—Half-way along the Central Buttress, passing over an obvious overhang in its upper part and cascading onto the Lower Pavement.

The Fourth Waterfall—At the back of a big wet recess at the more broken end of the Central Buttress.

The North Ridge—beyond the last waterfall is the broken North Face, the 300m ridge of folded rock strata overlooking the foot of Loch Dionard.

The Far North Wall—To the right of the North Ridge the face 'tails off' to become a triangular precipice.

The *Original Route* on the South Ridge was climbed by Messrs Glover and Ling over seventy years ago—'up the sky-line above the loch, (Loch Dionard), by ledges of heather with steep faces of rock between them; later there was bare, steep rock or sloping slabs with cracks, just enough to hold the side nails. The upper part was very steep, but good rock. The buttress is about 900 feet. A belt of turf and then scree led to the top of Creag Dionard, 2½ hours'. It was commented at the time that easier ways up exist, to the left.

Pantagruel—170m Severe (T. Sullivan and T. Abbey, 26th April, 1959) and *Gargantua*—180m Hard Severe (T. Sullivan and M. Denton, 26th April, 1959), both lie on the first clean white wall of the South Ridge, just to the right of the First Waterfall. Pantagruel starts up a stepped groove, left of the first corner of the cliff; Gargantua starts in the first corner, left of two conspicuous coloured streaks. Between these two lies *Whitewash*—165m Very Severe (B. Dunn and A. Paul, 11th August, 1976). The route starts at easy-angled slabs 20m left of the bottom of Gargantua and trends rightwards to finish next to Gargantua by way of the final corner (20m) avoided by the latter. One of the two natural lines which run the full height of the crag is *Chicken Run*—210m Hard Severe (I. G. Rowe and P. N. L. Tranter, 25th April, 1965). This takes the biggest of several dièdres on South Ridge, the second on the left from the Sickle Handle. The start is a rising traverse to the right, about 45m left of the true line of the dièdre, just right of a waterfall, thus avoiding a broken and unpleasant looking wall. The final 20m chimney gives a hard finish.

Crawlie Mouzie—255m Severe (D. Bathgate and W. Pryde, 8th July, 1967). The start is from the right-hand end of the tree terrace (midway between The Sickle and K.W.H.) following the easiest line up a pink wall and keeping well to the right of the obvious pinnacles and corners. The upper section takes a dièdre in the centre of a grey wall to the right of the upper part of Zig Zag and left of The Sickle Handle.

Iolaire—150m Very Severe (D. Broadhead and D. Rubens, 13th July, 1979)—starts about 60m left of the bay of Chicken Run, at the left end of a rocky terrace below a big roof. A crack leads to the roof, then a steep chimney and a corner lead to the final shelf.

Tortoise—255m Hard Severe (P. Nunn and C. Rowland, June, 1969)—lies to the right of Crawlie Mouzie throughout its length—crossing the line of Zig Zag at the middle terrace and carrying on up the front of a tapering tower between the Sickle and K.W.H. Start right of a rounded bastion to the right of the Sickle Handle, below and right of a slabby break in the steep wall.

K.W.H.—270m Severe (M. Galbraith and A. McKeith, 14th May, 1966). The first dièdre right of the Sickle Handle, the rightmost large dièdre on the South Ridge. This was found to be heavily-vegetated and left for clean, exposed arête higher up on the left. The rounded wall on the lower tier is climbed directly to start.

Zig Zag—300m Difficult (N. Drasdo and C. M. Dixon)—is the easiest and quickest line up the face of the South Ridge. Start to the right of K.W.H. taking a leftward-starting line upwards to cross that route on the terrace at mid-height, descending left along the terrace to cross over the lines of Tortoise, The Sickle and Crawlie Mouzie, then finish up the first left-slanting dièdre on the upper section.

Masha—270m Very Severe (D. Marshall and C. Rowland, May, 1972). This fine route was the first recorded V.S. route on the face. Start at the foot of Zig Zag and take a direct line of cracks and grooves up the cliff, leading eventually to a huge 35m open-book corner just below the top of the crag. This and the ensuing gully are climbed to the top.

Fingal—270m Mild Severe (T. W. Patey, 12th June, 1962). Starting up the rocks left of the bottom of the Second Waterfall, the route follows a virtually direct line up the crags, diverging left from the Second Waterfall, crossing two diagonal fault lines, and finishing up the right hand edge of a large V-depression in the top tier. This is a fine mountaineering route, one of the two natural lines taking in the entire height of the crag. Between Fingal and Masha are two less clearly defined routes;

The Veterans—300m Hard Severe (A. Howard and P. Phipps, June, 1969) 'ascends the rounded bastion left of Fingal, 45m left of the Second Waterfall, 30m right of a big rock at the foot of the face at a sharp, steep corner crack'. The route uses a chimney 'seen from the ground as a moon-shaped crack', finishing 'probably as for Fingal'.

Promiscuous Wall—(C. Ogilvie and M. Searle, 1975)—starts between Fingal and Masha, joins Fingal on the mid-way terrace and then follows that route briefly before traversing right to gain another upward line, probably utilising one or other of the two parallel crack-lines on the upper crag.

On the right hand side of the Second Waterfall lies *Boreas*—120m Mild Severe (A. R. M. Park and P. F. Macdonald, 25th April, 1965). The Lower Pavement is reached by a scramble up the small rock step just right of the waterfall, then continue up the next small step immediately above it. The climbing starts straight up the slab above, keeping as close to the right-hand side of the waterfall as is practicable to arrive finally on the Upper Pavement. Above the Upper Pavement is the very impressive 120m Summit Tier.

The *Original Route, Central Buttress*—Moderate (A. Parker and J. E. Young, 6th July, 1950) starts left of the lower part of the Third Waterfall, by a loose chimney to a shelf of heather and ash-trees, gaining the Lower Pavement after 60m. Follow this rightwards and a final right traverse across broken rock leads to a grassy rake which ends at the top of the crags. The *Right-Hand Route, Central Buttress*—105m Severe (L. S. Lovat, T. Weir, A. D. S. MacPherson,

15th June, 1954)—starts from the right-hand end of the Lower Pavement. A water-sprayed ledge is reached and followed rightwards to an awkward traverse round a bulge to a heather ledge. This is the crux of the climb. The route improves after climbing the vertical wall above.

Three Tier Route—270m Severe (H. and M. MacInnes, 1968)—starts left of the Fourth Waterfall (between two watercourses) on the rock face. The Lower Pavement was reached to the right of the Third Waterfall by way of a rightwards sloping shelf and a black waterfall chimney. The line above is by an obvious chimney on the left end of the face, to finish on the edge of the buttress. The route takes in as much of Central Buttress as is possible to do.

North Face Gully—240m (T. Weir and A. D. S. MacPherson, May, 1951). This is the name given by the original party to The Fourth Waterfall. An easy route on sound rock. *North Ridge*—300m Very Difficult (L. S. Lovat and T. Weir, 18th June, 1954). From the start at the lowest rocks beyond a large highly coloured outcrop, slabby Moderate rock gradually steepens. Climb fairly direct by short walls to the foot of a recess with a tree above. Climb the left wall to the tree and a mossy overhang. Continue up steep rock with much variation possible, 90m from the top the rock becomes broken and easier and other lines of a similar standard were considered possible.

A blitzkrieg assault during early February, 1979, produced a considerable number of new winter routes on Creag Urbhard. The party found that: 'Strath Dionard in winter turned out to be magnificent, both scenically and in the quality of climbing'. The waterfalls had become huge ice lines, as had large areas of slabs on the South Ridge. The most striking feature was the frozen Third Waterfall which had formed an enormous icicle reaching to a height of between 13m and 30m and a metre or so in diameter with a 3m drooping ice lip at the top.

Of the routes climbed (indicated below), the Second Ice fall and The Fly were considered to be the most significant. For purposes of identification, the icefalls were named after the Summer waterfalls. The Terrace is the broad terrace splitting the South Ridge at mid-height.

The winter routes recorded were as follows:

The First Icefall—135m Grade III (J. McKeown, C. MacLeod and B. Sprunt, 7th February, 1979)—the frozen First Waterfall between the left edge of Creag Urbhard and the First Dionard Buttress.

The Terrace—600m Grade III (B. Clough and A. Nisbet, 8th February, 1979)—an ascent of The Terrace, finishing up the snow gully above the Second Ice Fall. The Terrace was reached by a steep 15m ice pitch.

Thawr—120m Grade II (A. Nisbet and N. Spinks, 8th February, 1979)—follows the broadest of the ramps leading leftwards from The Terrace, starting about 135m past the huge corner of The Fly/Chicken Run.

The Fly—120m Grade IV (R. MacGregor and A. Nisbet, 12th February, 1979). The length is given from The Terrace—gained by climbing the initial ice-pitch. The main feature is an icefall depending from the huge corner of Chicken Run under the final pitch of Flyover. Follow the Terrace for 60m to reach the start—the icefall is reached by climbing diagonally left across heather and a short rock corner. The ice was climbed to a ledge which escaped leftwards from the main corner onto easier angled ice to finish.

Flyover—180m Grade III/IV (B. Clough and A. Nisbet, 10th February, 1979)—an obvious leftwards curving line which finishes along an undercut ledge overlooking The Fly/Chicken Run. The start is on the tree covered platform midway between the lower end of The Terrace and The Second Icefall.

The Second Ice Fall—180m Grade V (A. Nisbet and N. Spinks, 9th February, 1979). The frozen Second Waterfall—the length given is to The Terrace. The 70° preliminary ice-pitch was followed by 54m of easy snow leading to the foot of the main ice-fall which was climbed mainly on the left side.

Two routes to the right of the main crag are *The Green Knight*—105m Grade IV (A. Nisbet, 11th February, 1979)—a short, steep climb on a prominent green ice-fall high up and right of the North Buttress. *Gawains Chimney*—120m Grade III/IV (B. Clough, J. Elliot and A. Nisbet)—the narrow chimney to the left of Green Knight.

The complexity of Creag Urbhard has already been mentioned and, with the increase in climbing activity, there has often been some confusion over route identification and description. In an attempt to clarify this problem, a definitive article by P. F. Macdonald, which is well worth noting, appeared in the S.M.C. Journal, 1977. This not only traces the history of the development of climbing on this magnificent crag, but also puts across to the reader much of the unique atmosphere of the Strath—recommended reading.

7. *The Dionard Buttresses*—These lie between Creag Urbhard and Creag Alistair.

First Buttress is slabby and 'loaf-shaped'. It lies left of the First Waterfall. The first climb here *Toothache,* 78m Difficult (E. Buckley and G. Lee, 25th April, 1959) starts at the first line of weakness right of the prominent overhangs (cairn) facing the Waterfall. *Cengalo,* 210m Hard Severe (E. Howard and C. Rowland, June, 1969), takes a line up the right side of the buttress, left of the slabs of Toothache. Protection is poor and the route is considered serious for its standard. The start is in the gully used as a descent from Creag Urbhard at a point where small grey slabs form below an inverted L overhang. *Dialectic,* 240m Very Severe (P. Nunn, C. Rowland and R. Toogood, June, 1969) starts left of the centre of the buttress where steep walls cut through the overhangs. A difficult, magnificent climb with some loose rock. *Opportunist,* 420m Very Severe (P. Nunn and C. Rowland, June, 1969) has the same start as the previous route and follows the line for the first three pitches. The climb then continues rightwards to form a spiral girdle of the buttress.

Two winter routes are on record: *Incisor*—210m Grade III (R. MacGregor, A. Nisbet and N. Spinks, 10th February, 1979)—a broad, snowy ramp rises beneath the west face of the buttress to emerge at the top of the First Icefall (on Creag Urbhard). This route climbs the slabby face to the obvious skyline notch. *Plume*—120m Grade IV (R. MacGregor and N. Spinks, 11th February, 1979)—takes the impressive, sweeping icefall immediately behind the east end of Loch Dionard, to finish on a large diagonal terrace.

Second Buttress is really a long, low slanting wall which fringes the plateau and links the First and Third Buttresses. *Hugsy-Bugsy*—60m Very Difficult (Dr. and Mrs. A. W. Ewing, May, 1967). It starts at the lower end of the cliff where two converging grass rakes meet. A broken corner is climbed for 5m to the first rake. A traverse right for 3m leads to a series of short walls and mossy ledges, keeping to the left of the obvious crack. The angle eases at 25m, then trend rightwards to gain the crest of the buttress. There is considerable variation possible in the upper section. *Double Corner*—75m Very Severe (M. Boysen and P. Nunn. Alt. Leads, Whitsun 1973) takes a very smooth corner half way up the gully where the crag is seen to form a long escarpment, right cf a yellow buttress and invisible from below. The lower groove is climbed to a steep section (35m). Climb the corner to pass a bulging section on the left, then finish on slabs (40m).

Third Buttress and Fourth Buttress—These are fairly small and clean looking. They are separated by a deep gully down which ice avalanches in the spring. This is *Guinevere Gully*—300m Grade I/II (B. Clough and J. Elliot, 10th February, 1979). *Sigma*—180m Grade IV (B. Clough and R. MacGregor, 9th February, 1979) is on the Fourth Buttress. The route follows a sweeping ice line to the left of a large roof and rises steeply to a heather covered ridge. A step rightwards leads onto an undercut slab, then follow ice up a shallow gully to the top.

Fifth Buttress—Between the Fourth Buttress and Creag Alistair. Seen as a broken mass of rock set further back. *Gritstoners Revenge*—165m Very Severe (E. Howard and P. Phipps, June, 1969) starts left of centre of the face of the crag. Another route is reported here—*Smick*—200m Very Severe (C. Rowland and J. Smith, June, 1973). The location is none too clear and the climb is described as follows: 'The first of two parallel slabby ramps rising from bottom left to top right. After one pitch, the route transfers to the second ramp and follows this to the top, avoiding a bulge on the right'.

8. *Creag Alistair*—forms the east face of Plat Reidh, 1.5km to the south of Loch Dionard. This is the last significant cliff along the length of Strath Dionard and has slanting rakes of rock of moderate standard reaching to almost mid-height. Above that for 120m there is very steep rock, often overhanging. The earliest route here is *Left Edge*—270m Very Difficult (J. Brumfitt and B. Sproul, 20th May, 1967), starts at the lowest rocks of the arête which descends from the left side of the summit of the crag and forms the skyline when approached from Loch Dionard. It has easy rocks for 75m, then steeper rock to a belay in a corner below roofs and left of slab. Step out to the right, then up the slab to a terrace. Climb a further slab by a crack 6m from arête. Scrambling leads to the summit. *Succuba*—225m (T. Briggs, P. Nunn and J. Smith, Varied Leads. Whitsun, 1973)—takes the central crest of the crag between the gullies in the lower reaches and breaks through the overhangs more or less directly to climb the steep upper walls. Climb messy, loose rock right of the left-hand gully to a small ledge below better rock (peg belay 45m). The overhangs are reached after two pitches on the slabby front of the buttress. Climb a crack on the right to the overhangs. Cross a wall leftward and swing round an overlap on to a steep wall which is climbed to gain a vee-groove below a big roof. Move across left and swing round a second overlap to gain the edge of the overlaps. Go up

left to a small stance (40m). Finish right, then direct to the summit of the main buttress in two pitches, crossing a 'crevasse' on the second. Another route here is reported to have been climbed by M. Boysen and M. Richardson about the same time as the previous route. This started from the right-hand gully, whence a diagonal pitch led to a belay shared with Succuba. A second spectacular pitch led under the overhangs on the left to escape up the final continuation chimney of the prominent straight crack rising from the left hand gully. The climb is Very Severe.

The south fork of the track from Lone cuts almost due east for 13km through the centre of the southern part of the Reay Forest to Gobernuisgeach Lodge, crossing the Bealach na Feithe between Sabhal Beg and Mheall Garbh at a height of 449m. From Lone to the highest point of the pass is just over 6km and hills to the south form a pleasant hill walk, stretching for 13km to Loch Merkland. A similar circuit from the same point takes in the remainder of the tops to the north of the Bealach and from Creagan Meall Horn descends to join the north fork back to Lone, a distance of 11km.

Cranstackie (800m) and Beinn Spionnaidh (772m)

Cranstackie and Beinn Spionnaidh lie on the north-east side of Strath Dionard and are the highest points on the long grassy ridge of hills which drop gradually downwards to the coastline between Loch Eriboll and the Kyle of Durness. They offer pleasant hill walks and wide views across the Parph peninsula. The western slopes are steep and grassy and can be easily climbed from Carbreck, 4km past Gualin on the road to Durness. A car track goes into the croft at Rhigolter for 1.5km and from there less than 3km of ascent leads onto either top. A rough band of gneiss and quartzite is exposed along Cranstackie's long south-western flank above Strath Dionard but there are no prominent crags.

Legend has it that Robb Donn, the Celtic Bard, filled his beloved gun with tallow, and buried it in the rocks of Carn an Righe on Beinn Spionnaidh when his poaching days were over, rather than have it handled by anyone else. If he did, it could still well be there.

48. *Arkle from Achfarry*

TOM STRANG

49. *Ben Stack from the road to Laxford Bridge*

TOM STRANG

PETER MACDONALD

50.   *The Roost, Creag Shomhairlie*

51.   *The 200m cliffs of Clo Mhor near Cape Wrath*

52.   *Ben Hope*

TOM WEIR

53. *Ben Loyal*

TOM WEIR

54. *Ben Klibreck from Altnahara*

TOM STRANG

55.   *From Eilein na Roan, Kyle of Tongue to Ben Hope (Right) and Ben Loyal (Left)*

56.   *Looking west to the Kyle of Tongue and Whiten Head*

JACK SELBY

57.   *Dunnet Head on the north coast of Caithness, east of Thurso*

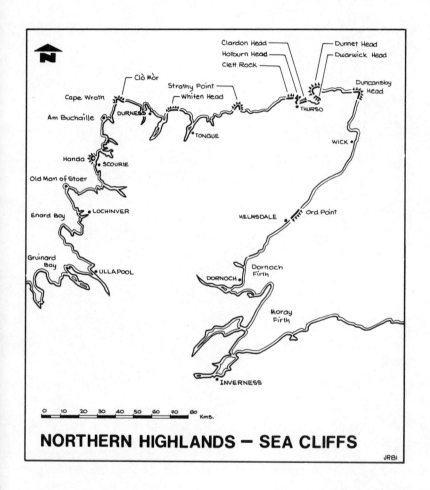

NORTHERN HIGHLANDS — SEA CLIFFS

THE NORTHERN HIGHLANDS

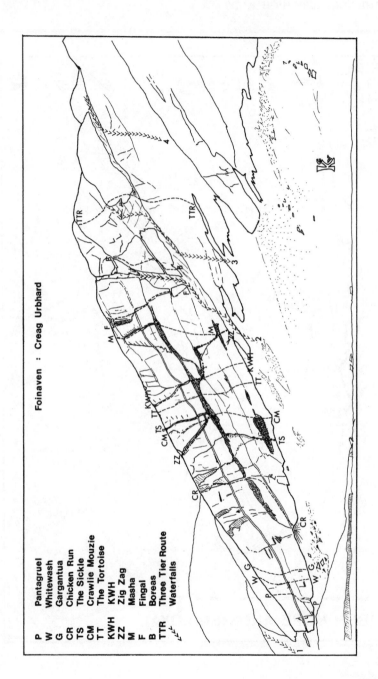

Foinaven : Creag Urbhard

P	Pantagruel
W	Whitewash
G	Gargantua
CR	Chicken Run
TS	The Sickle
CM	Crawlie Mouzie
TT	The Tortoise
KWH	KWH
ZZ	Zig Zag
M	Masha
F	Fingal
B	Boreas
TTR	Three Tier Route
⋀⋀	Waterfalls

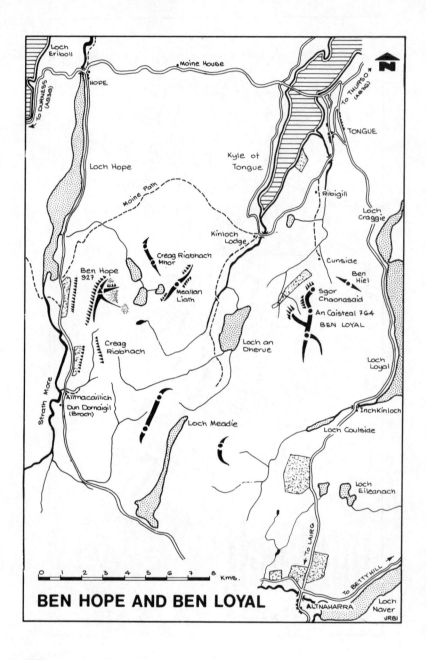

BEN HOPE AND BEN LOYAL

11

Ben Hope and Ben Loyal

Ben Hope (927m) N.C. 477502
Ben Loyal
(1) **An Caisteal** (764m) N.C. 578489
(2) **Sgor Chaonasaid** (708m) N.C. 579498
(3) **Sgor A'Bhatain** (700m) N.C. 575495
(4) **Heddle's Top** (741m) N.C. 576483
(5) **Carn An Tionail** (714m) N.C. 576477
(6) **Sgor A'Chleirich** (642m) N.C. 568488
MAP: O.S. 1:50,000 (2nd Series) Sheet No. 9—Cape Wrath. Sheet No. 10—Strathnaver.

These two fine mountains lie in the area immediately to the east of the Reay Forest, between Strath More and Strath Naver. The coastline stretches from Whiten Head on outer Loch Eriboll, eastwards to Torrisdale Bay at the mouth of the River Naver and is broken at its mid-point by the Kyle of Tongue, probing inland for almost 11km. The landward boundaries converge in the south on the village of Altnaharra, which is the road centre for the area.

From the cross-roads on the north of the village, three roads stretch out to meet with the north coastal road. The west road passes through Glen Mudale and Strathmore along the side of Loch Hope to Loch Eriboll. The east road follows Loch Naver through Strath Naver to reach the coast at the township of Bettyhill. A central route passes directly northwards to the village of Tongue on the east side of the Kyle, following the shore of Loch Loyal for part of its way.

From Loch Eriboll, the coastal road cuts eastward across the great peat-moss peninsula of a'Mhoine to the Kyle of Tongue. At Whitten Head, on the north-west corner, Loch Eriboll opens into the Pentland Firth. Here the 150m cliffs mark the end of the 192km long line of the Moine thrust plane, which, along with the great series of schists, has derived its name from the peninsula. Whiten Head, to the native Gael, was known as 'Kennagall'—the head-land of the strangers. The strangers were undoubtedly the Norsemen, who named the point 'Hvitr' or White Headland. From here to Loch Eriboll is to be found the only mainland breeding ground of the Atlantic Grey Seal.

Off-shore from Whiten Head stand two quartzite pinnacles, almost identical in height, and separated by a very deep channel. Collectively, these are known as *The Maiden,* first climbed (with tragic aftermath) in June, 1970. The eastern pinnacle, which has a cave cut through its base, was taken as the most promising. The approach is of necessity by boat. The landing is tricky and best done on the landward side. It would seem that the tide must sometimes cover the plinth. The route taken starts near the cave on the west side. The description is as follows: *The Maiden*—55m Very Severe (P. Nunn and T. W. Patey, B. Fuller, D. Goodwin and C. Rowland, June, 1970). Climb just above sea-level across sharp rocks to the left and over bulgy rocks up to a stance on the north side of the pinnacle (peg belay 20m). Move into steep groove but avoid overhanging crack by an airy traverse right onto limestone-like wall. This is climbed for 8m, then traverse right into the crack line and continue to good square ledge (peg belay 20m). Traverse shelf rightwards over loose blocks to bay. Climb left edge to stance below steep rocks (peg belay 18m). Move left and climb tottering flakes to the summit (20m). The descent is just possible in one rope length from the lower edge of the slanting top. The abseil is essentially free for 45m.

A different route was taken by W. March and J. Cunningham shortly afterwards. From the large platform on the landward side, a traverse left was made along a ledge to an overhang. This was climbed on large holds. The climb starts on the ledge above. Move right and climb the obvious overhanging crack by bridging. Continue to ledge at 15m. Traverse the ledge to the seaward side of the stack and climb straight up the obvious crack-line to the summit. This route measured 65m Very Severe.

The old road still winds round the head of the Kyle of Tongue but a recently constructed causeway and bridge now carries the main road directly across from the pier beside the youth hostel at Tongue Lodge, saving a distance of almost 15km. Tongue differs from the other communities in the north and west. It is rich and green and is well-wooded. The Gaelic name was Ceann-T-Saile A'Mhicaoidh—The Head of Mackay's Salt Water—and the ruined Castle Varrich west of the village was once a Mackay stronghold. Tongue House, north of the village, was built in 1678 by Lord Reay, chief of Mackay, but later passed into the hands of the Sutherland family. At the mouth of the Kyle of Tongue stand several islands. Eilean nan Ron, the largest of these, was inhabited until fairly recently, and on the sands of Rabbit Island, which can be reached by walking at low tide, the French sloop 'Hazard', carrying gold for the Jacobite Cause, ran aground and held fast.

Tongue itself is a busy holiday resort and provides a variety of tourist services, including good hotels, guest houses and a youth hostel. The bulk of the population is scattered in small communities along either side of the Kyle and on the coastal strip eastwards to Bettyhill. The crofting township of Melness, which owes its origin to the evictions from Strathmore, stands on the west side of the Kyle and can be reached by road from Tongue. The bleak peat-moss of A'Mhoine has few houses other than those connected to the estates.

The two mountains which lie within this area are similar only in the manner in which their appearance is enhanced by their isolation. Geologically, they are entirely different. Ben Hope is composed of rocks of the Moine series—granulite and horneblende schist. Ben Loyal is the only mountain of the igneous group of rocks to fall within the area of the Northern Highlands. It is largely composed of syenite which has many of the characteristics of the granite of the Cairngorms. The mountain has magnetic tendencies which can distract compasses and this was blamed for the aircrash which killed the Duke of Kent here in 1942.

Ben Hope (927m)

Ben Hope is the most northerly mountain in Scotland included in Munro's Tables. It rises from just 4m above sea level to the east of the roadside at the south end of Loch Hope. the name Hope is derived from 'hop', the Norse word for a 'bay'. This name has obviously worked its way inland from the bay on Loch Eriboll formed by the mouth of the River Hope, to both the loch and the mountain beyond.

Ben Hope rises in two great terraces from the loch side. The lower terrace has a fine natural birch wood covering which reaches 305m contour. The upper terrace starts at 610m and rises in a series of steep rocky ridges and buttresses. The west and north-west faces of Ben Hope are both steep and craggy but to the east and south-east the mountain slopes away more gradually. For the hillwalker, the long gently sloping south ridge gives the easiest approach to the summit, the northern ridge is both steep and narrow and requires greater care.

The two eastern ridges present no difficulty but are too remote to provide a useful means of ascent to the top.

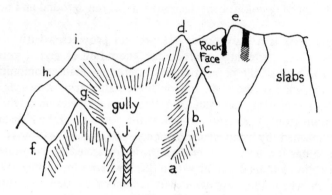

Fig. 7. North-west face of Ben Hope (the letters relate to text).

Ben Hope can be approached equally well from the north or from the south by way of the road from Altnaharra to Loch Eriboll, already mentioned. It should be noted that the road marked on the map from Loch Eriboll to the keeper's house at Cashel Dhu does not give access to Ben Hope. The ferry previously operating has long been out of use. From the south, this road passes by way of Glen Mudale into the broad valley of Strathmore. 3km down the Strath stands the Broch of Dun Dornaigil, which is one of the few structures of its kind of which part of the wall stands more than 6m high. The interior measures 8m in diameter and the wall is some 4m thick. An interesting feature is the large triangular lintel covering the outer opening of the entrance passage on the north- east side. The interior of the Broch is now largely blocked by fallen masonry.

From the Broch a track leaves the road by the scattering of houses at Altnacaillich, and follows the burn upwards into the Leiter Mhuiseil—the lower part of the south ridge of Ben Hope. The stream of the Allt na Caillich—the burn of the old woman—drops in a great waterfall above the houses—near here is the reputed birthplace of the Celtic Bard Rob Donn. The broad ridge can be followed directly up to the summit along the head of the western crags. The cliff edge is marked by several cairns but the summit cairn lies 135m north-east of the largest of these—from the Broch the distance is 5.6km.

An alternative route begins at a track rising from the south end of Loch Hope. This can be followed for a distance and then is left to climb steeply towards Dubh Loch na Beinne—the black loch of the Ben—which nestles on the first of the two terraces. The route now passes north-eastwards below the line of the rock cliffs onto the narrow north ridge which is followed to the summit. There is one 'bad' corner on the line of this ridge which requires care—especially on the descent. A possible, though longer, escape route to the east necessitates dropping into the corrie and then following the next ridge running due east-west onto the summit.

Rock climbing on Ben Hope to date has been found on the north-west face of the mountain. Seen from the loch side the main feature is a wide gully flanked by two rocky ridges. The accompanying diagram outlines the possibilities around this feature which was first explored by J. H. B. Bell in 1933. The south ridge was the most interesting and gave 240m of climbing from A to just below the summit. Some difficulty was found in the lower section AB, and a traverse was made across the face of the buttress to the right. From B to C excellent climbing rock was encountered, with occasionally difficult situations. C to D was pleasant and airy. Between D and E the ridge is narrow and has one exposed corner. The summit of Ben Hope lies just beyond E. The line FGHL was climbed in a gale and in bad conditions by H. M. Brown and D. Macnab, 22nd December, 1969. Under normal conditions the route would have been Grade I.

Another straightforward route on this face is *Petticoat Ridge* (S. and M. Johnstone). The ridge of Bell's climb is bounded on the left by a funnel-shaped gully and on the right by a steep grassy rake (a gully near its bottom) from which the right-hand wall of the ridge apparently rises in a series of steep slabby towers. One of these towers, on which lies a prominent square-cut pinnacle, rises on a ridge from the grassy saddle at the top of the rake, while a lower tower rises on a ridge from the rake about 60m below the saddle. This latter ridge was climbed. It proved to be moderately Difficult if the lower steep section is climbed and disappointingly artificial, as easy ground was always accessible on the right. The grassy rake was difficult of access. The Ben Hope crags are reported as coming regularly into good winter condition, providing numerous gully climbs of all standards. A number of new summer climbs has also been done, but information on these has not yet filtered through. It would seem that further exploration here would still be rewarding.

Ben Loyal

Despite its comparatively modest height, the isolated position and impressive profile of Ben Loyal, rising from the moorland to the south of the Kyle of Tongue, has earned it the title of 'Queen of the Scottish Peaks'.

To the north and east, only Beinn Stumanadh rises to any great height, while, to the west and to the south, its nearest rivals, Ben Hope and Ben Klibreck, both over 914m, lie 9.6 and 19km distant respectively.

The finest view is undoubtedly the one from the north. From this direction the full splendour of the ridge with its four granite peaks can be seen dipping and rising south-westwards from Sgor Chaonasaid. Seen from the east, Ben Loyal loses its clearly defined outline and while there is no difficulty in climbing onto the summit ridge from any point from the roadside along Loch Loyal, it is not recommended. From this direction the way passes across boggy moorland for over 3km and is unpleasant at any time of the year.

The best approach is from Tongue. The old road to Durness is left after 2.5km and a farm road followed to Ribigill. From here a good track leads for just over 1.5km to the shepherd's house at Cunside. Steep grassy slopes lead upwards onto Sgor Chaonasaid (708m) the northern top of the ridge. Alternatively, one can follow either of the two gullies which run to its highest point. Rock routes have been attempted in the past on the north buttress of Sgor Chaonasaid but the rock was not found to be very suitable and parties had to traverse off into the gullies. The most recently recorded route here is *Navytex Gully*—150m Very Difficult (H. M. Brown, June, 1968). From the north prow of Sgor Chaonasaid a burn comes down to the edge of the wood—Coille na Cuile. This is the line of the climb. At first the rock is clean, but higher up comes an unpleasant mixture of easy ground and incredibly loose walls.

The traverse of the ridge from Sgor Chaonasaid need present no difficulty and a circuit of the main tops and the return to Cunside covers a distance of 9.5km, with little intermediate re-ascent. A'Chaisteal (764m) the highest point of Ben Loyal, lies 800m south of Sgor Chaonasaid and drops in steep, smooth faces of up to 12m on its south side. The way to it passes the twin tors of Sgur a'Bhatain (The Boats), which lie slightly more to the west. A climb on the upper tor here is *Row Boat*—57m Mild Severe (K. Richardson and D. Dewell, June, 1959). The rock was found to be steep, impressive and sound;

the line taken probably the easiest on the main rampart of the crag. The route starts 1m left of the extreme bottom left-hand corner and follows the left-hand bounding ridge. Climb to the ledge immediately above the corner and continue up until the line of the ridge merges with that of the gully on the left (33m—belays). A prominent ledge crosses the main face giving a sensational walk. Climb on to it into a corner and climb the 5m left wall, continuing up a grassy groove to a belay (15m). Move right from the belay, step on to ledge on arête, and continue up easy rocks (12m).

Sgor a'Bhatain—Cirith Ungol—Very Severe (L. G. Brown and R. G. Wilson, June, 1969). This climb takes a line up the centre of the left-hand of two steep buttresses near the summit of Sgor a'Bhatain. The buttress is roughly triangular, with a smooth central section. Start at a broken vegetated groove just right of the centre of the crag. Climb towards a prominent overhang and pass it on the left by a groove. Leave this to cross a steep wall and climb a rib to reach a corner. Follow this to a bulge split by a thin crack. Climb this and the prominent overhanging crack above. Finally, climb a pinnacle and the overhanging crack above it, using slings for aid in the crack. The length of the route is not recorded.

From Sgurr a'Bhatain the ridge continues south for 800m over a top of 741m, which has been named Heddle's top, and then in another 800m to Carn an Tionail (714m), the featureless southerly point on the main ridge.

From Heddle's top, a branch ridge dips west-north-westwards onto the sharply defined peak of Sgor a'Chleirich (640m), undoubtedly the best crag on the mountain. The south-west face overlooking Loch Fhionnach gives a 255m Very Severe route, *Priest's Rake*. (D. D. Stewart and R. Tombs, 1958) described as follows: 'It is a rake ill-defined at first, rising from left to right across the crag, and another fault divides it in a vertical plane. Below the rake this second fault forms a groove, above it a steep, broken, dirty-looking dièdre. Start at a small cairn below the lowest rib, a few feet left of the dirty groove (piton, 30m). Traverse right here and climb into groove. Follow the groove until escape on the left leads to overhung grass patch. Exit on left out over exposed slabs to a larger grass patch which is the start of the defined section of the rake. Follow it up to the right to its highest point, whence a rib leads directly to the top of the crag. As far as the rake, the climbing is serious and difficult; the rake itself is narrow but easy and the final section is straightforward.' The climb occupied five hours and four pitons were used. The direct continuation from the rake up the steep dièdre was climbed by L. Brown and A. P. Turnbull, 14th June, 1969, giving a long and elegant route, *Marathon Corner*—280m Very Severe.

To the west, Sgor a'Chleirich drops steeply for almost 210m to a saddle which connects it with the 533m terminal cone of this branch ridge of Ben Loyal. The dip is only seen when the mountain is viewed from the north or from the road south of Altnaharra and is unapparent from the main ridge.

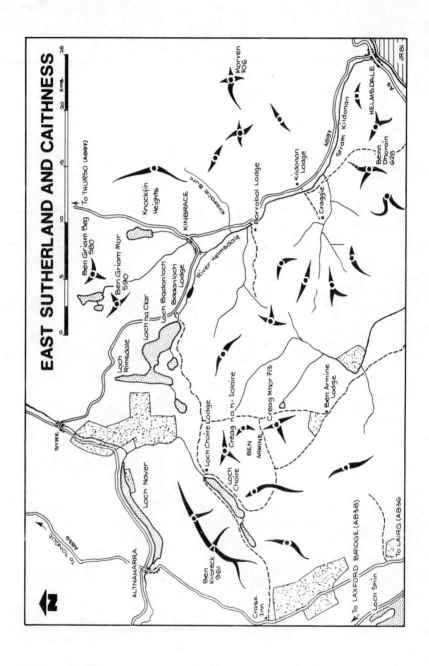

EAST SUTHERLAND AND CAITHNESS

12

East Sutherland and Caithness

(1) **Ben Klibreck** (961m) N.C. 585299
(2) **Ben Armine** (713m) N.C. 698240
(3) **Morven** (706m) N.D. 005286
(4) **Scaraben** (626m) N.D. 066268
(5) **Maiden Pap** (484m) N.D. 048293
(6) **Beinn Dhorain** (628m) N.C. 926156
(7) **Ben Griam Mor** (590m) N.C. 806389
(8) **Ben Griam Beg** (580m) N.C. 832412

MAPS: O.S. 1:50,000 (2nd Series) Sheet No. 10—Strathnaver. Sheet No. 11—Thurso and Dunbeath. Sheet No. 12—Thurso and Wick. Sheet No. 16—Lairg and Loch Shin. Sheet No. 17—Strath of Kildonan.

This chapter deals with the eastern part of Sutherland, which, together with the county of Caithness, forms the north-east corner of the area of the Northern Highlands. The area is bounded on the west by the main road from the head of the Kyle of Sutherland which passes north and north-eastwards through Lairg and Altnaharra to reach the coast at Bettyhill at the mouth of Strath Naver. The coastline, stretching more than 160km around the great headland of Duncansby, provides some of the finest sea-cliff scenery in the country.

Although the most northerly district on the Scottish mainland, Caithness is easy of access. 160km of good road travels the length of the east coast from Inverness. This is supplemented by a network of cross-country roads mainly connecting with the north coastal road which leads towards the north-west corner of Sutherland. A passenger service runs daily to the north from Inverness, and the track meanders through the centre of Sutherland before turning north-eastwards to Wick and Thurso. Use of the numerous request stops en route will open up the more interesting inland parts. One of the obvious advantages here of the oil development in the North Sea has been the vastly improved air links to and from the area. There is a busy airport at Wick, with regular flights from the South, and Dornoch, on the Kyle of Sutherland, has an authorised landing strip for private planes.

One important road bisects the area in a northwards direction from Helmsdale through Strath Kildonan and Strath Halladale to meet the north coast road by Melvich. This road is still in Sutherland but follows the old county border with Caithness which lies some 6.5km to the east, along the watershed. From Kinbrace Junction, at the head of Strath Kildonan, one other useful road passes north-westwards to Syre on Strathnaver, the only direct east-west road link in the area.

In the past, Caithness and Sutherland formed the Pictish province of Cat, or Cataobh, one of the seven provinces of Pictland, but, as the name implies, Caithness was at one time more Scandinavian than Highland. The Norsemen settled along the coastline and the fertile area which ran inland along the straths and here the place-names keep their Norse flavour. The terminal 'byster', common in many of the place-names, is the Norse word for 'farm'. On the inland heights the names are mainly the Gaelic of the native Celts who were pushed there by invaders.

Caithness has few characteristics in common with the rest of the area of the Northern Highlands, which it resembles only along its inland border with Sutherland. This can be accounted for when one looks at the geology of the area. Two main rock formations make up the surface of the county. The hilly inland region consists mainly of stratified schists and Cambrian quartzites—the lowland country stretching to the coastline is composed mainly of Old Red Sandstone. The lowland area of Caithness is similar in many ways to the Orkney Islands, Easter Ross and the country around the Morayshire coast. The underlying Old Red Sandstone breaks down to produce rich farming land, and agriculture plays an important part in the economy of the country. Like the Orkneys, there are few trees here, and the inland areas tend to be featureless and uninspiring. Inland, the gradually rising moorlands attain their greatest height along the south-west border and here, where the Archaean Metamorphic rocks prevail, the country consists of heather-clad hills, peat moss, lochs and bogs, in direct contrast to the cultivated flats of the north-east angle.

The coastline more than compensates for the uninspiring outlook across the flat farming lands and inland moors. Throughout its length it is indented with deep gorges or bays, lined with heather-topped cliffs and ending in great headlands of near-vertical, weathered, sandstone cliffs, the nesting grounds of countless varieties of sea-birds. Strange-shaped stacks have been isolated from the mainland by the action of the sea and, where this process is incomplete, great natural arches have been formed to add to the variety of the scene.

This whole coastline holds countless possibilities for the climber, and already there has been a fair amount of exploration. On the north coast, the headlands of Holborn and Dunnet enclose Thurso Bay, and further to the east around Clardon Head, Dunnet Bay with its 6.5km of golden sand. Dunnet Head is the most northerly point of Scotland. It stands some 122m above the sea, giving superb views of this whole northern coastline. Unfortunately the area is one threatened by the current oil boom—a mixed blessing from the point of view of preservation of the more beautiful parts of our national environment.

The Clett Rock, a 50m stack which stands off Holborn Head, is one which has been climbed in recent years. This gives *West Route*—50m Severe and A2 (R. Jolly, M. Willis and D. Young, 14th June, 1969). The stack is separated from the mainland by a 24m sea-channel, and, because of dangerous currents, it is strongly advised to seek expert local advice from the boatmen at Scrabster. Dwarwick Head—on the north side of Dunnet Bay (N.D. 200710)—is reputed to give the best available sea-cliff climbing in Caithness. It has been intensively investigated and a duplicated interim guide has been produced, the result of activity by the Caithness Mountaineering Club. Other scenes of climbing activity within the area are: Creag an Dherne—N.C. 540470; Strathy Point—N.C. 820690; Holborn Head—N.D. 109716; Duncansby Stacks—N.D. 400719. The headland of Duncansby, 3km east of John O'Groat's House, forms the tip of the north-eastern corner of Scotland. From here the view across the Pentland Firth towards the Orkneys, takes in the only island off the Caithness coastline—Island of Stroma. The south-east boundary of Caithness is impressibly marked by the great headland of Ord, whose 230m cliffs are breeding ground for sea-birds. The way to the Ord leads over the infamous Berriedale Hill, which in winter becomes a motorist's nightmare. On a Monday in the year 1513, the Sinclair Earl of Caithness, with 300 men, crossed the Ord by this route on his way to the ill-fated battle of Flodden. No one made the return journey.

The inland border of Caithness runs in a southerly direction from Drumholliston on the north coast, to the Ord Point, 1.5km north of Helmsdale on the A9. Pont's map of 1608 has the boundary along

Strath Halladale and Kildonan, but the watershed is the officially recognised line. The three highest mountains in Caithness lie within the extreme southern corner between the county boundary and the Berriedale water. This comes under the Braemore and Langwell Estate, a strictly preserved deer forest. The estate proprietors insist on permission being asked to enter the forest and this can be obtained from the Factor's office at Berriedale, 5km north of Helmsdale on the A9.

Morven (705m)

Morven, the highest point in Caithness, is one of the few mountains of Old Red Sandstone to obtain a height of over 610m. Its regular cone shape makes it a prominent landmark standing up from the surrounding moorland. It is best approached from Berriedale by a motorable road, up the Langwell water to Wag—a distance of 13km. The summit lies in a north-westerly direction from here and is easily climbed, although the last 305m are very steep. The way lies over wet moorland and it is best to make for the depression between the main top and the conspicuous knob of rock which is Morven's only irregular feature. Permission to use the road to Wag must be obtained as mentioned previously.

Scaraben (626m)

Scaraben lies 6.5km north-west of Berriedale and is a different type of hill from Morven. It consists of three smoothly rounded tops of quartzite of the Moine series. It is most easily reached from a track along the west side of the Berriedale river which also gives access to Maiden Pap (482m), almost 3km further north west. 3km to the east of Maiden Pap lies Morven.

The western part of the area of this chapter lies entirely within the county of Sutherland. The mountains here lie along the western boundary, the road from the south to Bettyhill and from these the land falls down gradually to the north and east coast along the sides of five great open straths. To the north—Strathnaver and Strath Halladale; to the south—Strath Kildonan, Strath Brora and Strath Fleet. The floors of the straths are rich in Archaeological remains dating back to the time of the earliest inhabitants but, of greater interest, is the underlying reason for the considerable number of more recently ruined settlements to be found along the now deserted upper valleys. This is the classic area of the Sutherland Clearances, which, by the middle of the 19th century, created an uninhabited wilderness where once there had been thriving communities. The story of the Clearances and the events leading up to them have produced a wealth of reading material and it is not the intention of this guide-book to examine the matter in detail. It is of interest to note, however, that the Clearances and the subsequent developments in the Highlands were included in the prophecy of Kenneth Mackenzie, the Brahan Seer, the Ross-shire soothsayer whose prophecies are still remembered over most of the Highlands.

'The day will come when the jaw-bone of the big sheep (Caoirich Mhora) will plough on the rafters. The bleating of sheep will cover the Highlands, great prices will be got, then they will go back until a man finding the jaw-bone of a sheep in a cairn will not be able to tell what animal it belonged to. The ancient proprietors of the land shall give place to strange merchant proprietors. Then the country is to be given over to deer and not a man left. The crow of a cock shall not be heard north of Druim Uachdair; the people will emigrate to islands now unknown but which shall yet be discovered in the boundless oceans, after which the deer and other wild animals in the huge wilderness shall be exterminated and drowned by a horrid black rain. The people will then return to take possession of the land of their ancestors.'

A great part of his prophecy is now historical fact. The sheep did come and the men were forced to leave to make way for them. The people did emigrate to lands overseas—New Kildonan was founded on the Red River in Canada by evicted tenants from Strath Kildonan and is now the city of Winnipeg. Some of the earliest settlers to New Zealand left from Brora. Whole communities left together for the growing lands of the new continents. Those who remained were resettled on the poorest lands of the coastal strip where they had to learn new skills to make a livelihood from the sea. This is the origin of many of the north and east coast communities still in existence at the present day. One example of these is the community of Bettyhill, at the mouth of the River Naver. Elizabeth, Marchioness of Stafford, set aside land here on which her evicted tenants from Strath Naver founded a township—named appropriately after its donor. Some of their previous homes can still be found in the pre-clearance villages at Grumore, Grubeg and Rossal.

The deer did oust the sheep in the latter part of the 19th century and saw the creation of the great sporting estates. These still exist, having been sold and re-sold through a succession of seasonal landlords.

With speculation rife on the future development of oil resources around the coastline of the north, perhaps the all-consuming 'black, black rain' is not so very far away after all.

BEN KLIBRECK (961m)

(1) **Meall nan Con** (961m) N.C. 585299
(2) **Creag an Lochan** (807m contour) N.C. 576281
(3) **Cnoc Sgriodain** (542m) N.C. 553271
(4) **Meall Ailein** (721m) N.C. 613315
(5) **Meall nan Eoin** (774m) N.C. 597293

Ben Klibreck rises from the east side of the road from Lairg to Altnaharra, between Loch Naver and Loch Choire. Together with the hilly tract which comprises Ben Armine, it forms the main mountainous mass of the area covered by this chapter of the guide. The main ridge of Ben Klibreck extends in a south-west to north-east direction with Meall nan Con, the highest point, at its mid-point. Three broad shoulders are flung out in a south-easterly direction to form a huge E shape. These enclose two large corries which drain into Loch Choire and its subsidiary, Loch a'Bhealaich. The mountain is a conspicuous landmark in this central Sutherland landscape, predominantly one of low-lying moorland, but it has few pronounced rock features. The western slopes are steep, but mainly heathery. The head walls of the south-east corries hold little continuous rock. The climb on to the ridge is usually made from the west side, either from Altnaharra or Crask Inn.

From Altnaharra the road from Lairg is left about 800m before reaching the hotel. From here a rough motor track leads in along the south side of Loch Naver for 1.5km to Klibreck Farm. A good track leaves the back of the farm and this can be followed easily for just over 3km onto the north end of the ridge. The traverse of the ridge from here presents no difficulty and the main 'Munro' top is reached in 3km.

The approach from Crask Inn, 21km north of Lairg, is equally straightforward. The little hotel lies at a height of 210m above sea level and the road here tends to be blocked easily by snow during the winter months. Its height is of advantage to the hill-walker; the 3.5km climb onto Cnoc Sgriodain, the western spur of Klibreck, involves only 305m of gentle ascent over moorland and heathery slopes. The main top is reached in 2.5km with only another 275m of climbing. The view westwards is across the whole range of Ben More Assynt. If one follows the central shoulder south-westwards to Meall an Eoin, there is a fine view down into the Loch Choire Forest and across over the rolling range of Ben Armine to the mountains of Caithness. It is now possible to descend to the shores of Loch Choire by way of either of the south-east corries of Klibreck and a path leads along the loch side over the Bealach Easach, then by way of Strath a'Chraisg to the Crask Inn across 5.5km of flat moorland.

Klibreck looks at its best in winter when the mountain can often be approached and ascended on skis, thus cutting out the otherwise long and rather uninteresting approach walks over the surrounding moorlands. This particular area holds snow early on most winters, giving the increased chance of good conditions for ski-touring. Transport difficulties to and from the mountain, because of blocked roads, unfortunately can present problems.

On the west side of Ben Klibreck, an area of rock rises onto the main ridge at a point just below the high top. It is easily located from the Lairg-Altnaharra road and can be approached more or less directly across the moorland from a point 5233, to by-pass Loch na Glaschoille. The nomenclature of the main features of the crag and descriptions of climbs on it are now clarified (H. M. Brown, S.M.C.J., 1971).

'The main feature of these rocks is Bell's Gully, which separates Eyrie Buttress to the north from broken slabby rocks to the south. There are four climbs recorded. *Bell's Gully*—150m Moderate (J. H. B. Bell and D. Myles, 1933). The gully is steep but the main difficulties can be avoided by flanking moves on the right. The Gully also gives a Grade II climb (H. M. Brown and D. MacNab, 23rd December, 1969). *Southern Crag*—105m Difficult (J. H. B. Bell and D Myles, 1933). It has a lot of broken rock and is not to be recommended. *Eyrie Buttress*—105m Difficult (J. H. B. Bell and D. Myles, 1933). This can be climbed almost anywhere. The steep lower section is difficult, the rest is pleasant and airy.' An eagle's eyrie is often to be found on the upper rocks, to which a descent can be made equally well from the ridge above.

BEN ARMINE

(1) **Creag Mhor** (713m) N.C. 6928240
(2) **Creag a'Choire Ghlas** (704m) N.C. 695273
(3) **Meall nan Aighan** (694m) N.C. 681289

(4) **Creag na H'Iolaire** (695m) N.C. 673289
(5) **Meall Ard** (634m) N.C. 666293

Ben Armine is the collective name given to the ridge of hills which runs in a line roughly south-south-east from the north end of Loch Choire towards the great straths which open onto the east coast of Sutherland. The hills lie entirely within the Armine Forest, part of the Sutherland Estates. The area is solely maintained for its sporting potential and enquiries about permission for access should be made at the Estate Office in Golspie.

There is no outstanding feature to catch the eye, but the wide expanse of rolling moorland rising gently upwards from the south, holds a peculiar attraction for those unaccustomed to such solitude. To the west, the outlying hills of the ridge drop steep heathery slopes into the Loch Choire basin and, to the east and north, the main ridge drops unexpectedly in a series of almost precipitous walls enclosing five large corries. The ridge drains southwards to feed the Rivers Blackwater and Brora which join at the head of Strath Brora and open into the North Sea. The fishing in the area is excellent.

A well-kept system of tracks encircles the Ben Armine ridge, connecting Ben Armine Lodge at the south-east end with Loch Choire Lodge on the north shore of the loch. These in turn connect with tracks leading westwards and south-westwards towards the Lairg road and provide a variety of possibilities for long but pleasant cross-country walking expeditions. This area is indeed one for the foot-traveller by virtue of the distance of the hills from main motor roads and the limitations of estate vehicle tracks serving the shooting lodges.

Three possible approach routes into the area can be suggested—

1. From Sciberscross, 16km inland along Strath Brora from the east coast. An estate track leaves the keeper's house on the west side of the road and travels 13km inland over the open moorland to Ben Armine Lodge, in Strath na Seilige. The gate at the road is seldom locked but drivers should note that only vehicles with high clearance should attempt this route. There is a fine unobstructed view to the north of Morven.

2. By way of Strath Kildonan or Strath Naver, leave the Syre-Kinbrace road at Loch Badanloch—6.5km from the remote Garbhalt fishing hotel. An estate road similar in condition to the road from Sciberscross reaches Loch Choire Lodge at the north end of the loch in 16km.

3. From the Lairg-Crask road, an estate road branches off at the river bridge, 8km north of Lairg. 6.5km inland lies Dalnessie Lodge and the road continues over to the River Brora for another 1.5km. A shooting path follows the east bank of the river for 2.5km and then cuts across country to meet the Ben Armine track at Greenface.

Two other hills of special interest are found within the area.

Bein Griam Beg (580m)

Bein Griam Beg, lying 5.5km west by south of Forsinard Hotel between Strath Halladale and Strath Naver, has on its summit the highest hill fort in Scotland. The remains consist of a stone wall about 2m thick which encloses an area of 150m by 60m at the top of the hill with an entrance on the north side. The remains of other walls are found on a lower level on the south flank of the hill. From Forsinard, it is possible most years to enjoy some skiing on the surrounding slopes.

Beinn Dhorain (628m) and Ben Uarie (624m)

Beinn Dhorain and Ben Uarie lie 9.5km west of Helmsdale. A rough track up Glen Loth is barely motorable. It leaves the A9 8km north of Brora and rises up along the eastern slopes of these two rounded hills of Old Red Sandstone to almost 335m at its highest point, before descending into Strath Kildonan to cross the railway line north, and the River Helmsdale, by a bridge near Kildonan Lodge. Glen Loth provides some skiing most winters.

Kildonan, in 1869, was the scene of a gold rush. The Kildonan and Suisgill burns yielded limited quantities but the rush eventually petered out. Recent mineral surveys in Sutherland have included the area in their work and there could still be a small fortune waiting here for some 20th century prospector.

APPENDIX I

Mountain Names and Meanings

The following list attempts to give the meanings of the Mountain names mentioned in the Guide. Gaelic spellings in the guide itself are those commonly used by the Ordnance Survey. In many cases these are found to be a corrupted form of the original Gaelic name, which add to the difficulty of accurate interpretation. It must be remembered that the original Gaelic names for the mountains are local names and often lose their aptness if taken out of context.

As has been mentioned in the text of the Guide, there is a strong Norse influence in several of the place-names in the Northern Highlands, and an attempt has been made to indicate this where it is applicable.

Many of the meanings are already well accepted but in the case of those where there is some doubt, either the most appropriate alternative has been given, or a blank has been left.

A'Chailleach: *The Old Woman*
A'Choinneach Mhor: *The Big Moss*
A'Mhaighdean(n): *The Maiden*
Arkle: *The Mountain of the level top*
Am Bodach: *The Old Man (Spectre)*
Am Buachaille: *The Shepherd (Herdsman)*
Am Faochagach: *The Wilk-Shaped Mountain*
Am Fasarinen: *The Talons*
An Cabar: *The Stake (or Antler)*
An Coileachan: *The Cockerel*
An Grianan: *The Sunny Place*
An Laoigh (Laogh): *The Calf*
An Liathanach: *The Grey Headed Man*
An Ruadh-stac: *The Red Steep Hill*
An Sgurr: *The Rocky Peak*
An Socach: *The Projective Place (The Snoot)*
An Teallach: *The Forge*

Baosbheinn: *The Wizard's Mountain*
Bealach or B(h)ealaich: *Pass*
Bealach an ar: *The Pass of the Slaughter*
Bealach nan Arr (Faradh): *The Ladder Pass*
Bealach na Ba: *Pass of the Cow*
Bealach Ban: *The White Pass*
Bealach na Bhiurich (Buirich): *The Pass of the Bellowing*
Bealach a'Chonnaidh: *The Pass of the Firewood*
Bealach a'Chornaidh: *The Pass of the Folds (Like the Folding of a Skirt)*
Bealach a'Chuirn *The Pass of the Cairn*
Bealach na Croise: *The Pass of the Cross*
Bealach Easach: *The Pass of the Waterfall (Marsh)*
Bealach na Feithe: *The Pass of the Bog Channel*
Bealach a'Ghlas-Chnoic: *The Pass of the Green Hillock*
Bealach Gorm: *The Green Pass*
Bealach na H'Imrich: *The Pass of the Removing*
Bealach na Lice: *The Pass of the Flat Stone*
Bealach nam Meirleach: *The Thieves' Pass*
Bealach Mhor (Mor): *The Big Pass*
Bealach a'Chomla: *The Pass of Meeting*
Beinn, Beinne, Beann: *Mountain*
Beinn a'Chaisgein Mor: *The Forbidding Mountain*
Beinn a'Chaisteil: *Castle Mountain*
Beinn a'Chlaidheimh: *Mountain of the Sword*
Beinn a'Chearcaill: *Circular Hill (The Mountain of the Girdle)*
Beinn a'Ghrianain: *Sunny Mountain*
Beinn a'Mhuinidh: *The Mountain of the Heath*
Beinn Airigh Charr: *The Mountain of the Rocky Shieling*
Beinn Alligin: *The Mountain of Beauty*
Beinn an Eoin: *Mountain of the Bird*
Beinn an Fhurain (Fhuarain): *Mountain of the Well or Spring*
Beinn Bhan: *The White (Fair) Mountain*
Beinn Damph: *The Mountain of the Stag*
Beinn Dearg: *The Red Mountain*
Beinn Direach: *The Steep Mountain*
Beinn Dhorain (Dhobhrain): *The Mountain of the Otter*
Beinn Eighe: *The Mountain of the Ice*
Beinn Enaiglair: *The Mountain of the Timid Birds*
Beinn Ghobhlach: *The Forked Mountain*
Beinn Lair: *The Mountain of the Mare*

Beinn Leoid: *The Sloping Mountain*
Beinn Liath Mhor Fannich: *Big Grey Mountain of Fannich*
Beinn nan Caorach: *The Mountain of the Sheep*
Beinn na h'Eaglaise: *The Mountain of the Church*
Beinn Spionnaidh: *The Mountain of Strength*
Beinn Stumanadh: *The Modest Mountain?*
Beinn Tarsuinn: *The Transverse Mountain (Lying Across, Oblique)*
Beinn Uidhe: *The Mountain of the Ford or Isthmus*
Ben Armine (Armuinn): *The Mountain of the Warrior*
Ben Griam Beg: *The Small Dark Mountain*
Ben Griam More: *The Big Dark Mountain*
Ben Hee (Shidh): *The Fairies' Mountain*
Ben Hope: *The Mountain of the Bay*
Ben Klibreck (Clibreck): *The Mountain of the Speckled Stone (of the Fish)*
Ben Loyal: *The Mountain of the Elm Tree*
Ben More Assynt: *The Great Mountain of Assynt*
Ben Stack: *The Steep Mountain*
Ben Strome: *The Mountain of the Current*
Ben Wyvis: *The Noble Mountain*
Bidein: *Pinnacle*
Bidein a'Ghlas Thuill: *The Sharp Peak of the Grey Hollow*
Bidein Toll a'Mhuic: *The Sharp Peak of the Pig's Hollow*
Bodach Mhor (Mor): *The Great Old Man (Spectre)*
Breabag (Braebag (beag)): *The Little Upland*
Cadha: *Pass or Steep Place*
Cadha na Beucaich: *The Pass (Steep Place) of the Roaring*
Cadha Amadan: *The Fool's Pass*
Cadha Ghoblach: *The Forked Pass*
Canisp: *White Mountain*
Carn, C(H)uirn, C(H)airn: *Heap of stones applied to a round rocky hill*
Carn an Fheidh: *The Deer's Hill*
Carn an Righe: *The Hill of the Slope*
Carn an Tionail: *The Gathering Hill*
Carn Ban: *The White Hill*
Carn Chuinneag: *The Hill of the Churn (Buckets)*
Carn Dearg: *The Red Hill*
Carn Gorm Loch: *The Hill of the Green Loch*
Carn na Criche: *The Boundary Hill*

Carn na Feola: *The Hill of Flesh*
Carn nan Conbhairean: *The Hill of the Greedy Ones*
Ceann Garbh: *The Rough Head*
Cearcall Dubh: *The Black Circle*
Cioch Beinn an Eoin: *The Breast of the Mountain of the Bird*
Cnoc Sgriodain: *Scree Slope*
Cona' Mheall: *The Enchanted Hill*
Corrag Bhuidhe: *The Yellow Pinnacle (Finger)*
Cranstackie: *The Rugged Hill*
Creag: Rock, *crag or cliff*
Creag a Choire Ghlais: *The Rock of the Green Hollow*
Creag a Duine: *The Rock of the Man*
Creag an Fhithich: *The Raven's Crag*
Creag Gorm: *The Green Crag*
Creag Ghrianach: *The Sunny Crag*
Creag, Liath, Braebag: *The Grey Crag*
Creag an Lochan: *The Crag of the Loch*
Creag nan Calmon: *Crag of the Dove*
Creag na Faoilinn: *Seagull Crag*
Creag na N'Iolaire: *Eagle Crag*
Creag na H'Uidhe: *The Crag of the Ford (Isthmus)*
Creag Rainich: *Bracken Crag*
Creag Riabhach: *The Brindled Crag*
Creag Ruadh: *The Red Crag*
Creag Shomhairle: *Samuel's Peak*
Creag Urbhard: *From Urabhallach—The herb 'Devil's Bit', found on hills*
Cul Beag: *The Little Hill-Back*
Cul Mor: *The Big Hill-Back*
Dun Caan: *The Fortress (of Caan)*
Eididh nan Clach Geala: *The Covering of the White Stones*
Fashven: *The Rise*
Fiachlach: *The Toothy One*
Fionn Bheinn: *The White Mountain*
Fuar Tholl: *The Cold Hollow*
Ganu Mor: *The Great Wedge*
Garbh Choireachan: *The Rough Circular Hollow (Cauldron)*
Glas Bheinn: *The Green Grassy Mountain*
Glas Leathad Beag: *The Little Green Grassy Slope*
Glas Leathad Mor: *The Big Green Grassy Slope*

Glas Mheall Liath: *The Green-Grey Hill*
Graban: *The Obstruction*
Iorguill: *The Battle Hill (of Shouting)*
Liathach: *The Grey One*
Maol Cheann Dearg: *The Bald Red Head*
Meall, M(Hill): *Lump (as applied to a rounded hill)*

Meall a'Aonaich: *The Hill of* $\begin{cases} \textit{The Heath} \\ \textit{Reconciliation} \end{cases}$

Meall a'Bhraghaid: *The Sloping Hill*
Meall a'Chrasgaidh
Meall a'Cleireach: *Hill of the Priest*
Meall an Eoin: *Hill of the Bird*
Meall an Fheadain: *Hill of the Whistle (Narrow Defile)*
Meall a'Ghuibhais: *Hill of the Fir Tree*
Meall Ailein: *The Beautiful Hill (of the Lawn)*
Meall Ard: *The Prominent Hill*
Meall Bad a'Mhuidhe: *The Hill of the Churn-Shaped Thicket*
Meall Beag: *The Little Hill*
Meall Dearg: *The Red Mountain*
Meall an Don: *The Brown Hillock*
Meall Each: *The Hill of the Horses*
Meall Gorm. *Green Hill*
Meall Horn (Fhir-Eoin): *The Eagle's Hill*
Meall an Liath Coire Mhic Dhugaill: *The Grey Hill of Dugald's Son's
    Coire*
Meall Mheadhonach: *The Middle Hill*
Meall Mheinnidh: *The Grassy Hill (The Solitary Hill)*
Meall nan Aighean: The Hill of the Hinds
Meall nan Bradhan: *The Hill of the Quern Stones*
Meall nan Ceapraichean: *The Hill of the Stumps, or Little Tops*
Meall nan Con:*The Hill of the Dogs*
Meall nan Cra (Crath): *The Hill of the Earthquakes*
Meall nam Peithirean: *The Hill of the Thunderbolts*
Meall na Saobhaidhe: *The Hill of the Fox's Den*
Morven: *The Big Hill*
Mullach, M(H)ullaich: *Top or Summit (Little Fort)*
Mullach an Rathain: *The Top above the Horns*
Mullach Coire Mhic Fhearchair: *The Top Above Son of Farquhar's
    Coire*

Mullach an Leathaid Riabhaich: *The Top above the Brindled Slope*
Quinag (Cuinneag): *The Water Spout (Bucket)*
Ruadh-stac Beag: *Little Red Peak*
Ruadh-stac Mhor: *Big Red Peak*
Sabhal More: *The Big Barn*
Sabhal Beag: *The Little Barn*
Sail: *Heel*
Sail Garbh: *The Rough Heel*
Sail Ghorm: *The Green Heel*
Sail Liath: *The Grey Heel*
Sail Mhor: *The Big Heel*
Scaraben
Seana Bhraigh: *The Old Mountain (Ridge)*
Seana Mheallan: *The Old Round Mill*
Sgribhis Beinn: *Rocky-sided Mountain*
Sgorr, Sgurr: *A rocky peak*
Sgurr a'Chadail: *The Peak of Sleep*
Sgurr Creag an Eich: *Peak of the Horse*
Sgurr a'Chaorachain: *The Peak of the Waterfall*
Sgurr a'Gharaidh: *The Peak of the Beast's Lair*
Sgurr an Fhidhleir: The Fiddler's Peak
Sgurr an Fhir Dhuibhe: *The Peak of the Black Man*
Sgurr an Tuill Bhain: *The Peak of the White Hole*
Sgurr Ban. *The White (Fair) Peak*
Sgurr Breac: *The Speckled Peak*
Sgurr Creag an Eich: *The Peak of the Horses*
Sgurr Dubh: *Black Peak*
Sgurr Fiona: *Peak of the Wine*
Sgurr Mhor: *The Great Peak*
Sgurr na Bana Mhoraire: *The Peak of the Lady*
Sgurr nan Clach Geala: *The Peak of the White Stone*
Sgurr nan Each: *The Horses' Peak*
Sgurr na Laocainn: *Peak of the Little Hero*
Sgurr Deas: *South Peak*
Sgurr nan Lochan Uaine: *Peak of the Green Lochs*
Sgurr Ruadh: *Red Peak (or Brown)*
Sgurr Tuath: *North Peak*
Sithean Mhor: *The Great Fairy Knoll*
Slioch: *The Spear*
Spidean a'Choire Leith:*The Peak of the Grey Coire*

Spidean Coire an Laoigh: *The Peak of the Calf's Coire*
Spidean Coire nan Clach: *The Peak of the Stony Coire*
Spidean nam Fasarinen: *The Pinnacle of the Teeth*
Sron Garbh: *The Rough Nose*
Stac Pollaidh: *The Peak of the Peat Moss*
Stob Cadha Goblach: *The Point of the Forked Pass*
Strone Nea: *The Nose of the Nest*
Stuc a'Choire Dhuibh Bhig: *The Peak of the Little Black Coire*
Stuc Loch na Cabhaig: *The Peak of the Loch of Haste*
Suilven (Norse): *The Pillar*
Toll Beag: *The Little Hollow*
Toll Mhor: *The Big Hollow*
Tom na Caillich: *The Old Woman's Hillock*
Tom a'Choinnich: *The Mossy Hillock*
Tom na Gruagaich: *The Maiden's Hillock*

Advice to Hill-Walkers

The Scottish Climbing Clubs consider it desirable to give advice to hill-walkers—especially to those with limited knowledge of conditions in Scotland. The present time is appropriate as an increasing number of people make use of the Scottish mountains in summer and in winter.

The Clubs are constrained to give this advice owing to the accidents in recent years which led to serious injury or death, caused trouble and anxiety to local residents called from their ordinary vocations, and to experienced climbers summoned from long distances to render assistance. Such assistance must not be regarded as always available, and it is only fair and reasonable that local helpers be paid adequately for their assistance.

The guide books issued by the Scottish Mountaineering Club describe routes which range from difficult climbs to what are in fine weather mere walks. It cannot be stressed too strongly that an expedition, which in fine weather is simple, may cease to be so if the weather becomes bad or mist descends. In winter, conditions on the hills change—what in summer is a walk may become a mountaineering expedition.

In many cases accidents are caused by a combination of events, no one of which singly would have been serious. Ample time should be allowed for expeditions, especially when the route is unknown. Further, before setting out on an expedition, parties should leave information as to their objectives and route and, without exception, have the courage to turn back when prudence so dictates.

In expeditions of any magnitude a party should consist of not less than three members, and they should never separate. If the party is large, two of the experienced members should bring up the rear.

If one member of the party is injured, another member should stay with him with all available food and spare clothing, while the remainder go to secure help. Great care should be taken in marking the spot where the injured man is left. Unless a conspicuous landmark is chosen, for example the junction of two streams, it is difficult to locate the spot, especially if the return is from a different direction or by night.

Some Common Causes of Difficulty are:

Underestimate of time required for expedition.

Slow or untried companions or members who are in poor training.

Illness caused through unwise eating or drinking.

Extreme cold or exhaustion through severe conditions.

Poor, soft snow; steep hard snow; snowstorms; mist.

Change in temperature rapidly converting soft snow into ice—involving step cutting.

Rain making rock slippery or snow filling the holds when rock climbing.

Frost after snow or rain glazing rocks with ice.

Sudden spates rendering the crossing of burns dangerous or impossible and necessitating long detours.

Hints—Equipment

All parties should carry:

Simple First Aid equipment, torch, whistle, watch, 1.50.000 2nd Series Ordnance Survey map, compass, and be able to use them.

Except in a few spots in Skye where the rocks are magnetic, the compass direction is certain to be correct even if it differs from one's sense of direction.

Ice axes should be carried if there is any chance of snow or ice, and a rope unless it is certain not to be required.

Clothing: At all times reserve clothing should be carried. Temperatures change rapidly, especially at high levels. Clothing should be warm; in winter a Balaclava helmet and thick woollen gloves should be carried. Well-shod boots should always be worn.

Food: Each member of a party should carry his own food. Climbers will find from experience what kind of food suits their individual need. Normally, jams and sugar are better than meat as they are more rapidly converted into energy. Most people will find it advisable to avoid alcohol on the hills, but a flask may be carried for emergencies. Light meals at frequent intervals are better than heavy meals at long intervals. In winter it may be advisable to make an early stop for food if shelter is found.

It is essential at all times to respect proprietary and sporting rights, especially during the shooting season, and to avoid disturbing game in deer forests and on grouse moors.

Issued with the authority of
Scottish Mountaineering Club
Dundee Rambling Club
Ladies' Scottish Climbing Club
Moray Mountaineering Club
Creagh Dhu Mountaineering Club
Edinburgh University Mountaineering Club
Cairngorm Club
Grampian Club
Lomond Mountaineering Club
Junior Mountaineering Club of Scotland
Etchachan Club

APPENDIX III

Bibliography

The literature relevant to the Northern Highlands is considerable. The following selection provides a useful source of information, and gives interesting general reading. It is only an indication of the basic texts. Those marked with an asterisk (*) contain comprehensive bibliographies, usually of a more intensive specialist nature.

General Guides

Bolton, G. D.—*Scotland's Western Seaboard*—Oliver and Boyd, 1953.

Campbell, M. F.—*Caithness and Sutherland*—C.U.P., 1920.

Dixon, J.—*Gairloch.*—Reprinted 1980 by The Gairloch Heritage Society. True X Press, Oxford.

Gardener, A.—*Western Highlands*—Batsford, 1947.

Gordon, Seton—*Highways and Byways in the West Highlands*—Macmillan, 1955

Gunn, Rev. A. and Mackay, J.—*Sutherland and the Reay Country*—1897.

MacCulloch, J.—*The Highlands and Western Isles of Scotland*—4 vols., 1824.

Macdonald, D. and Polson, A.—*The Book of Ross, Sutherland and Caithness*—Dingwall.

Maclean, C. I.—*The Highlands*—Batsford.

Macrow, B. G.—*Torridon Highlands*—Hale, 1969.

Miller, H.—*Sutherland and Sutherlanders*—1844.

Murray, W. H.—*Highland Landscape*—N.T.S., 1962.

Murray, W. H.—*Companion Guide to the West Highlands of Scotland*—Collins, 1968.

Pochin-Mould, D.D.C.—*The Roads from the Isles*—Oliver and Boyd, 1950.

S.Y.H.A.—*The Northern Highlands and Annual Handbook*—Stirling.

Weir, T.—*The Western Highlands*—Batsford, 1974.

Wainwright, A.—*Scottish Mountain Drawings.*—Westmoreland Gazette, Kendall.

Natural History

Collier, A.—*The Crofting Problem*—C.U.P., 1953.

Cowan, M.—*Inverewe, A Garden in the N.W. Highlands*—Bles, 1964.

Darling, F. F. (ed.)—*West Highland Survey*—O.U.P., 1955.

*Darling, F. F. and Morton Boyd, J.—*The Highlands and Islands*—Fontana New Naturalist Series, 1969.

MacKenzie, Sir G. S.—*General View of the Agriculture of the Counties of Ross and Cromarty*—1813.

MacNally, L.—*Year of the Red Deer. Highland Deer Forest.*—Dent.

*O'Dell, A. C. and Walton, K.—*The Highlands and Islands of Scotland*—Nelson, 1962.

Peach, B. N. and Horne, J.—*The Geological Structure of the North-West Highlands of Scotland*—London.

Peach, B. N. and Horne, J.—*Guide to the Geological Model of the Assynt Mountains*—1914.

Phemister, J.—*British Regional Geology. The Northern Highlands*—H.M.S.O. (3rd Edition 1960).

Sinclair, Sir J.—*General View of the Agriculture of the Northern Counties and Islands of Scotland*—1795.

St. John, Charles.—*The Wild Sports of the Highlands. Tour in Sutherlandshire.*—Published 1846.

Social History

Day, J. R.—*Public Administration in the Highlands and Islands of Scotland*.

Feachem, R.—*Prehistoric Scotland*—Batsford, 1963

*Gray, M.—*The Highland Economy, 1750-1850*—Edinburgh, 1957.

Grimble, I.—*The Trial of Patrick Sellar*—London, 1962.

Grimble, I.—*Chief of Mackay*—London, 1965.

Gunn, N.—*Highland River*—Faber and Faber.

*Haldane, A. R. S.—*The Drove Roads of Scotland*—Edinburgh, 1952.

Haldane, A. R. S.—*New Ways Through the Glens.*—David & Charles, 1973.

Johnson, J. B.—*Place Names of Scotland*—S.R. Publishers Ltd., 1972.

MacEwan, John—*Who Owns Scotland*—Polygon Books, 1981.

Mackenzie, A.—*The Prophecies of the Brahan Seer*—Golspie, 1970.

Mackenzie, A.—*A History of the Highland Clearances*—Glasgow, 1883, (2nd Ed. Rev. 1946).

Mackenzie, O.—*A Hundred Years in the Highlands*—London, 1965.

*Mackenzie, W. C.—*The Highlands and Isles of Scotland*—Edinburgh, 1949.

Macleod, D.—*Gloomy Memories in the Highlands of Scotland*—1857.

Macleod, D.—History of the Destitution in Sutherlandshire—1841.

Miller, H.—*Sutherland as it was and is, or How a Country may be ruined*—1843.

Mitchell, J.—*Reminiscences of My Life in the Highlands*—1883. (Reprinted in 2 vols. 1972).

Mitchison, R.—*Agricultural Sir John*—London, 1962.

Murray, J.—*The Dingwall and Ben Wyvis Railway.*—Monument Press, Stirling, 1979.

New Statistical Account of Scotland (By Parishes)—1835-1845.

Old Statistical Account of Scotland (By Parishes and written by the Parish Ministers) 21 vols. 1790-98.

Ordnance Survey.—*Place Names of Scotland.*

*Prebble, J.—*The Highland Clearances*—London, 1963.

*Richards, E.—*The Leviathan of Wealth*—London, 1973.

Sage, D.—*Memorabilia Domestica*—1889.

Swires, O. F.—*The Highlands and Their Legends*—Oliver and Boyd.

Temperley, A.—*Tales of the North Coast.*—Research Publishing Co. 1977.

Thomson, D. and Grimble, I.—*The Future of the Highlands*—London, 1968.

Watson, W. J.—*The History of the Celtic Place-Names of Scotland*—Edinburgh, 1926.

*Youngson, A. J.—*After the Forty-Five*—Edinburgh, 1973.

Mountaineering

Bell, J. H. B.—*A Progress in Mountaineering*—Edinburgh, 1950.

Bennett, D.—*Scottish Mountain Climbs.*—Batsford, 1979.

Brown, H.—*Hamish's Mountain Walk.*—Gollancz, 1979.

Cleare, J. S. and Collomb, R. G.—*Sea Cliff Climbing in Britain*—London, 1973.

Corriemulzie Mountaineering Club—*Rock and Ice Guide to Easter Ross and Foinaven Supplement*—1966.

Cambridge University Mountaineering Club—*Carnmore Guide Book*—1958.

Docharty, Wm. McK.—*A Selection of 900 British and Irish Mountain Tops*—1954.

MacInnes, H.—*Scottish Climbs* (2 vols.)—Constable, 1971.

MacInnes, H.—*West Highland Walks* (vol. I & II)—Hodder and Stoughton, 1979.

Murray, W. H.—*Undiscovered Scotland*—London, 1951.

Mountain Rescue Committee—*Cave and Mountain Rescue Handbook.*

Walker, J. H.—*On Hills of the North*—Edinburgh, 1940.

Weir, T.—*Highland Days*—London, 1948.

Weir, T.—*Scottish Lochs* (2 vols.)—Constable, 1972.

The Scottish Mountaineering Trust

The Northern Highlands District Guide—2nd Edition, 1936—W. N. Ling and J. Rooke Corbett.

The Northern Highlands District Guide—3rd Edition, 1933—E. W. Hodge.

Munro's Tables and Other Tables of Lesser Heights—Revised Edition, 1981—J. C. Donaldson and M. M. Brown.

Climbers' Guide to the Northern Highlands Area—Volume I—*Letterewe and East Ross*—I. G. Rowe—Volume II—*Torridon, Achnasheen and Applecross*—D. G. and R. W. L. Turnbull.

Scottish Mountaineering Club Journals, up to and including Vol. XXXII 1980.

APPENDIX IV

Estates

Within recent years, many of the old Highland Estates have changed hands, either wholly or in part. This list still attempts to keep up to date with the traffic in land, and indicates the landowners within the area of the text. On those estates where the proprietor is known to be resident more or less permanently, enquiries can be made direct. Names and locations of estate factors and/or estate offices are also included, where these are known, in the hope that they also prove to be of some assistance. Where foreign interests have taken over, information is often difficult to come by—where this is the case, it is usually best to make enquiries locally.

Chapter 1

APPLECROSS ESTATE—Major J. and Captain A. Willis.
   Estate Office—Shore Street, Applecross *Tel. No.* Applecross 209.
SHIELDAIG ESTATE—A. C. Greg.
   Balgy Lodge—Shieldaig *Tel. No.* Torridon 231.
COULDORAN ESTATE—A. B. Marsden-Smedley.
   Couldoran Lodge, Strathcarron *Tel. No.* Kishorn 227.

Chapter 2

SHIELDAIG ESTATE—A. C. Greg. As above.
NEW KELSO ESTATE—A. Macdonald.
   Torgorm, Conon Bridge, Ross-shire.
BEN DAMPH ESTATE—Major and Mrs R. B. Braithwaite.
   Stronvar, Inveralligin *Tel. No.* Torridon 265.
BEN DAMPH—COIRE FIONNERAICH—Sitze Kats.
   Per McAndrew and Jenkins, 5 Drummond St., Inverness.
ACHNASHELLACH ESTATE—Forestry Commission and Wills Estates.
COULIN ESTATE—Captain F. H. P. H. Wills.
   Per Manager's House *Tel. No.* Kinlochewe 224.

LEDGOWAN ESTATE—Trustees for G. E. and E. Ruggles-Brise.
Factor—Bingham, Hughes and Macpherson, Inverness.
Ledgowan Lodge *Tel. No.* Achnasheen 245.
GLENCARRON ESTATE—A. M. Sladen.
Glencarron Lodge, Achnashellach *Tel. No.* Achnashellach
216/217.

Chapter 3

TORRIDON ESTATE—The Nature Conservancy.
Fraser Darling House, 9 Culduthel Road, Inverness *Tel. No.*
Inverness 39431 or
Reserve Office, Anancaun *Tel. No.* Kinlochewe 254,
National Trust for Scotland, 109 Church Street, Inverness
Tel No. Inverness 32034 or
Inverness 32034 or
The Mains and Information Centre *Tel. No.* Torridon 221.
FLOWERDALE ESTATE—Gairloch and Conon Estate, Brigadier
W. A. MacKenzie
Estate Office (*Tel. No.* Urray 273).

Chapter 4

FISHERFIELD ESTATE—Ardlair and Kernsary.
P. Flentener Van Vlissingen, Factor—H. A. Bruce, Bank of
Scotland, Gairloch *Tel. No.* Gairloch 2015.
LETTEREWE ESTATE—Col. W. H. Whitbread.
Kinlochewe Lodge,
Estate Office—Incheril, Kinlochewe *Tel. No.* Kinlochewe 262.
GRUINARD ESTATE—Strathnashellag.
Lady McCorquodale.
Manager's House, Gruinard, Laide. *Tel. No.* Aultbea
240.
DUNDONNELL ESTATE—A. S., & M. M. Rogers.
Per. Innes and Mackay, Solicitors, Inverness.

Chapter 5

LOCHROSQUE ESTATE—P. C. G. Wilson.
Loanleven, Almond Bank, Perth.
LochRosque Lodge *Tel. No.* Achnasheen 266.
FANNICH ESTATE—Mulie-Goed. B. V. (Dutch Company).
Fannich Lodge *Tel. No.* Garve 227.

STRATHBRAN ESTATE—The Marquesa de Torrehermosa.
Strathbran Lodge, Achanalt *Tel. No.* Garve 202.
LOCHLUICHART ESTATE—The Rt. Hon. Spencer-Loch.
Manager's House, Forest Hill, Lochluichart (*Tel. No. Garve*

Chapter 6
WYVIS ESTATE—L. Gisselback.
TULLOCH ESTATE—Col. A. D. Vickers.
Bingham Hughes & Macpherson.
KILDERMORIE ESTATE—Lt. Col. D. Hignett.
Kildermorie Lodge *Tel. No.* Alness 882240.
GLEN CALVIE ESTATE—Benmore Estates.
Per Factor, Estate Office, Ardgay *Tel. No.* Ardgay 366.
Glencalvie Lodge *Tel. No.* The Craigs 232.

Chapter 7.
STRATHVAICH ESTATE—J. & H. Smith
Strathvaich Lodge, Garve *Tel. No.* Aultguish 226.
INVERLAEL ESTATE—Dr. S. M. Whitteridge.
Inverlael Lodge *Tel. No.* Lochbroom 262.
BRAEMORE ESTATE—Including Foich and Strone.
Dutch Owned.
Entrance Lodge, Braemore *Tel. No.* Lochbroom 222. or
Foich Lodge, by Ullapool *Tel. No.* Lochbroom 203.
LOCHBROOM ESTATE—L. W. Rolson.
Inverbroom Lodge, Loch Broom, by Garve.
RHIDDOROCH ESTATE—Major I. M. Scobie.
Estate Office.
North Kessock *Tel. No.* Kessock 212.
BENMORE ESTATES—Miss Godman.
Factor, Estate Office, Ardgay *Tel. No.* Ardgay 336.
CORRIEMULZIE ESTATE—Benmore Estates (see above).
LUBCROY ESTATE—Forestry Commission.
LANGWELL ESTATE—A. W. Fenwick.
Langwell Lodge, Strathkaniard *Tel. No.* Strathkaniard 321.

Chapter 8
STRATHKANAIRD ESTATE—Commander C. G. Vyner.
Keanchulish, Ardmair (*Tel. No.* Ullapool 2100).

BADEN TARBET ESTATE—Mrs. T. G. Longstaff.
Tel. No Achiltiebuie 225.
BENMORE COIGACH ESTATE—Royal Society for Nature Con-
servation.
The Green, Nettleham, Lincoln.
Local Field Officer-Mr. I. Campbell, Achiltibuie *Tel. No.*
Achiltibuie 363.
INVERPOLLY ESTATE—Rt. Hon. E. Davies.
Inverpolly Lodge.
Manager, Mr. C. MacDonald, Ardnahaird *Tel. No.*
Lochinver 252.

Chapter 9

ASSYNT ESTATE—E. H. Vestey.
Estate OfficeLochinver *Tel. No.* Lochinver 203.
BENMORE ESTATE—Estate Office Ardgay.
LOCH ASSYNT ESTATE—W. Philmore Sankey
Loch Assynt Lodge *Tel. No.* Assynt 216.
INCHNADAMPH ESTATE—E. H. Vestey.
Estate Office-Lochinver *Tel. No.* Lochinver 203.

Chapter 10

SCOURIE ESTATE—Mr. & Mrs. J. C. Balfour.
Per Factor—Bell, Strutt & Parker, Elgin.
KYLESTROME ESTATE—Lady Mary Grosvenor.
Factored by Westminster Estates.
Estate Office—Achfary (*Tel. No.* Lochmore 221).
WESTMINSTER ESTATE—Duchess of Westminster.
Estate Office—Achfary *Tel. No.* Lochmore 221.
Keeper's House—Ardchuillin *Tel. No.* Lochmore 223.
GUALIN ESTATE—Mrs. Ferguson.
82 Athol Road, Pitlochry, Perthshire.
Factor—Renton, Finlayson and Co., Aberfeldy.
MERKLAND ESTATE—Mrs. Garten.
Merkland Lodge *Tel. No.* Merkland 204.
ERIBOLL ESTATE—J. Elliott.
Balnakiel, Durness *Tel. No.* Durness 268.

Chapter 11

STRATHMORE ESTATE—Mrs. D. J. H. Gow.
Strathmore Lodge *Tel. No.* Altnaharra 248.

LOYAL ESTATE—Lt. Col. J. G. Moncrieff.
Loch Loyal Lodge, Tongue *Tel. No.* Tongue 220/291.

Chapter 12

ACHINTOUL & BERRIEDALE ESTATE—Braemore Estates
(Duke of Portland).
Factor—M. R. M. Leslie.
Estate Office—Berriedale *Tel. No.* Dunbeath 276.
BEN ARMINE ESTATE and
SUTHERLAND ESTATE—Countess of Sutherland.
Estate Office—Duke Street, Golspie *Tel. No.* Golspie 268.
KLIBRECK ESTATE—Sir M. Kimball.
Altnaharra Lodge *Tel. No.* Altnaharra 224.
LOCH CHOIRE ESTATE—D. Knowles.
North Dunslainsholme Farm, Northumberland, Loch Choire
Lodge *Tel. No.* Kinbrace 222.
FORESTRY COMMISSION TELEPHONE NUMBERS.

Conservancy Office Dingwall	Dingwall 62144.
Conservancy Office Dornoch	Dornoch 359.
Achnashellach Forest	Achnashellach 273
Shin Forest	Lairg 2478.
Lael Forest	Lochbroom 246.
Slattadale Forest	Achnashellach 273.

Recommended Routes

In any list of this nature, covering as it does in this case, a vast mountain area, it is inevitable that many fine climbs will be omitted. The following selection contains climbs which are generally agreed to be of some particular worth. It is hoped that the choice will fulfil a dual purpose, namely, provide a reasonable distribution of routes among the principal peaks, and cater for a width of difference in both standard and character. As far as possible a reference has been given to the appropriate S.M.C. Journal for route descriptions.

Applecross
Meall Gorm.   *The Blue Pillar*. Grade IV or Very Difficult.
                          SMCJ 1970/SMCJ 1954.
Sgurr a'Chaorachain.   *Sword of Gideon*. Very Severe. SMCJ 1962.
                          Swordstick. Severe. SMCJ 1970.
                          The Cioch Nose. Very Difficult. SMCJ
                          1961.
                          The Maxilla. Very Severe. SMCJ 1970.
Beinn Bhan   *March Hare's Gully*. Grade IV. SMCJ 1970.
                          Mad Hatter's Gully. Grade V. SMCJ 1976.
                          Silver Tear. Grade V. SMCJ 1977.

Achnashellach
Fuar Tholl.   *Enigma Route*. Severe. SMCJ 1953.
                          Investigator. Hard Severe. Vol. II.
Sgurr Ruadh.   *Raeburn's Buttress Direct*. Grade IV. SMCJ
                          1969.
                          Robertson's Gully. Grade IV. SMCJ 1976

Torridon
Beinn Eighe.   *Junior, West Buttress*. Hard Very Severe.
                          SMCJ 1977.

	Piggott's Route. Central Buttress. Mild Severe. Vol. II.
	East Central Ribs. Severe. SMCJ 1955.
	Ordinary Route. East Buttress. Difficult. Vol. II.
	Boggle. Very Severe. SMCJ 1962.
	Groovin' High. Hard Very Severe. SMCJ 1974.
	The Pineapple Chimney. Very Severe. SMCJ 1974.
Liathach.	*The Northern Pinnacles.* Grade II. SMCJ 1894
	Poacher's Fall. Grade V. SMCJ 1978.
Beinn Alligin	*Deep North Gully.* Grade II. Vol. II.
	Deep South Gully. Grade I. Vol. II.

Loch Maree to Loch Broom

Tollie Crags.	*The Trip.* Hard Very Severe. Vol. I.
	Cocaine. Hard Very Severe. SMCJ 1971.
	The Hand-Rail. Severe. Vol. I.
Beinn a'Mhuinidh.	*The West Climb.* Severe. Vol. I.
	Stoater. Severe. SMCJ 1973.
	Vertigo. Hard Very Severe. SMCJ 1973.
Beinn Lair.	*Butterfly Gully.* Grade II. SMCJ 1979.
	Wisdom Buttress. Very Difficult. Vol. I.
Beinn Airigh Charr.	*The Beanstalk.* Very Severe. SMCJ 1973.
Carnmore Crag.	*Fionn Buttress.* Very Severe. SMCJ 1957.
	Dragon. Hard Very Severe. Vol. I.
	Gob. Hard Very Severe. SMCJ 1961.
	Black Mischief. Very Severe. Vol. I.
	Balaton. Extremely Severe. SMCJ 1967.
Torr na h'Iolaire	*Hieroglyphics.* Very Severe. Vol. I.
A'Mhaighdean.	*Ecstasy.* Severe. SMCJ 1957
	Dishonour. Very Difficult. SMCJ 1957.
	Pillar Buttress. Difficult. Vol. I.
An Teallach.	*Lord's Gully.* Grade II. SMCJ 1959/SMCJ 1980.
	Hayfork Gully. Grade I/II. SMCJ 1959.

The Fannichs
Sgurr nan Clach Geala. *Gamma Gully*. Grade IV. Vol. I.
Delta Gully. Grade IV. SMCJ 1973.

Easter Ross
Alladale. *Rumble*. Very Severe. Vol. I.
Whigmaleerie. Severe. SMCJ 1963.
Tane. Very Difficult. Vol. I.
Tother. Very Difficult. Vol. I.

Beinn Dearg and Corriemulzie
Beinn Dearg. *Penguin Gully*. Grade III. Vol. I.
Tower of Babel. Very Difficult. SMCJ 1963.
Fenian Gully. Grade III/IV. SMCJ 1970.
Emerald Gully. Grade III/IV. SMCJ 1971.
Seana Bhraigh. *Sunday Post*. Grade III. Vol. I.
Pomegranate Gully. Grade II. Vol. I.
Diamond Edge. Grade III/IV. SMCJ 1979.

Coigach.
Sgurr an Fhidhleir. *The Fiddler. Direct Route*. Very Severe and
Grade V. SMCJ 1970/SMCJ 1981.
North West Face. Grade III. SMCJ 1979.
Stac Pollaidh. *West Buttress*. Difficult. SMCJ 1957.
Jack the Ripper. Very Severe. SMCJ 1965.

Assynt
Quineag. *The Waste Pipe*. Grade II. SMCJ 1970.
Stoer Point. *The Old Man of Stoer*. Very Severe. SMCJ
1967.

The Reay Forest.
Foinaven. *Cengalo*. Hard Severe. SMCJ 1971.
Dialectic. Very Severe. SMCJ 1971.
Tortoise. Very Severe. SMCJ 1971.
Zig-Zag. Difficult. Vol. I.
Fingal. Severe. SMCJ 1963.
The Second Icefall. Grade V. SMCJ 1979.
Pobble. Severe. SMCJ 1973.
Pilastre. Hard Very Severe. SMCJ 1974.

Creag Shomairle.   *The Ramp*. Very Severe. SMCJ 1970.
                        The Roost. Very Severe. SMCJ 1980.
Ben Hope.   *Bell's Route*. Difficult. Description in this
                          Guide.

N.B.—SMCJ Refers to the *Scottish Mountaineering Club Journal*.
Vol. I and II refers to the *Climbers' Guides to the Northern Highlands*
published by the Scottish Mountaineering Club.

Index